Transforming Atonement

"Since the mid-1970s, a significant ecumenical literature has emerged that sees the theology of the cross as a provocative and necessary alternative to the religious triumphalism (*theologia gloriae*) of the Western Christian establishment, as well as the sentimentalism and personalism of American pietism. In its quest for new ways of articulating the meaning of the cross for today, and especially its insistence upon the 'theopolitical' character of this theological tradition, Professor Jennings's book is a valuable contribution to this growing literature."

Douglas John Hall, C.M.
Professor of Christian Theology Emeritus, McGill University, Montreal

Transforming Atonement

A Political Theology of the Cross

Theodore W. Jennings Jr.

Fortress Press
Minneapolis

All Scripture quotations unless otherwise marked are the author's own translation.

Scripture quotations marked NRSV are taken from the New Revised Standard Version Bible, copyright © 1989 from the Division of Christian Education of the National Council of Churches of Christ in the United States of America and are used by permission. All rights reserved.

Cover image: *To Study the Body of Christ,* by Jean-Michel Alberola, 1992. Copyright Artist Rights Society (ARS), New York. Photo: Philippe Migeat © CNAC / MNAM / Dist. Réunion des Musées Nationaux / Art Resource, N.Y.
Cover design: Ivy Palmer Skrade
Book design: PerfecType, Nashville, TN

Library of Congress Cataloging-in-Publication Data

Jennings, Theodore W.
  Transforming atonement : a political theology of the Cross / Theodore W. Jennings, Jr.
      p. cm.
  Includes bibliographical references (p.   ) and index.
  ISBN 978-0-8006-6350-6 (alk. paper)
  1. Jesus Christ—Crucifixion. 2. Political theology. 3. Atonement. I. Title.
  BT453.J36 2009
  232'.3—dc22
                              2008053707

The paper used in this publication meets the minimum requirements of American National Standard for Information Sciences—Permanence of Paper for Printed Library Materials, ANSI Z329.48-1984.

Manufactured in the U.S.A.

CONTENTS

For Kunitoshi Sakai

PREFACE

Unlike many of my friends in and out of the church, I have always been drawn to the cross of Jesus. It has always seemed something to which I wanted to be loyal. Yet it has also perplexed me, as so many of the ways of speaking about the cross seemed inadequate or unintelligible. I knew it was of basic importance but was not sure in what way or why. This book grows out of living with that perplexity.

I first wrote about the cross when I was teaching in Mexico. It was the first thing I wrote in Spanish. Perhaps it was living with a suffering and struggling people that made this theme feel so urgent for me. It was published in Holy Week while my wife, Ronna Case, and I were in Nicaragua as it was subjected to the Contra War, funded by the United States.

Over the years, I developed a number of Bible studies for laypeople, seminarians, and clergy on the question of the theology of the cross. This book took shape in the course of a regularly offered seminar at the Chicago Theological Seminary. The subsequent response of students from various parts of the world has pushed me to bring this project to a certain completion. Without their questions, their yearning for comprehension, their enthusiasm, and their encouragement, I could not have written this book.

Although it would be fitting simply to list the names of those who, over the years, have been part of this seminar, I will mention only two whose own work on this theme may eclipse mine (this is as it should be, for that is the whole point of teaching): Adam Kotsko, whose expert help has been invaluable in the completion of the manuscript, and Kunitoshi Sakai, whose passion for the cross has made us friends.

I am grateful to the editors of Fortress Press, to Neil Elliott, whose own work on Paul has been a source of inspiration, and to Michael West for his enthusiasm for this project.

CHAPTER ONE

Rethinking Atonement

I f one were to visit most Protestant churches during what is called Holy Week, one would find the churches unusually filled on Palm Sunday and Easter, but little happening in the course of the week. Some churches have Good Friday services, but they tend to be sparsely attended. As a consequence, the congregants will hear a great deal about Christ's triumph but little of his agony, much of resurrection but little of the cross.

To be sure, in some churches one hears a good deal about the cross as something like a payment for the sins of the worshippers, who are thus assured of being in the good graces of God (often in contrast to those who are not present in this or similar congregations). And most churches still have a place for a cross on their altar as a kind of obligatory decoration (usually in faux gold). It thus serves as a type of identity marker: this is a Christian church as opposed to, for example, a mosque or synagogue. But beyond this simple assertion of identity, the meaning of this adornment is seldom if ever explored.

Thus, on the one hand, churches that seem to be "mainstream" have little if anything to say about the cross, while churches that have a more conservative bent may say a great deal, but often of a sort that seems maudlin or masochistic or just plain unintelligible to others.

One illustration of this divide comes from the reaction to Mel Gibson's movie *The Passion of the Christ*. Many of the more conservative churches sent busloads of adoring congregants to swell the ranks of the conventional seekers of entertainment, while many churches of a more "progressive" persuasion decried the movie's violence, gore, and anti-Semitism.

In many denominations styled "mainline" as well, there is today a vigorous debate about how, if at all, the cross is to be understood, with conservative caucuses pushing a particular interpretation of the cross (sometimes called substitutionary atonement) as the only true view of the matter, while others are somewhat embarrassed about how to give an account of the cross at all. Indeed, some seem to have concluded that the standard ways of talking about the cross only serve to encourage anti-Judaism or to glorify violence and gore and a view of God that all too often licenses abuse of the innocent and helpless.

Clearly, the cross has become something of a bone of contention among Protestant Christians. Is there any way to affirm the centrality of the cross of Jesus without falling into reproducing the many problems that have been associated with traditional accounts of its significance? This book is an attempt to do just that, for I am persuaded that a Christianity without the cross is salt that has lost its savor—it has become tasteless, innocuous, without point or pertinence. On the other hand, I agree that many of the available ways of speaking about the cross have either become unintelligible or acquired meanings that are pernicious, destructive of the very gospel they intend to "defend."

My intention in this book is to present a way of understanding the cross that makes it intelligible for contemporary people without losing the most important insights of scripture and tradition. In order to do this, however, it will be necessary to attend closely to some of the ways that talk of the cross may have become unintelligible for us, and to some of the problems that must be faced in attempting to reconstruct an understanding of the cross for modern Christians. On that basis I will suggest the outline of a way forward that will be developed in the remainder of this book.

Worn-out language

One of the basic problems we often have when we try to speak of the significance of the cross of Jesus is that much of the language that we have inherited from tradition seems alien or foreign to us. Although we may continue to repeat that Christ died for our sins, or that Christ came into the world to save sinners, or that he made peace by the blood of the cross, we are often hard pressed to say what we mean by these terms.

There is a very good reason for this difficulty. Much of this language is borrowed from contexts that are themselves no longer intelligible to us. For example, in the Middle Ages, when feudalism was in flower, St. Anselm attempted to express the meaning of the cross in terms of the key concepts of the feudal system, especially in its idealized terms of chivalry. The result was what is often called the satisfaction theory of atonement. According to this view, the sin of the creature offends the honor of the creator, in much the same way that the rebellion of the serf offends the honor of the lord. Honor must be restored, especially since the one dishonored is the true Lord over all. But the insult to the honor of God, because the one involved is God, requires an infinite satisfaction. This the creature, as finite, cannot repay, even by eternal punishment. Only one who is himself divine can pay what will restore the balance and thus restore the divine honor. For this reason the Son suffers the punishment of death, paying what we cannot possibly pay (for our life is finite). Thus, the honor of God is restored and the creature is released from this infinite debt.

What Anselm achieved by this was to show the significance of Jesus' death on the cross in terms that made sense—that were plausible—within the framework of the medieval world. It was a masterstroke of theological reflection. But when people no longer regularly interpret their world and experience in terms of chivalric notions such as honor and satisfaction, then the interpretation of the cross in terms of this worldview no longer makes much sense. Either we have to turn our attention to trying to make sense out of this unfamiliar worldview, going into long explanations of these feudal concepts and then trying to get people who never use these notions in everyday life to still use them in church; or we conclude that the whole thing is unintelligible and turn away from an attempt to understand the cross at all, focusing instead on things such as the importance of being good and decent people. Either way is, however, catastrophic. For if we follow the second path and shrug off talk of the cross as unintelligible, then it is difficult to make any sense of the place given this event in the New Testament; it becomes difficult to say in what way it can be good news. But if we try simply to impose this worldview of feudalism, then we run into the problem that the language of faith becomes a kind of museum piece, or a private language, that no longer speaks to everyday experience. We use the slogans, perhaps, but we seem to ourselves to be talking a mysterious language, a strange dialect that we no longer know how to apply to everyday life.

The example I have just used is from the Middle Ages, but we could find a similar problem with the language of the New Testament. Another example may be helpful. Much of the religious life of the Hellenistic world was steeped in the practices of temple sacrifice. This was equally true for Jews and gentiles. An elaborate sacrificial system centered in the temples ensured that whether or not people participated in this practice, they would understand well enough how it worked.

One of the central notions of sacrifice was the substitution of a scapegoat for those making the sacrifice. Thus, if the people seemed to be in trouble with their divinity, the way to deal with this anger was to deflect it onto another object. In order to do this, the other object would somehow be identified with those making the sacrifice. Sometimes this meant choosing a representative person, in some cases the king, whose death then would become a substitute for the people as a whole. Or one might choose an unblemished victim (the notion of the sacrifice of the firstborn or of a virgin, and so on).

Of course, this is all rather costly, so many found ways to invest less valuable members of the community with the faults of the people. Hence the use of a (literal) scapegoat in Israel, or of unblemished animals. The Greeks even found ways to use disfigured prisoners for this purpose. The point is that the death of the sacrificial victim would appease the divine wrath and so bring good fortune to those who engaged in this ritual process.

Because this system was widespread, and because it was impressive (temples, priests, and so forth), it seemed to the people of the time to make a good deal of sense. It was right there waiting to serve as a vehicle for making sense of the gospel, and it was employed for just this purpose. No doubt it made sense to the hearers of the message; that is why it was used.

However, the problem is that we are no longer familiar with this language, because we are no longer familiar with this practice. There are still parts of the world where the use of temple sacrifice is common, but this is no longer true in the world where Christianity is widely practiced. There is a reason for this: Christianity abolished the system of sacrifice. The early Christians were accused of being atheists, in part because they did not engage in temple sacrifice—neither that of the Jews, nor that of the pagans, nor a new system of their own. Indeed, the Letter to the Hebrews is an essay that largely aims at the destruction of the notion of sacrifice. To be sure, it does this by saying the need for this system is abolished because Jesus is the final sacrifice. That is, it uses the language of the sacrificial system in order to abolish it.

The language about Jesus as sacrificial victim, then, depends on the plausibility of the sacrificial system and at the same time abolishes this system. The rub is that the documents that are responsible for ending this practice still make reference to it. This is a problem for those subsequent Christians who, precisely because they are Christians, no longer know what to make of this language. One response of the church was to introduce a new, but modified, sacrificial system: the Mass. Here, the sacrifice of Christ could be repeated regularly. In this way the language of sacrifice would continue to make sense even if it was limited to this one event.

However, the Protestant Reformation maintained that the sacrifice was done once and for all, and so it need not, and cannot, be repeated by mere priests and rituals. There is neither need for, nor even the possibility of, a repetition of the sacrifice. This has the advantage of continuing the work of eliminating the sacrificial system that had been begun in the New Testament, but it also robs this biblical language of its one remaining context. Now we have to explain the sacrifice of Jesus to people who have no idea what a cultic sacrifice is. The result, again, is that our language no longer connects with people's everyday reality. We repeat the slogans in church (at least at Communion services), but we can't say what we mean. We take it "on faith," which now means we are bewildered by it. We suspect it is important but we can't say why.

Often, because we can't explain this language, even to ourselves, we decide that it is simply something to be discarded, and we wind up with no way to speak of the importance of Jesus' cross, of how the event of Jesus makes any difference to anyone at all, and so we have to fall back on things like going to church as a good way to get child care or find friends.

Another type of discourse within which it was possible for the early church to express the significance of the cross was that of the "mystery cult." In the Hellenistic world of the first century, there were a number of cults that were based on the ancient fertility rituals of Near Eastern religions. Earlier traditions had emphasized the pattern of the seasons as the framework for ritualization. Thus, the aim of the religious practice of temple, altar, priest, and ritual was to assure a good harvest for the social group.

In the Hellenistic world, however, elements of these cultic traditions were separated from their original agricultural setting and transposed into the new situation of the Hellenistic world of empire and city. Instead of representing the dying and rising divinity as the prototype of the seasonal transition from winter to spring, or from rainy to dry season, these cultic forms were adapted to the common human plight of death itself. Thus, the cults were loosened from their agrarian setting and their original geographical and cultural context in order to appeal to the culturally rootless urban peoples of the empire.

These cults appear to emphasize the initiation of persons into the fate of a divinity who passed through death in order to be reborn into immortality.[1] Since these cults closely guarded their initiatory rites and the mystery into which adherents were initiated, we can only reconstruct the barest outlines of their practice. But we do know that these cults were very widespread, especially in urban settings—the very place where Christianity took root in the first century.

There are a number of themes that permitted some transposition into Christian discourse. The initiatory function of baptism, especially as this could be interpreted as assimilation to the fate of the dying and rising God, appeared a natural point of contact for the interpretation of the gospel. An idea of what is involved here can be glimpsed in some of the hymns that we still occasionally hear: "There is a fountain filled with blood"; or "washed in the blood of the Lamb." These hymnic formulations seem to recall the cult of Mithras, in which the initiates were placed beneath a platform on which a bull stood. When the bull's throat was slit, the initiates were literally washed in blood. In this way, they received the life force of the animal that represented the divine and so were initiated into immortality.

A number of New Testament passages that refer to the cross also appear to echo some of the ideas of initiation into the dying and rising God. Thus, Paul can ask, "Do you not know that all of us who have been baptized into Christ Jesus were baptized into his death?" (Rom 6:3 NRSV), and then go on to say, "If we have been united with him in a death like his, we will certainly be united with him in a resurrection like his" (6:5 NRSV). We shall see in subsequent chapters, however, that this sort of language typically has in view not some mere cultic act, but a sharing in the historical reality of persecution and suffering.

Certainly, we find ourselves in the situation in which the language of participation through initiation into the mystery of the dying and rising God no longer has the ability to link Christian proclamation to publicly intelligible discourse. There are, of course, still secret societies, like the Masons, that make a great deal of initiatory practices and the acquisition of secret knowledge. But these societies in general no longer focus upon "salvation" from the fate of death as the aim of the initiatory practice. Rather, they aim at a kind of secular advantage: fellowship, a sense of belonging, and mutual aid in economic, political, and social life (rather like some contemporary forms of Christianity). Thus, they no longer depend upon the mystic participation in the fate of the divine hero in order to confer the benefits sought by their adherents.

This being so, the terminology of the mystery cult that could serve in the first century to make the centrality of the cross intelligible to the urban masses of the Roman Empire no longer connects with widespread thought and practice. Rather than making the gospel intelligible to people, this language serves to make the gospel seem weird—indeed, rather barbaric.

As in the case of the sacrificial system, so here in the case of the mystery cult, the disappearance of this language and practice owes much to Christianity itself. In the first place, as a message directed to all people, Christianity was at odds with the basic perspective of the mysteries. Rather than being an esoteric cult, Christianity represented an exoteric public message and community. Moreover, as we shall see, the participation in the fate of the divine hero of the mysteries was "demythologized" by the way in which participation in the fate of Jesus normally meant a literal, rather than cultic, sharing in his fate: being persecuted, arrested, tried, and even executed. Further, the ethical dimension of the contrast between the old and the new life meant that instead of a secret cult initiation, what was emphasized was a public style of life. In all of these ways the mystery cult language, while being appropriated, was also being dismantled.

A third discourse that early Christianity could appropriate for the purposes of making the gospel intelligible to first-century contemporaries was that of a cosmic battle between good and evil. This language seems to have originated in the religious traditions of Persia, represented in the first century by the Parthian Empire, stretching from India into Iran. This was a second empire alongside the Roman Empire, and the world of Hellenistic culture was divided between them. Although they were politically separate, they were nevertheless part of the same cultural sphere.

The distinctive feature of the religion of Persia, descended from the prophet Zoroaster (Zarathustra), was the notion of a cosmic battle between the forces of the benevolent divinity (Ahura Mazda) and the malevolent divinity (Angra Manya). The rich symbolic code of this tradition had already strongly influenced the emergence of apocalyptic literature in the Judaism of the Second Temple period.

In terms of the interpretation of the cross, we should note that this language offered several possibilities. One was to interpret the cross in terms of the defeat of Satan, which had the effect of releasing humanity from thrall to mortality and corruption. This became one of the favorite themes of fourth-century Christian theology, and I will have to give an account of this language later in the book. This interpretation was often based on New Testament themes dealing with the overthrow of principalities and powers through the cross. Another interpretive possibility was in the mythopoetic transformation of the struggle of this small movement against the apparently overpowering might of Rome. This seems to be what is going on in the images from the Revelation of John concerning the Lamb slain from the foundation of the world at the head of God's conquering armies. In any case, this sort of language plays a role in early Christian talk of salvation and is incorporated at certain points into what Gustav Aulén called the classical view of the atonement.[2]

However, the general utility of this language for Christian faith was limited by a number of factors. First, Christianity rejected the dualistic presuppositions of this discourse. The crisis for this interpretation came during the struggle with Marcionism in the second century, and with Manicheanism (a descendant of Zoroastrianism) in the fourth and fifth centuries—most notably in the struggles of Augustine in his turn from Manicheanism toward something like orthodox Christianity.

The proclamation of the gospel also made it difficult to sustain a belief in the continuing power of Satan and his minions. Already in the Gospel of Luke, Jesus says that he has seen Satan's fall from the heavens as a consequence of the mission of his followers (Luke 10:18). By the time of Athanasius, it was possible to say that the demons simply flee at the sign of the cross.[3] Once again, we see that Christianity was able to make use of a given discourse to render its own claims intelligible to those who found the discourse intelligible. But in the process of expropriating this discourse, Christianity robbed it of its power so that it no longer could stand on its own. In consequence, the only place we encounter dualistic language (or Satan/demon language) is in the very place where it is being robbed of its power. Thus, attempts to recuperate this language are doomed to failure and frustration.

This brief preliminary survey indicates something of the difficulty that faces us in the work of understanding the language that served to make the cross intelligible in early Christianity. Many of the ways of speaking about the cross that served to make it intelligible in the first century (and other epochs as well) serve only to make the cross seem unintelligible today.[4] This is typically a sign not of the failure but of the very success of the work of those earlier theologians who made use of available discourses in such a way as to rob them of their independent power.

As we have seen with respect to each of these discourses, Christianity borrows a language that was generally intelligible and plausible to wide sectors of the Hellenistic world. It uses this language to express the meaning of the cross. This meaning, however, so transforms the language in which it is "explained" that the language is itself overthrown. Sacrificial institutions are abolished, mystery cults are robbed of their power, and the triumph of God means that dualism is no longer plausible. When, many centuries later, we find that these languages no longer have meaning for us, this is not a sign of failure but of success. It would surely be an odd move to try to get people to believe in demons when the message of the cross itself has made such belief impossible. The same is true of sacrificial systems and other institutions and languages that Christianity both borrowed and utterly transformed.

The way forward, then, will lie not in attempting to give these now impotent forms of discourse life again, but rather in attempting to do in our time what they succeeded in doing in their time: render intelligible and persuasive the claim that the cross of Christ is the decisive turning point in the history of the earth and the decisive ground of a radically new form of existence for those who adhere to the way of the cross.[5]

However, in order to do this properly, we will not simply ignore the attempts of previous generations to give meaning to the cross, but rather seek to learn from them how this task may be prosecuted today.

The contemporary problematic

In our own day there are two major challenges to the development of an understanding of the centrality of the cross that must be taken into account in articulating a plausible interpretation. On the one hand, in the aftermath of the attempt to exterminate Judaism, and the resultant Holocaust or Shoah that took place in the center of Christianized Europe, we have to ask whether it is even possible to emphasize the cross of the Christ without becoming complicit in the ways this theme has been employed to license lethal anti-Judaism. On the other hand, contemporary feminist thought has made it imperative to reconsider traditional ways of thinking about the cross that have seemed to make it a license for an abusive God, one who employs violence and victimization as the means of salvation. Either of these considerations alone presents us with formidable challenges in reconstructing a theology of the cross, and both come to bear upon the question of whether the cross licenses violence and victimization. Accordingly, I will attend to each of these in turn.

The cross of Judaism

No responsible Christian theology can be done today without taking into account the ways in which Christian theology has been implicated in the unimaginable horrors of the methodical attempt to exterminate the covenant people of God. The Holocaust, or Shoah, in which six million Jews were exterminated, cannot be understood apart from the history of European Christian anti-Judaism. This is all the more true with respect to the theme of atonement and the cross. From fairly early on, Christian theology and popular piety have held the Jews responsible for the death of Jesus. The notorious charge that the Jews were killers of the Christ has served to license religious violence against the Jewish people. While it may be true that Martin Luther, in an especially powerful way, emphasized the theology of the cross, it is also the case that his virulent anti-Judaism—as illustrated in his infamous text entitled "The Jews and Their Lies"—was even more influential in the subsequent history of Europe. Disastrously, these two themes were connected in Luther's thought.[6] As a consequence, a Germany steeped in the legacy of Luther also became home to the most virulent form of anti-Judaism ever seen, an anti-Judaism that became a concerted attempt at the genocide of the Jewish people.

Any attempt to think about the theology of the cross today must therefore take with absolute seriousness the ways in which this theme has become complicit in the most unspeakable evil, an evil that permanently stains the history of the West and of Christianity. In the aftershock of this earthquake, Christian theologians have increasingly recognized the urgency of rethinking the whole of Christian doctrine with an eye to how it has been complicit in this evil. This reconstruction is at no point more urgent than in an attempt to rethink the significance of the cross.

One of the ways this atrocity has been made possible is by a rather simple displacement of the blame for the death of Jesus onto the Jewish people and away from the manifest agent of that death, the military rule of the Roman Empire. This is obvious from the manner of Jesus' death: he was not stoned to death as a blasphemer, as was customary among the Jews, but instead was crucified as a subverter of Roman rule. Of course, it is easy to see how this inversion could have come about. In the early days of Christianity, there was an understandable desire not to invite the wrath of Rome against a small sect whose leader had been executed by Roman authority in a way that was reserved for escaped slaves and for rebels against Roman rule (for example, the "bandits" who are crucified along with Jesus in the passion stories of Matthew and Luke). Even in the Gospels, one can detect attempts to ameliorate the implicit attack upon Roman "justice" and rule contained in a message concerning the crucified. Once Christianity seemed to succeed in allying itself with Rome, following what is called the conversion of Constantine, the political critique of the Roman Empire became largely a thing of the past. Over time, then, the cross was emptied of its concrete historical significance as an instrument of Roman torture and became simply a cipher for unjust death. And if the Romans must not be blamed, then the Jews provided a convenient scapegoat.

It is a classic case of deflection. The real culprit is too powerful, so instead of blaming him we will shift blame onto one who has no real power. Hence the recollection of the death of Jesus becomes the occasion for the promotion of a virulent attack upon the "Christ killers." As we shall see, this is but one of the ways in which traditional atonement theory has been involved in the sort of blame-shifting that makes the innocent suffer in the place of the guilty.[7]

Changing this situation will mean that a consideration of the significance of the cross must begin by taking the cross itself with more than metaphoric seriousness. This in turn means that we will have to anchor reflections on its meaning or significance in the historical reality that it evokes: the execution of the enemies of Rome, and hence the enemies of empire and of military rule.

The cross of women

One of the most important features of contemporary theology that distinguishes it from all previous eras of Christian history is the emergence of increasingly acute theological voices that bring into question the masculine domination of theological discourse. Although there have been significant women's theological voices across the centuries, never before have the voices of women theologians had such an impact on the form and content of theological construction. Slowly but surely, theology may be emerging from the shadow of patriarchal domination.

As women enter more fully into theological discussion, the insights and experiences that shape their own lives have a greater chance of being heard and honored within theological reflection. One of the ways that this has been especially important in recent years has been the question of whether traditional interpretations of the significance of the cross might be understood as portraying a theologically sanctioned form of child abuse.[8] If God the Father consigns his Son to suffer and die, then even if the Son is a willing participant in this drama, it would count as abuse. In the sad stories of such abuse, it is often the case that the victims refuse to blame their abusers, but seem almost willing to suffer, if that is what "he" wants.

Does God engineer the death of Jesus so as to actually bring his suffering about? Could this possibly be an act of love? Even if it is said that God does this in order to save others, does this not still seem to bless the violence done by the powerful (God) against one who is less powerful (in this case, the Son)?[9]

The question of the justice of God in relation to what is said about the cross has long troubled theologians. In the early developments of orthodox atonement theories, it was supposed that the incarnation of God in Jesus was a sort of trick that persuaded the devil to overstep his bounds in causing the innocent (and divine) Son to suffer and die. But those who formulated some of the versions of this so-called ransom theory of atonement also sought to clear God of the potential charge of acting unjustly toward the devil![10]

In the Middle Ages, Anselm formulated the "satisfaction" theory of atonement, in which he tried to show that it was actually in accordance with reason that God the Son should have become human in order to pay the debt owed by humanity through his own death. It is this version of the theory of atonement that is often criticized by feminist theologians. But Anselm himself was aware of the danger that his view would make a mockery of the divine justice: "For how can it be just to make the innocent suffer in place of the guilty?"[11] This same question forced Abelard, a century later than Anselm, to develop quite another view of the meaning of the cross,[12] suggesting that the limitless love of God manifest there was such as to convert humanity from violence to virtue.

The point here is not to tease out all these different ways of trying to think through the significance of the cross, but only to show that the question of divine justice has always been an acute and important question within any attempt to think through the significance of the cross.

The nub of the problem is this: Does God desire or intend the suffering and death of the Son? On the other hand, if the passion of the cross is not intended by God, how then can it be or become the divinely sanctioned means for the benefit or salvation of humankind? If it is an accident or a miscarriage of justice, then how can it have any significance whatsoever, let alone saving significance for all? Does saying that the cross has become God's way of transforming the world mean that God meant this to be the outcome all along?

These are the very sort of questions that often arise in the ordinary experience of the faithful. Something terrible happens—the sudden death of a child, for example. An instinct that one often encounters is to say that God intended this. The person who says this is often simply trying to say: This is not sheer meaninglessness and absurdity; there must be some meaning here. If, some years later, people who have experienced such a loss find that their life has been changed by the experience of grief, so that they are able to be more caring and compassionate, they may again be led to say: This was God's doing. God meant this for my good. It turned out well, and therefore it was what God had in mind all along.

To one standing outside of experience, it may seem that this is simply monstrous. It makes God into one who can do the most horrifying things (cause the death of a child, for example) in order to provide some benefit for someone else and, as a surplus benefit for himself, also get the thanks and loyalty of the person thus benefited.

However, I don't think that this is what people mean when, as they are drowning in a sea of unimaginable grief, they seize the plank of assuring themselves that God is in this somehow, that God has not lost control of the world so completely as to allow these terrible things to happen. But the price paid for this assurance is to make God both cause and agent of the terrible things that happen.

This is the structure that we also encounter in the ways of thinking about the cross. We must find a way to speak of the meaning of the cross without turning that meaning into a justification for unjust suffering.

The way forward

We have seen that there are a number of formidable challenges that await one who would seek to make the message of the cross intelligible and helpful for people today. On the one hand, many of the ways of explaining the cross to people in earlier times and cultures simply won't work for us today. The languages are themselves no longer intelligible. On the other hand, we are increasingly aware of ways in which traditional language about the cross has been implicated in the very violence and violation that are counter to the message of the divine love, grace, and generosity. It is not without reason that many people simply suppose that there is therefore nothing to be said about the matter, that we will have to make do without an intelligible, plausible, helpful, and illuminating theology of the cross.

That is not my position. I believe that the cross can be understood in ways that can illuminate and transform life in all its dimensions today—that the cross can once again become world-transforming good news. I should explain how I intend to go about finding such an interpretation of the significance of the cross.

A characteristic feature of traditional treatments of the cross in Christian theology is that these discussions tend to separate the fate of Jesus (cross and resurrection) from the mission and ministry of Jesus. One can detect in much modern theology a great divide between those who emphasize cross and resurrection (and hence atonement) and those who emphasize the words and deeds of Jesus, especially as these are represented in the Synoptic Gospels. In general, "liberal" Christians tend to emphasize the latter, while "orthodox" Christians tend to emphasize the former. It sometimes seems to come down to a division between Jesus and Paul, one of the standard clichés of modern theology.

As a result, the cross of Christ seems utterly unrelated to the mission and ministry of Jesus, while the words and deeds of Jesus seem to have no connection whatever to his fate. This is an extraordinary situation. This modern situation, however, is not without connection to the long tradition of Christian reflection on the significance of cross and atonement. Whether in the early orthodox reflections on the incarnation, death, and resurrection of the Son, or Word, as the overcoming of death and corruption (Athanasius, Gregory of Nyssa, and others), or in the medieval development of the idea of substitutionary atonement (Anselm), one notable feature of these perspectives is the way in which they largely ignore the accounts of the mission and ministry of Jesus. (Ironically, we shall also see that that they ignore the specific features of Jesus' actual death as crucifixion.)

More than a century ago, Wilhelm Wrede characterized the Gospels as passion narratives with longer or shorter introductions. Although Wrede's characterization may require revision, it remains the case that the Gospels seek to relate the ministry of Jesus to his fate at every point. I have shown in *The Insurrection of the Crucified* how this is particularly true of what is arguably the earliest Gospel, that attributed to Mark.

The close connection between Jesus' mission and ministry on the one hand, and his execution on the other, was initially emphasized in powerful ways in Latin American liberation theology, especially as it became increasingly clear that those who imitated Jesus' mission among the poor and despised were also regularly exposed to the violence of the state and its allied death squads. Thus, the fate of the one who preached good news to the poor was a daily reality in many parts of Latin America. One important document clarifying this connection was Jon Sobrino's *Christology at the Crossroads*.[13] The ground had been prepared for this connection in the theological reflections of Jürgen Moltmann, who, in his *Crucified God*, had already shown something of the connection between Jesus' fate and his mission, particularly in his discussion of the historical trial of Jesus.[14] This connection was subsequently made even more explicit through Moltmann's Christological reflections in *The Way of Jesus Christ*.[15] My own work on the theology of the cross is greatly influenced by these rediscoveries of the historic significance of the cross of Jesus.

It is therefore one of the most distinctive features of the following reflections on the significance of the cross that I will emphasize at every point the connection between the death of Jesus and his mission and ministry. It is simply not the case that an adequate understanding of the execution of Jesus can be developed that does not, at the same time, pay attention to the characteristic features of his life as reflected in the accounts of the Gospels. Indeed, what is sometimes called the "mystery of the cross" is often the consequence of severing this connection, so that the death of Christ seems to come out of nowhere. Because it seems arbitrary and unmotivated, it then becomes necessary to provide Christ's death with arcane explanations unrelated to history and experience. Perhaps it was for this reason that the Gospels were written—to anchor the death (and resurrection) of Christ in the history and experience of Jesus and those with whom he was remembered to have interacted. Without this anchoring, the death of the Messiah could become an arcane and esoteric "fact" without connection to the life and experience of those who were drawn to his message and his story.

In important respects, this incorporation of Jesus' life into the emphasis upon the significance of his death goes some way in the direction of what Bonhoeffer called a nonreligious interpretation of the most basic perceptions of Christian faith. Put another way, the problem with "religious interpretation" is that it restricts the significance of the Christ event to the narrowly religious sphere, making of it a cultic or mystic datum unconnected to the rest of life and history. This is deeply contrary, I believe, to the character of the earliest Christian testimony, which saw in the cross a message that related to the whole of human life—not a private and "interior" reality, not one that relates only to the sphere of worship and devotion, but one that reshapes human history and reality in all their dimensions.

Accordingly, we may speak of the historical reference of the cross in two related senses. On the one hand, the interpretation of the cross must be anchored in the actual fate of Jesus as this is recalled in the Gospels and in the letters of the "apostles." On the other hand, the interpretation of the cross must be related to our own history, to the wider world within which our faith must be situated and make sense.

This last point is important precisely because the message concerning the cross was never supposed to be something that could be hidden away in some sort of religious corner of our imagination and practice. Whatever the cross means, it must mean that reality has been changed. The reality that has been changed is not simply the inward one of our relation to God, or of God's relation to us, but a change in the world itself, and even in God. The cross was a public event with public significance. That is why it was so important to early theologians to make use of the various languages available to them in their own cultures in order to express its meaning and centrality. We too must seek to do this today.

But the result of recontextualizing the thinking of the cross in the way that I am suggesting is that what comes into focus more and more clearly is what might be called the theopolitical significance of the cross. As we shall see, thinking about the cross entails coming into confrontation with the principalities and powers that seek to rule the earth. In the first century, this meant Rome and its collaborators. In our time of what Hardt and Negri call Empire,[16] it means confrontation with the way in which the entire globe is subjected to the rule of avarice and violence, often blessed by the inheritors of the crucified Messiah.

Outline of the project

In the chapters that follow I will attempt to clarify several dimensions of the interpretation of the cross not only as the central reality of Christian faith, but also as an event that has in view the transformation of human reality as such. In every case I will seek to anchor these reflections in the narratives and central metaphors of early Christian thought, especially of the New Testament. In this biblical reflection, it will be important to keep attention focused on the interrelationship between the death by crucifixion of Jesus and the typical features of his mission and ministry as recalled in the Gospels. And in each case, I will indicate how the dimensions of the cross, thus opened up, entail the fundamental transformation of our world. Since this will also mean a transformation of the way in which we think about the cross, I will have to show how in each case this would mean a transformation of the way that Christian community is formed and transformed, as a community constituted by the proclamation of the cross.

In the next chapter, I will focus on what I believe to be the most basic characteristic of the cross as a public event: that Jesus was executed by authorized representatives of the Roman Empire, as a threat to the military-political rule of that empire. In many ways, this is the most obvious yet, at the same time, the most neglected aspect of the meaning of the cross, since the cross was precisely the instrument of Roman rule by terror. Only with the emergence of Latin American liberation theology does the cross's basic meaning come into focus within the history of theology. I will not contend that this is the whole meaning of the cross, but I will contend that only by beginning here will it be possible to anchor theological reflection on the cross in its historical and public reality. All other reflections on the cross will have to take their bearings from this dimension if they are not to get lost in hazy speculation and mythopoiesis. If we begin here, we will also be able to see how it is that the message concerning the cross could plausibly have the potential effect of transforming the public, and to that extent political, reality in which our contemporary lives are situated.

Jesus was executed by the executors of Roman imperial rule. What leads to this execution is the repudiation of Jesus on the part of those who understood themselves to be the authorized interpreters of God's privileging of his own people. While historically this meant that many of the leaders of the Judean people condemned Jesus and handed him over to the Roman rulers, we must be aware that the defense of religious particularity, privilege, and prerogative is an ingredient common to all religious traditions. It is not something that is peculiar to Judaism, as the long history of Christian attack upon those regarded as undermining Christian particularity and privilege amply attests. What is at stake here is the way in which the cross of Jesus is related in the Gospels to his breaking down the barriers that separated the elect people of God from the outsiders, as well as the reflections of writers like Paul on surmounting the basic religious distinction (and relative privilege before God) of Jew and gentile. But this breaking down of walls of separation extends well beyond the "religious sphere" to include the abolition of distinctions between slave and free, male and female. That the world (and the church) is structured by similar exclusions even today demonstrates that the message of the cross has yet to be taken with full seriousness, even by communities that identify themselves with the Crucified One. At the same time, the abolition of such divisions would entail a radical restructuring of our social reality.

Whether as sacrifice or as substitution, the cross of Jesus has regularly been associated, at least in Western theology, with the idea of the forgiveness of sins. Is it possible to make contemporary sense of this long-prevalent idea that is associated, as we have seen, with forms of thought that no longer have any purchase on the public world within which Christian faith must express itself? Attention to the mission and ministry of Jesus shows that he is remembered as one who was in solidarity with those who were identified as sinners. This identification includes those who are branded as outlaws by the political order and as outsiders by the structure of religious privilege. But it also includes those who in other respects are regarded as transgressors of the divine law. By living in solidarity with sinners, Jesus' ministry anticipates the fate by which, as crucified, he is made out to be sin, sin itself, separated and abandoned by God, the very form of the accursed. That the one so accursed and condemned is "without sin" means, then, that the power of the law to accuse and condemn is forever broken—"there is therefore now no condemnation" (Rom 8:1)—and the community of the Crucified is characterized by the refusal to accuse or condemn the other. That Christianity has instead become an institution characterized by accusation and condemnation of others as sinners illustrates how far that community is from demonstrating that solidarity with sinners that characterized both the ministry and the fate of Jesus.

Jesus' radical solidarity, in his ministry and in his death, with those who are the victims of structures of domination, division, and condemnation brings him also into solidarity with all who suffer. The meaning of the cross has often been related to the fate of those who suffer from these unjust systems, but also to the fate of all who suffer the encroachments of death into life. Accordingly, it is important to see how both the ministry of Jesus and his passion and death transform the situation of those whose lives are menaced by the power of death, whether in sickness and in suffering, or in the apparent final victory of death itself.

The four dimensions of the cross that we have thus considered also point us to the ways in which humanity is estranged from God. In the final chapter of part 1, therefore, I will turn to the cross as the announcement of reconciliation with God. It is essential, however, to reverse the way this reconciliation has typically been understood in Western theology. Traditionally, it has been supposed that it is God who must be reconciled, who must be brought to accept humanity. But the biblical language that we examine from the New Testament makes clear that it is humanity that is characterized by enmity and anger toward God. For God is the one who is generally supposed to be on the side of systems of domination and division, the one who condemns and afflicts with suffering and death. Those who suffer these things must be alienated from God. However, the message of the cross is that instead of being the one who visits these calamities upon humanity, God is the one who, in the mission and fate of the Messiah, is "at one" with the victims of such systems. The message "Be reconciled to God" has the concrete significance that humanity is enabled to turn toward God with confidence and trust because God is in solidarity with all who are the victims of such structures.

In part 2, I will turn to a somewhat different set of dimensions of the cross, those that deal with the ways in which the cross, or the message concerning the cross, is regarded as having specific effects in the world. Here again we will reverse our method, beginning with Paul, who emphasized the effects of the cross, and then verifying the way these effects are anticipated in the Gospel narratives concerning the mission and fate of Jesus.

New Testament language about the effect of the cross is, to an extent not generally recognized, devoted to the sort of community that is formed by those who are the adherents of the Crucified. Accordingly, I turn first to the way in which Paul and others insist that the primary effect of the cross is a transformed community or society of persons. This emphasis on the social is quite different from the traditional emphasis upon the individual who is to be crucified with Christ. But as we shall see, this language in the New Testament, especially in the works of Paul, points to the sort of persons we become as those who are fitted to participate in the community of the Crucified. That is, the corporate, rather than the individual, is the most basic form of transformed existence. Hence, I will deal first with the cruciform community, the community that is constituted as the body of the crucified Messiah. Then I will look at what is said concerning dying and rising with Christ, insofar as this deals with persons who are members of this new corporate (and thus social or political) reality.

Perhaps the most radical significance of the cross is the suggestion that the crucifixion of the Messiah, or Son of God, transforms the very character of the divine. It is precisely in an attempt to give an account of the cross as entailing an event "in" God that the Christian understanding of God as triune has been developed. In this concluding reflection, I will attend briefly to this, as well as to the modern form of asserting a radical transformation in God through the death of the Messiah, or Son of God, under the heading of the pain, the pathos—indeed, the death of God. In what way is the cross also the cross of God?

PART ONE

The Cross against the Principalities and Powers

CHAPTER TWO

Cross and Domination

I f we are to make sense of the cross in our time, we cannot begin with the traditional theories of atonement. Rather, we must begin by basing all such theories in the historical fate of Jesus, who was understood by the first Christian witnesses to be the Christ, or Messiah of God, and whose mission was to announce and enact the coming of divine rule in history. The messianic mission of Jesus comes to its apparent end in his execution at the hands of Roman imperial authorities. It is this cross, the cross of history, the cross as a public fact related to this messianic mission, that must be the basis of our reflections. This is the literal and historical significance of the cross upon which all other interpretations must be built, and which must be their constant point of reference if we are not to get lost in clouds of metaphysical, mystical, and mythic speculation. By beginning here, we will be able to understand anew the many ways in which the cross has been interpreted and may be interpreted today. That is, we begin here not in order to say that this is "all there is," but in order to anchor our subsequent interpretations firmly in the historical reality attested by the texts of the New Testament. Thus, we begin with what is, in a way, the most obvious reality of the cross, but at the same time that dimension of the cross that has most often receded from view in the history of its theological interpretation.

When Bultmann wrote his *Theology of the New Testament*,[1] he dealt with Jesus not as a first theologian, or as one whose teachings provided the first theological perspective, but as the presupposition of New Testament theology. Critical examination of the Gospels had persuaded him that about all that could be said with any certainty about the career of Jesus was reducible to the fact of his having been executed by means of crucifixion.

Bultmann did not draw the conclusion from this uncomfortable fact that the basic meaning of the cross should be sought at this level of historico-political significance. Instead, he turned to an explication of Pauline theology, which he interpreted in existential terms by focusing on its meaning for personal existence. In this way, he sought to give meaning to the cross in a context in which the realm of political or public history seemed to have disintegrated into the chaotic calamities of the first half of the twentieth century.

Only in the second half of that century did the public, political, or historical significance of the cross take center stage. This happened, above all, in the reflections of certain Latin American theologians who were confronted by the struggle of the impoverished laity in their churches against deeply unjust social, economic, and political orders that ruthlessly suppressed all dissent or movement for change, through the imposition of what was called the "national security state," and through the deployment of death squads in a type of state-sponsored terrorism (sometimes called low-intensity warfare). This was also the context within which these same people and their priests and theologians began to read the Bible, there to find testimonies to the way in which the messianic mission of Jesus among the poor and marginalized of Palestine had also been met with the brutal force of crucifixion and subsequent persecution. When this was combined with the great importance that had been placed upon the celebrations of Holy Week, often characterized by public processions of "the way of the cross" and identification with the fate of the Crucified in passion plays also enacted in public, the way was prepared for a reconfiguration in theological understanding of enormous potential. What emerged was a new manner of seeing the public significance of the historical cross in which Jesus' messianic mission culminated.[2]

In order to comprehend what a significant breakthrough in theological perception is entailed by such recognition, it may be helpful to examine two standard interpretations of the significance of the cross that seem rather bewildered about what to make of its historical reality. Athanasius in the fourth century and Anselm in the eleventh century shape the whole tradition of theological reflection on the meaning of Jesus' cross, yet, as we shall see, they seem perplexed when it comes to the actual fact of death by crucifixion.

At the beginning of his remarkable treatise "Against the Nations," which serves as a preface to *On the Incarnation*,[3] Athanasius remarks that the whole objection of the pagan world to the message of Christianity focuses on the fact of the cross: "The pagans . . . have nothing other than the cross of Christ to cite in objection," he says—even though, as he remarks, "its power has filled the world."[4]

What Athanasius sets out to demonstrate is that the cross is indeed "not the ruin but the salvation of creation" ("Against the Nations," §1, p. 5). In order to do this, he begins his reflections on the "incarnation of the Word" with what he takes to be the presupposition of the significance of the cross, namely, that God has entered fully into the human Jesus so that his death will have the result of overthrowing the power of death and conferring upon mortal humanity the blessing of immortality. The bulk of his argument comes to be focused on the incarnation of the divine Word as the fitting way for God to redeem humanity. Yet hovering in the background of this argument is still the question of the death of Jesus, and more particularly, the precise sort of death (the cross) that has been the chief objection of the pagan critics of Christianity. Ultimately he can no longer delay the force of this question and so turns to explicate why precisely it is fitting for Christ to die. This seems intelligible, if the human problem is that of mortality. By sharing this fate, the divine can transform it: "The death of all was fulfilled in the Lord's body, and also death and corruption were destroyed because of the Word who was in it" (§20, p. 185). This will get him as far as suggesting why actual bodily death was appropriate or fitting. But why this sort of death? Athanasius then seeks to demonstrate why it would not have been appropriate for this death to have been private (as opposed to publicly witnessed by all) and why it could not have been due to sickness or suicide. The closest he can bring himself to get at the precise form of death is to wrestle with the question of why death at the hands of others could not have been the less shameful death by beheading, which was the way in which citizens of Rome were executed (§24, p. 195). However, he simply cannot bring himself to comment on the actual death by crucifixion. Finally, he gives in to a purely symbolic interpretation: Jesus dies with arms outstretched in order to signify the inclusion of all, and suspended between earth and heaven in order to indicate the comprehensiveness of the significance of his death (§25, p. 195). It is an important image, but it removes the cross from the very earth that it is supposed to transform. The cross is left hanging in midair, adrift from its anchor in the specific reality of death by execution, of death by crucifixion. And there the cross will remain, suspended in midair, for much of the subsequent history of theological reflection.

In the eleventh century, when Anselm sets out to demonstrate why the "Godman" was necessary, and above all why the death of this man was necessary,[5] he barely even mentions the cross. As we saw in the introduction, the aim of his explication was to situate the death of Christ within the context of medieval notions of honor. The human has offended the honor of God and so cannot justly be saved unless the infinite debt contracted by this offense is repaid. This debt can only be repaid by one who is both God and human. And the manner of repayment is the death of one who does not deserve to die (because he has not sinned) and is also divine so that the payment is itself infinite. The nearest Anselm comes to focusing attention on the actual manner of death of the "Son" is in the following passage:

> Do you not understand that by enduring with gentle patience the injuries and insults and death on the cross with thieves—all brought on him, as we said above, by his obedience in maintaining justice—he gave an example to men, to teach them not to turn away from the justice they owe to God on account of any trials which they can experience?[6]

The cross becomes simply a sort of insult that does not prevent Jesus from acting in accordance with justice. However, there is no indication that Jesus acts in accordance with justice in any way other than by persevering in the process that will make it possible to accomplish his mission: to die for the guilty. There is, then, nothing specific to the cross (it could have been death by hanging, for example) nor any role attributed to political or military authorities (it could have been the result of mob violence, for example).

These two examples, drawn from among the most important texts in the history of atonement theology, indicate what a significant transformation is entailed by the simple recognition that any reflection on the meaning of the cross ought to begin with taking the cross itself seriously as a historical reality. But because this foundational reality of the cross of Jesus has so seldom been made the starting point of theological reflection on the significance of the cross, it will be necessary to attend to it in some exegetical detail.

The historical reality of the cross

Jesus was by no means the first—or the last—to be crucified. Indeed, crucifixion was an all-too-common fate for those who ran afoul of the Roman Empire. Those who resisted its military force were regularly crucified. This was the fate meted out to the rebel gladiators who flocked to the banner of Spartacus; it was also the fate of the citizens of Corinth who had held out against Rome's imperial ambitions. Near the hometown of Jesus' youth, scores were executed in this way in order to make clear that no rebellion would be tolerated. The cross, then, was the standard means of imperial control.[7] Like all empires, Rome ruled by what we might call "shock and awe." It did not have at its disposal an enormous military machine. The whole Roman military numbered not much more than about 400,000, and this force was not only the military force of the empire, but its engineering corps as well. Such a relatively small force, stretched from Britain and Spain to North Africa and Syria, had to be able to apply ruthless force in order to make revolt unthinkable. Ruling as it did over such a vast realm, with so many different peoples who had to be persuaded to accept the benefits of Roman rule—populations that in many cases were composed of a majority of slaves, who moreover had become slaves by being defeated by Rome—Rome had to ensure that the price of rebellion or resistance would be high indeed.

The chief means for enforcing the rule of Roman military law was the use of an especially dramatic and ferocious method of public execution: crucifixion. This was by no means the fate for just any sort of crime. Roman citizens, should they be convicted of a capital offense, could not be crucified. If they did not consent to take their own lives, they could at worst be beheaded. And non-Romans could better be pressed into the voracious maw of the slavocracy—a society built upon slavery always needed more victims. However, those who were deemed to be a threat to Rome's domination were crucified.

The point of this means of execution was prolonged torture and public humiliation for the malefactor, and a shocking display of Roman ruthlessness and awe-inspiring force for the public. After the miscreant had been stripped and publicly beaten, the naked and bleeding body was stretched out on a preconstructed cross that could be elevated so that all could see the dying agony of one who had been deprived of every vestige of human dignity. The death itself was a long-drawn-out spectacle of anguish that could last several days, until the rib cage collapsed and suffocation ensued.[8] Bodies were typically left to rot and be eaten by carrion birds.[9] In the case of an imagined or real uprising, scores, even hundreds, of crosses could be raised along the roadside. The stench and the sight would warn all who traveled of the terrible power of Roman rule.

It actually worked rather well as a deterrent. Every reader of the Gospels in the first few centuries knew perfectly well what this form of execution was like. Everyone had seen it done and would remember all too well the bodies covered only in feces, urine, blood, and flies, groaning out labored breath until they died and began to rot. No form of execution had been devised that was more humiliating, excruciating, devastating—or more effective. This is what people of the first several centuries of our era would know about crosses: not a piece of jewelry, not a brass decoration, but the grisly fate of those who were imagined to be a threat to Roman rule. And this was the fate of the one called the Messiah of God. It was precisely this fate that had to be made sense of by those who claimed him not only as Messiah but as the divine "Son."

If we are to make sense of the cross, we must begin here, where Jesus' earliest followers had to begin, by seeing the cross in terms of its function within the context of the military-political rule of the empire in one of Rome's most rebellious provinces. While our focus is on the cross of Jesus, we will not be able to understand it in isolation from the thousands of crosses that Roman rule required, for this is the context within which it was necessary for the earliest Christians to come to terms with this particular cross.

The execution of Jesus

Because of the ways in which attention is focused in the Gospels on the indecisiveness of Pilate, the meaning of Jesus' execution within a military-political context has often been obscured in subsequent interpretation. While this may have seemed a necessary strategy to mitigate somewhat the appearance of subversion on the part of Christians, the writers still leave no doubt about the cross as firmly rooted in the structure of military domination. We will first look at some of the elements in the Gospels' portrayal of the cross that make this context clear, before turning to a consideration of the ways in which Jesus' mission and ministry are depicted as anticipating, and even provoking, precisely this outcome. This will then set the stage for considering how Paul and other apostles of the cross came to terms with the character of the cross in the context of imperial structures of domination.

When Jesus is executed, he is not alone. In Matthew and Luke we are told that he is executed among bandits. Although there is an attempt in subsequent interpretation to make these companions in misery into relatively harmless "thieves," the crucifixion of mere thieves is not attested in the historical sources. They are, rather, "bandits" in the same way that we identify those who engage in guerilla tactics as bandits. It is because their activity, whether as "highwaymen" or as engaged in ambush, is regarded as a threat to the order maintained by the military occupation of the province that they are subjected to this form of execution. In Matthew, we are told that they join in reviling Jesus. That is, they resent the notoriety that is implied in the sign posted over Jesus' body: "The King of the Jews." They then seek to bring him to the same level as themselves. And that, of course, is precisely where he is. His fate is identical to theirs. In Luke, only one of the bandits curses Jesus. The other defends him. But in either case we have solidarity among bandits, either negatively ("You're no better than us") or positively ("let him alone"). At this point we are not concerned with the differentiation of these types of solidarity, only with the fact that the solidarity exists.

We should also note that Jesus himself seems to equate his fate with that of a "bandit" when he is taken captive in Gethsemane, saying in all three gospels, "Have you come out with swords and clubs to arrest me as though I were a bandit?" (Mark 14:48 NRSV and parallels). Thus, the texts make clear that Jesus is to be understood as suffering the fate of bandits, of those who are in some way rebellious against the rule of Rome.

A second and related feature of the Gospel narratives is that much is made of the substitutability of Jesus for Barabbas. Pilate offers to substitute one for the other. Here again, we are not concerned with the historicity of this proposed exchange or of the purported custom that makes it possible (the release of a captive on the Passover). Of concern here is that the fate of Jesus is identical to that of one who was an assassin in an uprising, presumably in Jerusalem itself. If tradition has converted bandits into ordinary thieves, Barabbas is a bit more difficult to hide. The relation between Jesus and Barabbas is even more striking because they share the same name or title. Barabbas means "son of the father." And there is some evidence that Jesus also regarded himself, or was regarded by others, as in some way the son (*bar*) of the father (*abba*). The symbolic name of the "terrorist" in parallel to the understanding of Jesus transmitted by the narrators makes it clear that Jesus and Barabbas belong together in some odd way.

It really doesn't matter how far we seek to distinguish the strategy of Jesus from that of Barabbas. Jesus himself does not condemn Barabbas, even if he does seem to embody a different way of confronting the imperial authorities. Instead, he dies in his place. If Jesus' death may be literally said to be a ransom for another, that other is first of all none other than Barabbas, the terrorist, the assassin.

The execution of Jesus as a military-political act of the occupying imperial power is made evident, as well, in the prominent role played by the soldiers of Rome. This role has a number of parts that, taken together, make clear that this is a military act.

In Matthew and Mark, Jesus is made sport of by the soldiers who make him a caricature of imperial authority: this is "the whole cohort."

(A cohort is composed of six centuries of about eighty men each, or 480 soldiers, including at least six centurions. This is possibly the military unit either stationed in Jerusalem or that accompanies Pilate.) He is stripped and covered with a scarlet robe, given a crown of thorns and a reed scepter, treated with mock "worship" as befits a king or emperor—then struck, spat upon, and mocked. This charade seems double-edged. On the one hand, it carries forward the charge of royal pretension. On the other hand, it burlesques the very structure of rule that the soldiers uphold. Do the soldiers in this way also give subconscious vent to their own resentment against those who wear crowns and purple?

In any case, they are depicted as carrying out the execution. They are there to guard against any attempt at forcible rescue on the part of his partisans. They cast lots for Jesus' clothes, perhaps a legendary act, but it makes clear that he has now been definitively stripped. He is naked, not decorously draped. The soldiers who guard against his followers' rescuing him from the cross are later said to be posted at his tomb. In the narrative, the care taken suggests that Jesus (and the group of adherents to his cause) is depicted as one who is a danger to military rule.

In spite of the ambivalence attributed to Pilate himself, the narratives make very clear that the execution of Jesus is an act of military rule. It is not what might be termed an ordinary act of civil or criminal justice, but an affair of the military dictatorship operating through military force.

The Gospel of John adds, or rather underlines, the supposition that Jesus is charged as rebel against the emperor: "If you free this man, you're not the emperor's friend! Every self-appointed king is in rebellion against the emperor" (19:12). And the same Gospel reports that it is Pilate who writes or has written the notice in three languages: "Jesus the Nazarene: King of the Judeans" (19:19).

The death of Jesus as depicted in the Gospels is unmistakably an episode in the rule by terror that characterized the Roman policy of occupation and domination. The bandits, the assassin, the soldiers, the proconsul—all underline the location of the cross within a specific strategy of military rule.

The policy of Jesus

How does Jesus come to meet such a fate? Is this all a terrible misunderstanding? Or have there been aspects of his mission that have ineluctably brought him into conflict with the frontline servants of empire? Although the Gospels have very different ways of depicting Jesus' mission, they all suggest that the implicit conflict between Jesus and the Roman Empire was there from the very beginning. The end only makes the conflict manifest. Whatever else may be true, Jesus came announcing the impending arrival of quite a different empire, one that was not the allegedly divine empire of Rome, but one in which God was coming to establish quite a different sort of empire: God's own rule or reign. The truly divine empire he announces will not rule by ruthless force and terror, but it will be the direct rule of the God of true justice and mercy within human history. This is not, as Luther would subsequently suppose, a kind of parallel empire that leaves the kingdom of cruelty in place while seeking only an invisible and barely detectable inner reign. The Gospels will make clear that they are contrary, indeed opposing, forms of rule. This is not, however, a rule that will be brought about by force of arms. Jesus already rejects that temptation in the desert before his mission begins (Matt 4:8-10). He declines the title "son of David," which would make him a king of the same sort as David (Mark 12:35-37; Matt 22:41-46; Luke 20:41-44). In a way, this seems to distinguish Jesus' messianic role from that of a Davidic king or military commander.[10]

Jesus is reported as saying that his kingdom is not of this world (John 18:36). But here it would appear that Jesus again distinguishes his kind of rule, or that of God, from that which is worldly; that is, from that which rules by violence or by "force" of law. At the same time, Jesus seems to deliberately court the idea that he is a menace to society, to the established social order. We see this first in the ways in which his story is told, especially by Mark.[11]

One of Mark's most elaborate and intriguing stories is the tale of Jesus and the Gadarene demoniac. This story is exceedingly complex, but the one element that was often overlooked in the past is that the demon that drives the man crazy is called "Legion." This is merely the name of the occupying army of this part of the world. It is not a byword for multiplicity, but the name of the army division that occupies all of the surrounding region of what is now called the Middle East. Such a military division would be composed of about 5,400 soldiers. Normally, only one such legion would have been stationed in the whole of "Syria." It is this division that is "cast into the sea," thereby cleansing the territory of its occupying power. In this way, Mark signals to the readers, under cover of humor and magic, the anti-imperial agenda of the Jesus movement.

Another of Mark's stories containing a latent political critique of imperial politics is the oft-repeated story of Jesus feeding the multitude. This multitude itself may be understood as a counterpart to the legion (which, as we have seen, was composed of about 5,400 soldiers) since it is said to number about 5,000, is divided into companies of 50s and 100s (like the militia of Israel), and is pointedly said to be made up of males. However, what brings this episode most clearly into the political sphere is Jesus' remark that the people are like sheep without a shepherd (Mark 6:34), a prophetic description of the people of Israel when their king and aristocracy are corrupt (Jer 27:6). Although Jesus divides the "males" into military companies (50s and 100s), he does not do this in order to assume military command. Rather, he does what leaders in the new order should do: he feeds the people rather than taxing them, bringing plenty rather than starvation. Moreover, he does not do this by way of a single-handed miracle (changing stones into bread, for example, as Satan suggested), but by having them share what little they have. It is this economy of sharing and thanksgiving, rather than the economy of exploitation and expropriation, that constitutes the new divine rule that his ministry announces and enacts.

In its Markan context, Jesus' description of the multitudes as sheep without a shepherd may contain an implicit critique of Herodian rule. The frequently recalled association between Jesus' ministry and that of John the Baptizer places Jesus in solidarity with one who was executed by Herod, who was himself a client of the Roman emperors. In Mark, the beginning of Jesus' ministry is linked to the arrest of John (1:14), and the narrative of John's execution (Mark 6:12ff.) is connected by the narrator to the sending out of Jesus' disciples into the towns of the Galilee. Luke's Gospel even has Jesus brought before Herod, who is thereby brought into alliance with Pilate (23:8-12).

We have seen that Jesus was executed among the bandits and that he was regarded as substitutable for Barabbas. However, it also appears that at least in the Gospel of Luke, Jesus' inner circle included one who belonged to the party of guerilla warfare against Roman occupation: the Zealots. Simon the Zealot is named both in Luke 6:15 and in Acts 1:13. (Mark and Matthew call him Simon the Cananaean.) One of the most remarkable features of the Jesus movement is that its inner circle included both collaborators (tax collectors) like Levi/Matthew and revolutionaries like Simon the Zealot. The presence of the latter among those of Jesus' inner circle makes clear that from early on, Jesus does not insist on a radical separation of his movement from those who were "bandits" and guerilla fighters.

To what extent is an alternative political order being prefigured in the Jesus movement? We have already seen the substitution of feeding for policies that induce starvation, as Jesus functions as the shepherd-king of the masses. Furthermore, we have detected a different sort of politics as well in the association of Levi and Simon, that is, the association of collaborators and violent opponents of the military occupation. That is a politics beyond what we might term ideology.

An even more striking image of alternative politics is contained in Jesus' saying that his followers are not to imitate the leadership style of the gentiles (that is, the Romans) who seek domination and subjugation. Rather, whoever seeks honor among them does so by becoming the menial servant of the others (Mark 10:41-44). In this way, the Jesus movement seems intent on developing a counter-politics, a counter-empire, which by its very existence is a telling critique of state and empire.

We have seen that there are indications in the mission and ministry of Jesus of a counter-imperial politics that associates itself on its own terms with others who sought the overcoming of existing political and military structures of domination. This becomes far more intense with the march on Jerusalem.

The provocation of Jesus

One of the most successful instances of exegetical legerdemain has deprived Jesus' ride into Jerusalem of its political character, in spite of all that the narrators could do to make this crystal clear. As Christianity became the religion of empire, it was important to defuse this remarkable piece of subversive street theater.

The Gospel of Mark makes clear that this is by no means a spontaneous welcome of Jesus on the part of the inhabitants of Jerusalem, but a carefully managed operation that is carried out exclusively by the mobs who come with Jesus to Jerusalem from Galilee under the direction of Jesus himself. It is Jesus, for example, who directs the search for the horse (*polos*) of Judah. In the blessing that Jacob gives to his sons in Genesis, the blessing associated with Judah is his rule or governance (Gen 49:10-11). It is said that the scepter (the sign of rule) will not depart from Judah "until he comes to whom it belongs." To this is added the detail, of which Mark's account makes a good deal, "binding his foal to the vine and his colt to the choice vine." It is precisely this colt that Jesus commandeers for his ride into Jerusalem.

In Mark it is a horse; in Matthew it is an ass or onager (Matt 21:2). In neither case is it a donkey. In Matthew, the reference is to a prophecy concerning the victorious ride of a new emperor who, unlike other emperors, associates himself with the cause of the humiliated, the poor, and so on, and so is not arrogant (Matt 21:5 = Zech 9:9). For Matthew as well, this ride indicates a counter-politics that is nonetheless a politics. In both cases it is a mount for a king. Subsequent Christian art delights in picturing Jesus riding a small donkey or burro as a sign of his apolitical stance. It is seldom asked why, if it was Jesus' intention to appear humble (in the sense of looking just like everyone else), he doesn't just walk into Jerusalem as he otherwise always does, and as all the others do? Why is he mounted? Why this "man on horseback" symbolism?

In addition to the echoes of ancient hopes for an authentic kingly rule in this depiction of Jesus riding into Jerusalem, there is also the business of the robes thrown on the ground by Jesus' followers to mark the route of his passage. This seems to be a deliberate replay of the most famous coup d'état in Israel's history (2 Kgs 9:13). The only biblical account that parallels this odd action is the coup launched under Jehu that results in a bloodbath in which the descendants of the tyrant Ahab (as well as the despised Jezebel) are massacred and the worshippers of Baal are slaughtered. All this, of course, had been set in motion by YHWH's decision, communicated first to Elijah and then passed on to Elisha, that a new king was required in Israel. But now it is Jesus, not

Jehu, who rides on the capital, surrounded not by soldiers but by the multitudes who have accompanied him from Galilee, a multitude that, moreover, sings the freedom chants borrowed from the psalms that depict the ride home of the king of the Judeans after the successful conquest of Judea's enemies.

The entire episode, then, is one that anticipates the title that will appear over the head of the executed Jesus: the king of the Judeans. That title does not appear out of nowhere or out of the ironic imagination of Pilate: it is a direct reading of what Jesus is doing in his march on Jerusalem. It is this march that dictates the terms under which he will be executed.

The act of Jesus with his understudies and the mob appears as a direct provocation that precipitates a fundamental transformation in the arrangements of power. To be sure, it seems more like a piece of street theater than like an actual coup d'état. This is because Jesus does not come at the head of a military force, but at the head of the poor and the sick and the crazy who have been given new hope and wholeness in and through his mission and ministry. And all this makes clear that even this ministry is political in character, as we have seen in the case of the feeding of the five thousand.

Once in Jerusalem, the provocations do not come to an end. Another text of obvious political import that has been depoliticized by tradition is the question addressed to Jesus in Jerusalem by the Herodians and others concerning the payment of taxes to Caesar (Mark 12:13-17 and parallels). This is an astonishing bit of theater as well. They ask the trick question, will he agree to a tax revolt and so become an obvious enemy of the state, or will he support the taxes and so lose his popular support? But Jesus has no coin. He is not one who is concerned in this matter. Nor apparently do his disciples have coins. He then asks for a coin. The Herodians have coins, coins that bear Caesar's image and inscription. Jesus acts like he has never seen one before: Whose image and likeness is this? Caesar's, of course. The reply of Jesus is devastating: Give to Caesar that which bears his image. Give to God that which bears God's image. That is, the human being belongs to God; let Caesar keep his money. Now, was that a yes or a no? Characteristically, Jesus has deprived Roman rule of its legitimacy without, however, falling into the trap of anything quite as ordinary as a simple tax revolt.

The radical political implications of this subversion of Roman authority are not missed by those who witness it, even if they are regularly
missed by subsequent imperial interpreters of these episodes. Luke will
inform the readers of that Gospel that Jesus is accused of forbidding
the people to pay taxes: "He subverts the people, forbids paying taxes,
and makes himself a king" (Luke 23:2) is the charge brought against
him. Now in a certain way, this is a misunderstanding, but not so great
a misunderstanding as that which refuses to see the political challenge
that Jesus has thrown down against Roman imperial rule.

In all the Gospels, we are told of the presence of a sword among
Jesus' followers when he is arrested as a bandit in Gethsemane. In John,
we are told it is Peter who wields the sword. (If we were in Luke, we
would expect it to be Simon the Zealot.) But where does the sword
come from? In Luke's Gospel, the disciples have swords because Jesus
told them they needed some (Luke 22:36). The disciples announce
that they have two swords. Jesus says that is enough. Enough for what?
He says it so that he will be treated "like a criminal" (22:37)—but two
swords are certainly not enough to arm an uprising. Again this appears
as a sort of street theater, but an exceedingly dangerous form of street
theater. However different the Jesus movement is from an armed uprising, it certainly courts the impression that it is like one.

If Jesus can be understood as undertaking something like a symbolic
coup against the Roman occupying forces, we may wonder why he seems
to be so docile in relation to these authorities when he is arrested and
brought to trial.[12] How is this related to the forceful challenge represented by his march on Jerusalem, or his careful association with bandits?
While this has often been interpreted in such a way as to either entirely
depoliticize the challenge that Jesus poses to imperial rule ("My kingdom is not of this world") or downplay the conflict with Rome for other
reasons, there is another explanation. Such an explanation would have to
take into account that the writers of these documents are well aware that
conflict with political power is inevitable for the followers of Jesus.

What seems to be involved here is something like a policy to prevent the Jesus movement from being simply another small-scale rebellion against imperial power that Rome knows only too well how to
crush. The aim is, on the one hand, to be plausibly mistaken for such a
movement but also, on the other hand, to be decisively different. Jesus'

surrender to the authorities and the acquiescence to his fate seem as if they served the political purpose that is at work here. That is, they serve to separate Jesus from the mob that is all too ready to engage in suicidal uprisings. Perhaps they point to a way that actually robs the empire of its legitimacy, forcing it to show its violence without oneself resorting to violence, and thus breaking the cycle of reciprocal violence.

This interpretation at least is consistent with what we are told in the narratives, namely, that Jesus concluded that this was the only way to be faithful to his own mission of inaugurating a very different rule: that of justice and mercy. This may also be what was in view in the stories of Jesus' agony in Gethsemane as he prepared himself for the excruciating and humiliating fate that was in store. And this may find expression in the references of Paul, both to the faithfulness of Jesus or Messiah (Gal 2:16; Rom 3:22, 26) and to his adherence to the way that led to the cross (Phil 2:8).

Unfortunately, this has also lent itself to much later interpretations that link the death of Jesus directly to the will of God. This is simply not possible in the Gospels, in which the activity of Jesus that heralds the in-breaking of the divine rule and demonstrates that the divine will is in every case opposed to human suffering as such.

What is at stake, then, is a strategy for overcoming a structure that causes the suffering of "many," but doing this not through inflicting suffering upon the rulers, but rather through confronting them with their own violence.

Albert Schweitzer had already seen that the willingness to be executed for the sake of the reign of God could be understood as a desperate gamble.[13] In this I think he was partially right. But the gamble was of a different order. It was to take the risk that a new political reality would emerge not from armed rebellion or a simple suicidal uprising of the masses, but from the act that exposes the violence, and so the illegitimacy, of those who hold power.

The cross against empire (Paul)

Although the perspective of Paul is often read in an entirely nonpolitical way that emphasizes the purely "spiritual" significance of his theology of the cross, this seems to be increasingly untenable. Indeed, whatever other dimensions to the significance of the cross may be brought out by Paul, and there are many of these as we shall see, they all depend upon or presuppose this historical and political reality of execution at the hands of the political and military structures of the empire.

Paul's most extended direct discussion of the significance of the cross for his message comes in the first two chapters of 1 Corinthians. Here he will maintain that he had resolved to know nothing but "Messiah, and him as crucified" and to insist that it is precisely the message concerning the execution of the Messiah that opens the way to the new relationship both to God and to one another that Paul takes to be the way of salvation.

That Jesus is crucified rather than stoned must surely point us toward the question of the legitimacy of Roman law and Roman judgment, something actually foregrounded by Paul when he writes that the "rulers of this age" crucified "the Lord of glory," as he does in 1 Corinthians 2—immediately after he has maintained that he has focused his proclamation precisely on the crucified Messiah.

It is helpful to attend a bit more closely to this text. In a situation marked by contention among factions in the Corinthian community, Paul reminds his readers that he "decided to know nothing among you except Jesus Messiah, and him crucified" (1 Cor 2:2). This assertion that Paul's "knowledge" was limited to the executed Messiah of God is what he terms his proclamation: "We proclaim Messiah crucified" (1:22). This proclamation, Paul admits, is weakness and folly by the standards of his world. That is, it appears to contradict what passes for wisdom and strength. While Paul will maintain that this proclamation is actually divine wisdom and strength, it is not of the sort that is understood or possessed by the "rulers of this age." These rulers, Paul says, "are doomed to perish" (2:6 NRSV). Oddly, commentators rarely ask themselves who the rulers of Paul's age might be. That they might be the very ones in whose name and on whose behalf the penalty of crucifixion was routinely administered by the military forces—who pledged vows of personal loyalty to none other than the emperor— seems seldom to occur to post-Constantinian readers of Paul. Centuries of attempts to depoliticize the reading of Paul have meant that even the most obvious connections get lost in a kind of mythic haze. But Paul leaves us no room for doubt about the connection when he expressly states that if the rulers of this age had possessed true, as opposed to merely human, wisdom, "they would not have crucified the Lord of glory" (2:8 NRSV). In Paul's view, moreover, the execution by crucifixion of the Messiah results in a sentence of death upon the empire: God chose what is low and despised in the world, things that are not, to reduce to nothing (or nothingness) things that are (1:28). Thus, the very instrument (the cross) by which the imperial order terrorized the world into submission becomes the instrument of its undoing.[14]

This makes possible Paul's subsequent argument, at the beginning of Romans, that subverts the claims of Roman law and judgment by demonstrating the injustice of the Roman social order that "imprisons the truth." Of course, this depiction of Roman injustice has generally been transformed into simply a list of bad behaviors, usually understood as individual vices. This is particularly true in English, where injustice (*adikia*) is translated as "wickedness." But Paul's frame of reference is made clearer when we read his indictment: "For divine wrath is revealed from heaven against all ungodliness and injustice of those who by their injustice imprison the truth" (Rom 1:18). That the truth is jailed is something that may be seen in many (imperial) social orders, but was quite sharply focused in the arrest, torture, and execution of the Messiah. Paul's indictment of Roman society will lead him to demonstrate that those who administer Roman law are, as representatives of that same social order, condemning themselves when they pass judgment on one they consider to be a criminal (2:1). His indictment then aims at disqualifying Roman "law" and Roman "justice": "They were filled with every kind of injustice: evil, covetousness, malice; full of envy, murder, strife, deceit, craftiness, they are perjurers, slanderers, God-haters, insolent, haughty, boastful . . . foolish, faithless, heartless, ruthless" (1:29-31). Paul concludes: "They know the divine decree, that those who practice this deserve to die" (1:32). The death sentence passed on Roman social (dis)order is strikingly like what Tacitus will also say a few decades later, as he writes about this same period of Roman history. "I have to present in succession the merciless biddings of a tyrant, incessant prosecutions, faithless friendships, the ruin of innocence, the same causes issuing in the same results, and I am everywhere confronted by a wearisome monotony in my subject matter" (*Annals*, bk. 4, 33). He also reports that "the force of terror had utterly extinguished the sense of human fellowship, and with the growth of cruelty, pity was cast aside" (*Annals*, bk. 6, 19).

However much Paul will seek to adapt his message concerning the cross to other dimensions of its meaning, the cogency of Paul's arguments concerning the significance of the cross depends upon the way these reflections are anchored in the historical and *political* reality of the cross itself.

The cross of the disciple

The cross of the Messiah can be emptied of its significance if it is separated off from the fate of the follower. Indeed, one of the ways that the cross of Jesus as a historical reality has come into theological focus recently has been precisely in the recognition that the fate of those who bear the brunt of military, political violence, most especially in Latin America, mirrors the fate of the Messiah. However, this was something that was already quite clear in the emergence of the Jesus movement, which took it for granted that the disciples, understudies, or followers would similarly find themselves in deadly conflict with the crushing power of the empire. Thus, the cross of Jesus did not stand alone but also anticipated and modeled the fate of the follower. In order to make this clear, we will look first at the Gospels, then at the Epistles, particularly those of Paul, and finally at the ways in which this was understood, especially in the second century when Christians, as they then began to call themselves, experienced sporadic but lethal persecution at the hands of the imperial guarantors of the social, economic, and political order.

The Gospels

The Gospels are constructed not as stories of Jesus alone but as stories of Jesus and his understudies or apprentices. What he does, they are also to do. Thus, they are commissioned to announce, heal, and cast out demons (Mark 3:14-15; 6:7, 12-13). They are included in the work of forgiving sins (Mark 2:10). In Matthew, it is made clear that this is not Jesus' deed alone (Matt 9:8). In John, as we will see in a subsequent chapter, this is made a specific commission to the understudies (John 20:20-23). Moreover, it is the freedom of the disciples with respect to the rules of the sabbath that provokes Jesus to say that the "human" is lord of the sabbath (Mark 2:23-28). In the last two instances (forgiveness of sins and lord of the sabbath), what appears is that the disciples are included in the collective "Human One"—that is, the new humanity that is taking shape in the mission of Jesus.[15]

With respect to Jesus' apparent strategy of confrontation and provocation of the imperial authorities, it is crucial to see that the political character of Jesus' cross is connected to the disciple. That is, the strategy applies not only to Jesus but to his apprentices as well. This is somewhat in keeping with Rita Nakashima Brock's insistence that the Christ is inclusive of community,[16] even though "community," as we shall see, may be the wrong way of designating this collectivity of Jesus and his understudies. We may be closer to Dorothee Soelle's emphasis on representation rather than substitution, in that the action of Jesus holds open the space for his followers/apprentices to move toward mature responsibility.[17]

This is made even clearer in the three passages that are sometimes called "passion predictions," Mark 8:31ff.; 9:31ff.; and 10:32ff. In each case, we have a depiction of the confrontation between the human and the authorities that is made explicitly into a theme also for the understudies. Indeed, as I have tried to show elsewhere,[18] the pattern of conflict that emerges is one that includes the Baptizer as well.

Let us begin with the most startling image of all.

First, Jesus says, "The Human One was destined to suffer a great deal and be rejected by the elders and the ranking priests and the scholars and be killed, and after three days rise" (Mark 8:31). It is here that we have the famous interchange with Peter, who is opposed to this strategy and gets called "Satan" for his trouble (8:33). Then Jesus clarifies and applies: "Those who want to come after me should take up their cross, and follow me" (8:34).

The image of the cross that Jesus uses here has been rendered harmless in much subsequent Christian preaching and theology, but as we have seen, the cross was not a symbol but a gruesome fate reserved for those deemed subversive of the empire. To be Jesus' understudy is to take on his strategy, and so his fate—to be prepared to die in this way "for the sake of the good news."

Thus, after the third prediction, the one that conforms most closely to that which will be narrated concerning Jesus ("The Son of Man will be handed over to the chief priests and the scribes, and they will condemn him to death; then they will hand him over to the Gentiles; they will mock him, and spit upon him, and flog him, and kill him" [Mark 10:33-34 NRSV]), James and John are told that they will drink the same cup and be baptized with the same baptism as Jesus (Mark 10:38-39): that is, they will suffer the same fate at the hands of the authorities.

Later, in his apocalyptic discourse, Jesus makes clear to his followers that they, like the "Son of Man," will be brought before councils and synagogues, before governors and so on (Mark 13:9). This is precisely what had been said in 8:31 concerning the Son of Man.

It appears, then, that Jesus has come to the view that a strategy of confrontation that may end in martyrdom is the way of God in the world that ushers in the divine reign. Thus, the fate that occurs to the prophets and to John is transposed into a basic pattern that is attributable to the in-breaking of the reign of God. Jesus seems to adopt this strategy deliberately. It is not something that will come out of the blue, but is something that will be deliberately provoked so as to turn imperial power against itself. And finally, Jesus trains understudies to adopt precisely the same strategy so that it becomes self-perpetuating beyond the death of Jesus, or the death of other leaders of the movement.

This at least is the picture that emerges from Mark and is amplified and variously modified by the other writers of narratives concerning Jesus and his understudies. It is, of course, possible that this is the product of Mark's coming to terms with the execution of Peter and Paul and then reading it back into the Jesus movement. If so, it is an exceedingly effective piece of theological invention, since it is impossible to see how the Christian movement could have survived without this understanding of martyrdom.

We thus seem to have a deliberate and provocative strategy that serves to unmask the pretensions to power of the military-political empire. It is a way, as Ched Myers suggests, of binding the strong man.[19]

The persecuted community

It is not only in the Gospels that we have inscribed the commonality between the fate of the Messiah and that of his followers. We also find in the Epistles, particularly those of Paul, a clear recognition that the fate of the community is exemplified by the fate of its leader or head.[20]

There are a number of texts where Paul presupposes the inevitability of persecution as a sharing in the fate of Jesus. In the first place, this is regularly related to the experience of Paul himself: "I will boast all the more gladly of my weaknesses, so that the power of Messiah may dwell in me. Therefore I am content with weaknesses, insults, hardships, persecutions, and calamities for the sake of Messiah" (2 Cor 12:9-10). In writing to his beloved community in Philippi, Paul (who appears to be imprisoned) writes, "I want to know Messiah and the power of his resurrection and the sharing of his sufferings by becoming like him in his death, if somehow I may obtain the resurrection from the dead" (Phil 3:10-11). Clearly, Paul supposes that to share in the resurrection of Jesus entails also sharing in the fate of his particular form of death, that is, death that comes as a consequence of the opposition of the very imperial authorities who have imprisoned Paul.

However, this is also applied to the experience of the communities that Paul has founded. Already in the first of Paul's letters, we are told that the Thessalonian believers have become imitators of the Judean congregations: "You suffered the same things from your own compatriots as they did from the Judeans, who killed both the Lord Jesus and the prophets" (1 Thess 2:14-15).[21] Apparently Paul has already told them that they are destined for persecution (3:3-4). But now their persecution at the hands of the Thessalonian authorities mirrors the fate both of the prophets and of the Messiah, as well as that which is currently experienced by their Judean companions. That the follower of Jesus is to expect to share in his death as well as his resurrection is also presupposed by Paul in Romans, where he writes, "For if we have been united with him in a death like his, we will certainly be united with him in a resurrection like his" (Rom 6:5 NRSV).

This view does not seem to be restricted to Paul. In 1 Peter, we also find an attempt to encourage a community that is suffering greatly at the hands of the dominant pagan culture (2:21-24; 3:17; 4:1, 13), by reminding them that Jesus was also humiliated and caused to suffer, and that therefore their suffering brings them into solidarity with him. In the case of this text, we are informed that the unjust suffering that they undergo may actually turn their tormentors[22] into allies, if the community is careful to make clear that the suffering has no grounds.

The care suggested by the author of this epistle to ensure that the opponents have no grounds for their opposition, however, may later be taken to be a recommendation that Christians simply accept the given sociopolitical order. This is also the fate of similar recommendations made by Paul in Romans 13:1-8, in which he seems at pains to prevent the Christian challenge to imperial order from being mistaken for something so "trivial" as a simple tax revolt. (This is something that, as we have seen, is also of concern in the Gospels.) Paul's statements here about rule coming from God have been regularly turned into a justification for obedience to any sort of rule, in spite of the fact that Paul himself situates this exhortation within the context of persecution (Rom 12:14-21).[23]

Although some early Christian writers seem to downplay the opposition between the messianic communities that are constituted through loyalty to the Messiah and the imperial order within which they are formed, the experience of persecution in the second century revives this solidarity between the fate of Jesus and that of his disciples in quite dramatic ways.

The martyrs

Although the term *martyr* refers first of all to a "witness," that is, to one who gives testimony in court, during the second century it comes increasingly to be associated with those whose public testimony or witness leads to their being sentenced to death at the hands of the imperial authorities. The attempt to understand and interpret this experience of ferocious opposition on the part of the military-imperial authorities was something that concerned both Jews and Christians in this period.[24] For Christians, this occurs by way of reflection on the commonality between the fate of Jesus and the fate of those later followers of Jesus singled out by the empire for torture and execution, precisely on account of their loyalty to their crucified leader.

The material that would be relevant to our theme from this period of the emergence of Christianity is quite large. Here, I will only point to two instances of the attempt to draw a connection between the fate of Jesus and that of the martyrs: the letters of Ignatius at the beginning of the second century, and the reflections of Irenaeus at the end of that century.

In his letter to the Ephesians, Ignatius, an early bishop of Antioch, writes as he is being transported to Rome to be executed (during the reign of the emperor Trajan, 98–117): "On hearing that I came bound from Syria for the common name and hope, trusting through your prayers to be permitted to fight with beasts at Rome, that so by martyrdom I may indeed be the disciple of Him 'who gave himself for us, an offering and sacrifice to God' [Eph 5:2]."[25] Ignatius makes a strong parallel between his own fate and that of Jesus; it is his martyrdom that makes him in truth a disciple. The common element here is not the precise manner of death (being consumed by wild beasts in the arena versus public execution through crucifixion), but rather the common agent of that death, namely, the imperial "justice." We should also note that his citation of Paul's letter to the Ephesians ("who gave himself for us, an offering and sacrifice to God") effectively transposes what might seem to be the cultic language of sacrifice into the language of political judgment. In this way, the cultic language is, as it were, demythologized. It is changed from a religious to a political and historical reality. We might even say that what Ignatius reveals is that the cultic terminology may actually only serve as a kind of code for the reality of conflict with the empire. It is precisely this fate that Ignatius can describe in a letter under the same circumstances to Roman Christians (those who are at the site of his destination): "Permit me to be an imitator of the passion of my God."[26] Ignatius is seeking to forestall any attempt on the part of Christians at Rome to rescue him from his fate as one condemned to die at the hands of the imperial authorities. He says that his only request is "that I may not be merely called a Christian but really be found to be one."[27]

In the letters of Ignatius, we find striking confirmation of the way in which identification with the fate of Jesus as the executed Messiah is understood to be not simply symbolic or cultic (and thus not merely "religious"), but rather historico-political, that is, placing the follower in the same situation of conflict with imperial policies of domination.

Nearly a century later, we find something similar in the writing of Irenaeus, whose work *Against Heresies* was composed in Lyons following a massacre of Christians there. The fate of the followers of Jesus is anchored by Irenaeus in the call of Jesus to "take up your cross and follow me." Irenaeus continues: "For these things Christ spoke openly, He being Himself the savior of those who should be delivered over to death for their confession of Him, and lose their lives."[28] That Jesus is the Savior does not mean here that he makes it unnecessary for his followers to die, but that he gives them an example of how to die: "He did not speak of any other cross, but of the suffering which he should undergo first and his disciples afterward."[29] It is quite evident that the execution of Jesus is the pattern for his disciples. To say that Jesus dies "for us" is to say that he dies in order to demonstrate how to die. In this respect he can refer to Stephen, the first "martyr" who dies, as Irenaeus says, "copying in every respect the Leader of martyrdom."[30]

One of the features common to Ignatius and Ireneaus is the insistence on the real suffering and death of Jesus, over against those who found such a fate to be unseemly for one who is held to be not only the Messiah, but the Son of God. Ignatius, for example, writes: "But if as some without God, that is, the unbelieving, say that he only seemed to suffer . . . then why am I in bonds? Why do I long to be exposed to the wild beasts? Do I therefore die in vain? Am I then not guilty of falsehood against the [cross of] the Lord?"[31] And in a similar vein, Irenaeus writes: "For if He did not truly suffer, no thanks to Him, since there was no suffering at all; and when we shall actually begin to suffer, He will seem as leading us astray, exhorting us to endure buffeting and to turn the other cheek, if He did not Himself before us in reality suffer the same."[32] Thus, there is a close connection between insisting on the actual suffering and death of Jesus and that to which the followers are also exposed at the hands of the same imperial authorities.[33]

This confirms Dorothee Soelle's understanding of the role of Christ as the representative, as opposed to the substitute. Jesus does not replace us in these perspectives, but rather dies in a way that is exemplary of our own conflict with structures of domination. He represents us rather than substitutes for us. And this further indicates why "substitutionary theories of atonement" may be fundamentally misleading when they focus upon the cross of Jesus to the exclusion of the cross of the follower. Even when the urgency of a reflection on martyrdom begins to fade as certain forms of Christianity find favor with imperial authorities, Athanasius will still be able to use the fearlessness of men, women, and children in the face of death as proof of the efficacy of the cross of Jesus.[34] But already, in what will come to call itself orthodox or catholic Christianity, Christianity no longer finds itself in opposition to imperial policy, but becomes the religious legitimation of that policy, and so martyrdom will recede in favor of something more like mortification of the flesh (the need for food, drink, society, and even sex[35]) as a form of alleged solidarity with the Crucified. In a subsequent chapter, on dying with Christ, we will have to see to what extent, if any, such an interpretation of the cross is warranted. For this interpretation of the cross to become dominant, however, it will be necessary for the cross itself to be emptied of specific historical meaning, and it is to the beginning of that process that we will next attend.

(De)coding the cross (patristic perspectives)

We saw at the beginning of this chapter that the historical and concrete meaning of the cross had already begun to recede from understanding by the time of Athanasius, whose difficulty in identifying the specific features of death by crucifixion is symptomatic of what would follow in the Christian tradition. One of the ways this was made possible was through a process of what might be termed a cosmic "encoding" of the cross. The cross of Jesus was transposed into the scale of a cosmic event whose relation to political reality would become less and less apparent over time. Accordingly, we should attend to some of the features of this encoding, for this helps to understand the loss of a political meaning for the cross, while at the same time permitting a subsequent decoding that will help to verify the truth of the original political meaning of the cross.

We noted in our reading of Paul's language in 1 Corinthians 2 concerning the "rulers of this age" that subsequent readers have engaged in a mythologizing of these references to make them refer not to the

actual rulers of the Roman Empire, but to rather vaguely imagined cosmic powers. This "mythologizing" of such references is carried forward
in some New Testament texts and continues into the patristic period.
At the same time, we will see that even when transposed onto the level
of cosmic powers, there remains a strong sense in which the political
undertones allow themselves to be heard, even in this register or "key."

In Colossians, the writer (who may or may not be the same Paul
as the writer of 1 Corinthians and Romans) writes: "[Christ] disarmed
the principalities and powers and made a public example of them, tri-
umphing over them in [the cross]" (Col 2:15). While "principalities and
powers" may be read as referring to cosmic rather than political powers,
this is also a rather clear reference to the very strategy that we have
seen referred to in relation to the cross of Jesus, namely, that it turns the
tables on those who enforce Roman law, and so makes a public spectacle of those who sought to make a public spectacle of Jesus, so that
their violence and illegitimacy are exposed in the cross. One could even
say that the apparent cosmic reference is but a more or less transparent
coding of the political reality, a coding that may have enabled the letter
to survive scrutiny by imperial agents.

Certainly, scholars have long since recognized such a strategy in the
Apocalypse of John, where references to the beast, the whore of Babylon, and so on, are rather transparent codings of the imperial power and
its agents, just as the "Lamb that was slain" appears to be a coding of
the cross of Jesus.

In Ephesians, this process of coding may appear to break loose from
its historical moorings: "For we are not contending with flesh and blood
. . . but principalities and powers, against world rulers of the present
darkness" (Eph 6:12). Again, however, it is by no means necessary to
remove the historical reference, since one could just as easily suppose
that our struggle is not against individual men ("flesh and blood"),
in which case one might simply hope for a new and better emperor,
but against the entire structure of the political or imperial world (the
"world rulers of the present darkness").

If we move forward to the time that Christianity (or its soon-to-be
dominant form) is beginning to find itself a home within the imperial
order, then we discover that the political reference of the cross becomes
less direct. We have already seen how Athanasius has some difficulty in

writing about the historical significance of the cross. What he does do, however, is transpose this into a kind of allegory that will continue to be important in attempts to understand the significance of Jesus' cross. Thus, he writes in explanation of the fittingness of God (the Word) intervening in history through the incarnation: "For if a king has constructed a house or a city and brigands attack it through the negligence of its inhabitants, he in no wise abandons it but avenges and rescues it as his own work, having regard not for the negligence of its inhabitants but for his own honor."[36] Still later he writes: "Furthermore a king—who is a man—does not permit the realms which he has founded to be handed over and become subject to others and escape from his power, but reminds them with letters, . . . and if there be need he himself goes to them to win them over by his presence, only lest they become subject to others and his work be in vain."[37] What is significant here is that the dominant allegory or metaphor remains political and historical: the coming of the true king to overthrow the rule of the interloper.

In the case of Gregory of Nyssa a generation later, this allegory is both more "cosmic" (in reference to Satan) and more pointed: "In consequence that angelic power, which had been given the governance of the earth, took it amiss as something insufferable that, out of the nature subject to him, there should be produced a being to resemble the transcendent dignity."[38] The act of God, then, is to recover the humanity imprisoned by this arrogant and deceptive power. This happens through getting that evil power to overstep its bounds by attacking (consuming) the divine Word/Son, and so being forced to disgorge imprisoned humanity. In the development of this analogy, Gregory is concerned to demonstrate that it all happens in accordance with justice, that God does not act with violence toward the evil power, but rather simply brings that power to demonstrate its true injustice: the divine justice then is manifest "in His not exercising an arbitrary authority over him who held us in bondage."[39] God thus contrives "a just and not a dictatorial method" to redeem humanity.[40] This "just method" functions to overpower that evil power.[41] Thus, there remains the image of an imperial figure who rules humanity unjustly by force, and in contrast, the divine strategy that wins by apparent weakness and persuasion (and so justice).

Even though these interpretations of the cross might be understood as an evasion of the concrete, and thus political, reality of the cross of Jesus, I believe that they may also be understood as pointing toward an extrapolation from that concrete reality, an extrapolation that, however much it may have evaded the historical cross, nevertheless bears within it the dangerous memory of that historical reality and transposes it onto the wider canvas of cosmic reality. They suggest to the reader that these imperial forces are but the visible expressions of a sort of cosmic force or structure. Thus, it is not simply a question of this or that emperor, but rather of the character of human rule as such. It is not a matter of changing emperors, nor even of changing empires. For even with a change in empire, the same structures of domination and division, of avarice and violence, still prevail, as the sad history of Israel with the imperial orders of Egypt, Assyria, Babylon, Persia, Greece, and Rome would testify. In this sense, it is not a question of "flesh and blood," of these individuals or those nations, but of what seems to be the basic form and forces that govern human history.

For many people of the first century, there would be an inherent plausibility in naming these basic structures as elemental structures of the cosmos, and in some cases, personalizing these forces as demonic or Satanic power. If this way of generalizing the basic forces of domination and division no longer has a hold on the imagination of many of those who inhabit our world of science and technology, this need not alienate us from what seems to have been the central concern of these writers: to point beyond the particular features of this or that emperor, this or that empire, to designate what seems to be the way of domination and division as such.

Thus, the transformation that is heralded in the proclamation concerning the cross is not the passing of a particular emperor (Caligula or Nero, for example), nor the passing away of the Roman Empire. Rather, it is the uprooting of the whole structure of domination and division, and its replacement by a completely new kind of sociality grounded in openness to the other, in welcome without reserve, in generosity, and so in justice that brings peace and joy to the whole of creation.

Even if this "encoding" of the cross begins to create a forgetfulness of the dangerous memory of the execution of Jesus, it is nevertheless the case that for several centuries, the recollection of the cross seems to have had what might be termed political "effects" in the way in which Christians understood themselves with regard to the basic institutions of the empire.

We have already seen that the implicit conflict between the gospel and the empire could come to a head in the experience of martyrdom. But there were also other "effects" that need to be noted.

When discussing the effects of the cross as evidence of the truth of Christian proclamation, Athanasius not only notes the readiness of the martyrs to die, but also points to the cessation of violence and wars wherever people respond to the Christian gospel. In "On the Incarnation," he notes that in the time of idolatry, "Greeks and Barbarians used to war against each other." The world before the coming of the cross was one of constant warfare fueled, he supposes, by superstition. Yet when they are converted to the gospel, "they put from them the savagery of murder and no longer have thoughts of war, but all their thoughts are henceforth of peace and the desire for amity."[42] This limitation of violence has at least two implications for Christians of this period. One is that Christians were generally prohibited from participation in the use of military force. Thus, for several centuries, Christians were prohibited from joining the Roman Legion. This of course made sense so long as it could be recalled, however vaguely, that the legion had crucified Jesus. What is even more remarkable is that Christians were also prohibited from participating in the legal institutions of the empire. Lactantius, in the *Divine Institutes* (6.20), writes:

> For when God forbids us to kill, He not only prohibits us from open violence, which is not even allowed by the public laws, but He warns us against the commission of those things which are esteemed lawful among men. Thus it will be neither lawful for a just man to engage in warfare, since his warfare is justice itself, nor to accuse any one of a capital charge, because it makes no difference whether you put a man to death by word, or rather by the sword, since it is the act of putting to death itself which is prohibited. Therefore, with regard to this precept of God, there ought to be no exception at all; but that it is always unlawful to put to death a man, whom God willed to be a sacred animal.[43]

Even as the cross seemed to be abstracted from the historical reality within which it occurred, it is remarkable that Christians retained for so long the strong sense that they could not be a party to the violence of the imperial political institutions (even if the specific connection to the cross could be lost, as here in Lactantius, where what is at stake is an understanding of the prohibition of murder). This would be forgotten for many centuries as Christianity came more and more to associate itself with the successors of Constantine and to honor the cross upon his flag rather than the one who had been crucified "under Pontius Pilate." Only with the radical Reformation of the sixteenth century do many Christians seem to become aware again of the political meaning of the cross that had been so effectively hidden when it had been coded into the scale of cosmic (rather than) political confrontation. And this "decoding" gathers a certain momentum in the latter part of the twentieth century.

The cross against the violence of domination today

As we have seen, it is in the context first of Latin American theology, then of multiple struggles of Christian peoples against various forms of violent domination, that the historical and political significance of the cross rises out of the Christian unconscious to become again more fully conscious. What does it mean today to again take seriously the historical cross of Jesus as the turning point in human history?

Here we may notice a supreme irony, that the followers of a messiah executed by the minions of military rule and imperial hegemony are often today, at least in the United States, found to be staunch advocates of the death penalty, of the militarization of our involvements with other nations, of preemptive military invasion of other countries, and of a policy of American hegemony.[44] Only a complete subversion of the gospel could explain such a thoroughgoing inversion of evangelical values. When this happens, then, the cross must somehow have been rendered "safe," transposed into mythology, or sentimentalized— or even become the sign of conquest.

That Christendom has betrayed the cross is obvious. But does that mean that its meaning has been utterly lost? One of the things I have learned from Thomas J. J. Altizer is that the movement of God into the world cannot be stopped, even by the church. If there is to be a future for humanity, it will be a future of the cross, of nonviolent confrontation that aims to win over the whole earth to the way of nonviolence, to the way of the abolition of force.

Now let us suppose for a moment that the cross had not been hijacked. What would it mean that a movement of militant nonviolence is launched that renounces force yet topples the legitimacy of military-political rule? What would history be like if this movement had held to the basic and most obvious reality signified by the cross as the military-political execution of the Messiah of God?[45]

Had Christianity retained clarity at this point, the horrifying distortion of the cross into the emblem of anti-Semitic and anti-Jewish rhetoric would not have been made possible. It would have been clear that Jesus is executed by the military and imperial powers of the nations (gentiles), of which at most it could be said that the religio-political leaders of Judea were collaborators. And this would have signaled that it is exceedingly dangerous for those who call themselves Christians to similarly collaborate with these same sorts of forces and powers, for then it is also clear that we become those who collaborate in the death of Christ.

It is precisely when the cross is stripped of its relation to concrete human history that anti-Semitism becomes possible. And those who today continue to promulgate a "satisfaction" theory of atonement must beware of the latent anti-Semitism that lurks behind such formulations.

Since Augustine reluctantly concluded that it was necessary to accept the military support of the empire to respond to the Donatists in North Africa, Christianity has found itself ensnared in alliances with military powers of force and domination. Indeed, this force has often been most ruthlessly deployed against other Christians, from the Donatists, to the crusades against the Cathari and Waldenensians, to the early modern wars of religion and the flagrant persecution of the Anabaptists. Even more recent history in Northern Ireland and the Balkans presents us with the same ghastly picture: in the name of one who was executed by political and military violence, limitless violence is unleashed, even upon fellow Christians.

Clarity concerning the historical reality of the cross would entail a Christian renunciation of violence, including the alliance with state-sponsored military force. As Erasmus already realized,[46] it should be impossible for Christians to take up the sword, to resort to military force. In this respect the historic peace churches are surely far closer to the truth of the cross than are the dominant forms of Christianity.

But the historical reality of the cross does not simply suggest pacifism as the most appropriate stance. For the cross is not simply the consequence of a refusal to engage in violence, a theme strongly emphasized by Matthew's Gospel, but it also represents the culmination of a deliberate strategy of resistance to, and indeed provocation of, those who wield the force of empire. One of the most suggestive ideas of Jacques Derrida is of a historical "process of Christianization which seems to have no more need for the Christian church."[47] In this he was speaking of a process whereby nations confess their crimes against humanity and, by extension, the very emergence of the idea of crimes against humanity that are regarded as if they were crimes against "God-become-man."[48]

What may be even more impressive historically in this regard, however, is the proliferation of movements that seek liberation or emancipation from structures of political domination through nonviolent militancy. In the twentieth century, this took initial form in the struggle by Gandhi, first in South Africa and then in his native India, a struggle in part inspired by Tolstoy's interpretation of the gospel. The effect of such a struggle was to expose the illegitimacy of imperial power and colonial rule by provoking these forces into displays of violence that unmasked their true character.

In the United States, the civil rights movement, under the leadership of Martin Luther King Jr. and many others, similarly laid bare the unjust violence of structures of racial domination in ways that stripped them of any cover of legitimacy, and so resulted in considerable strides toward freeing our polity of the stain of official or legal racism. These same strategies took hold as many nations sought deliverance from Soviet hegemony during the time of the collapse of the Soviet Union, a collapse that was indeed brought about by the militant nonviolence of people in Poland, East Germany, Czechoslovakia, Romania, and so on. To be sure, not all such movements succeed, at least in the near term.

For a variety of reasons, similar earlier attempts in Hungary (1956) and in Czechoslovakia's "Prague Spring" (1968), as well as the later nonviolent resistance in Tiananmen Square (1989), did not produce immediate transformations in the social orders within which they took place. And today's struggles against the most pernicious forms of what is called globalization, as well as global protests against America's pre-emptive war strategy, have not yet succeeded in their aims. What is impressive, however, is the demonstration in this last century of the efficacy, however limited, of the very strategy of nonviolent provoca-tion that in the first century was seen by early Christians as inaugurat-ing the collapse of Roman imperial might (the rulers of this age) and the coming of the divine reign of justice and mercy.

It is as if we were witnessing a more or less secular unveiling of the historical significance of the execution of the Messiah of God, an unveiling that is demonstrating the power of this reality of the cross to utterly transform human history. While many, both inside and outside the church, may regard this way as folly and weakness, it may be show-ing itself to be the way in which the reality of the cross can remake the very conditions of human history. After lying dormant for more than a millennium and a half, the message concerning the cross may yet be disclosing itself as the power and wisdom of God that overthrows the rulers of this age.

In the meantime, movements to abolish torture and assure bodily integrity as a basic human right, movements to end the death penalty, to resist war as a means of resolving disputes between nations or other groups, to oppose violence in all its forms, even when these are or seem to be entirely secular movements, may be understood to be the histori-cal effects of the message concerning the cross.

In this connection it is also important to emphasize that this does not mean that Jesus "had to die." Even at the end of Jesus' path, there are glimpses of another possible outcome. Jesus' executioner, the centurion—who was bound by an oath of personal loyalty to the emperor—is the first to call Jesus "Son of God" and serves with Joseph of Arimathea—a member of the same circle of Judean leaders that had denounced him—as the witness to his death before Pilate. What these glimpses foreshadow is that the human beings who are in the service of the structures of domination, indeed, the enforcers of these structures, may be persuaded by the way of nonviolent militancy to abandon their role and to become instead agents of a new order of persuasion rather than force, of justice and mercy rather than violence and ruthlessness; or as Paul says, those who were formerly "instruments of injustice" might become "instruments of justice" (Rom 6:13), something that in his own way Paul himself knew something about. If the way of Jesus is truly the way of God in the world, then the logic of violence and domination may be overcome in history by the message and lifestyle of justice and mercy. It is only if the logic of violence does not renounce its own force that the cross becomes the inevitable outcome of the way of justice and mercy. But even then, that outcome is overturned by the resurrection from the dead, which demonstrates that God wills not death but life, true life, life delivered from the threat and power of death.

CHAPTER THREE

The Cross and Division

The cross as the event that strips the powers of domination and violence of their pretended legitimacy, and demonstrates the unequivocal solidarity of God with the oppressed and the humiliated, is the most obvious, but also the most often obscured, meaning of the cross of Christ. The literal significance of the cross as an event in political or public history leads us to stress this dimension of the cross as the basis of all others. Without the historico-political cross of Jesus, there can be no talk of its wider or symbolic significance.

However, the cross as God's identification with the oppressed, and so the overcoming in principle of the powers of oppression, by no means exhausts the significance of the cross of Jesus. Just as Jesus is executed by the Roman imperial power, so also his death is the consequence of his being handed over to this power by the guardians of Israel's exclusive identity and relationship with God. This lies at the foundation of the Christian assertion of the cross as an instrument of reconciliation, as the event that overcomes the separation between Jew and gentile, and so makes universal the announcement of the gospel.

In this chapter I will focus on the cross as the event of reconciliation in the sense of overcoming structures of division.[1] Here again we are concerned to show in what way the cross of Jesus may be understood as the pivotal event or turning point in planetary history. We are not concerned here with myth but with history. This means that we will have to see how the cross of Jesus functions to break down divisions between persons and groups, and how this event of the cross thus understood is really based in the ministry and mission of Jesus.

We may first remind ourselves of some of the ways this dimension of the cross of Jesus is expressed in the New Testament. There are a number of summary assertions of the reconciling effect of the cross. In 2 Corinthians, Paul writes, "God was in Christ reconciling the world to Godself" (2 Cor 5:19). In Ephesians, written if not by Paul then by one of his associates, we are told that it was God's plan "to gather up all things in him, things in heaven and things on earth" (Eph 1:10 NRSV). This is echoed in Colossians, where the connection to the cross is made quite explicit: "Through [Messiah] God was pleased to reconcile to Godself all things whether in earth or in heaven by making peace through the blood of his cross" (Col 1:20).

These assertions are comprehensive; they emphasize that the reconciling effect of the cross is absolutely universal. But we may wonder: what is the basis for this sort of assertion? Does it have any historical meaning that we can grasp in nonmythological language? What actual divisions between persons or communities are overcome or reconciled through the cross?

The reconciling function of the cross comes to more concrete expression in the assertion of the overcoming of specific forms of division: "There is neither Jew nor Greek, there is neither slave nor free, there is neither male nor female, for you are all one in Christ Jesus" (Gal 3:28). And in a similar statement from Colossians that seems to extend the specific divisions that are to be overcome: "Here there cannot be Greek or Jew, circumcised and uncircumcised, barbarian, Sythian, slave or free; but Christ is all in all" (Col 3:11).[2] These programmatic assertions signal the direction of the overcoming of specific divisions, of concrete barriers between persons. We will have to return to these statements to see how they indicate the dramatic effects that are attributed to the cross of Jesus. In the meantime, we may still wonder how this function is related to the historical cross of Jesus.

Perhaps the most decisive statement of this theme, and one that also links it unequivocally to the cross of Jesus, is to be found in Ephesians:

Therefore remember that at one time you Gentiles in the flesh, called the uncircumcision by what is called the circumcision, which is made in the flesh by hands—remember that you were at that time separated from Christ, alienated from the commonwealth of Israel, and strangers to the covenants of promise, having no hope and without God in the world. But now in Christ Jesus you who once were far off have been brought near in the blood of Christ. For he is our peace, who has made us both one, and has broken down the dividing wall of hostility, by abolishing in his flesh the law of commandments and ordinances, that he might create in himself one new humanity in place of the two, so making peace, and might reconcile us both to God in one body through the cross, thereby bringing the hostility to an end. And he came and preached peace to you who were far off and peace to those who were near; for through him we both have access in one spirit to the Father. So then you are no longer strangers and sojourners (aliens and refugees), but you are *fellow citizens* with the saints and members of the household of God, built upon the foundation of the apostles and the prophets, Christ Jesus himself being the cornerstone, in whom the whole structure is joined together and grows into a holy temple in the Lord; in whom you are also built into it for a dwelling place of God in the Spirit. (Eph 2:11-22; emphasis added)

This passage, which serves as a kind of summary of important aspects of Paul's thought (even if it was not written by Paul himself), affirms that the cross of Jesus serves to abolish the separation, and so the hostility, between Jew and gentile, between the near and the far off, between the circumcision and the uncircumcision. It does this by way of seeking to include the gentile or pagan into the covenant of God from which the gentile had previously been excluded. It is the breaking down of this barrier, I will suggest, that is the model for the breaking down of other forms of division, and that in turn leads to the acclamation of Jesus as the one who abolishes all forms of division and so reconciles the world to God.

Thus, in order to understand the comprehensive character of reconciliation, it is necessary to begin with the overcoming of the division between Jew and pagan, between insider and outsider. And we must ask how this barrier is broken, or is seen to be broken, in the cross of Jesus.

The basic issue that is in focus here is what we might call an ideological privilege of one group relative to another. Asserting a kind of ideological privilege serves, then, to set up structures of division and exclusion. In Israel, this takes the form of identifying one people as the sole chosen people of God, and thus as being uniquely favored by God. The signs of this special relationship were the sabbath, circumcision, and the law in general. These all had the function of making Israel a distinctive people who, as such, were the unique and exclusive recipients of the divine promise. This makes of the nations or peoples of the earth (the "gentiles") a category of outsiders, of those who are not similarly included in the divine history, the divine promise and blessing. Thus, the ideological or, in this case, religious privilege of one group results in the division between it and the "others" who are then, in principle, excluded from the same privilege or "blessing."

Before proceeding further, it is well to remind ourselves that the claim to be the specially chosen of God, the special people of God, is a fundamental dynamic of human history. It is at the heart of tribalism and nationalism. It is well known to us in the form of patriotism, in the name of which the nations of Europe entered into the First World War confident that God was on their side—Germans and French, Italians and English alike. The role of this sense of being God's special people is also well known in the life of the American people, who are all too happy to understand themselves as having a certain manifest destiny, or as being the "indispensable" or even the "exceptional" nation. But for the history of the West, the election of Israel serves as the exemplary case of this sense of being the people uniquely and thus exclusively favored by God. Most other subsequent structures of division and exclusion come to be modeled upon an expropriation of the specific features of Israel's exclusive election.[3]

Here our issue is how it happens that, in Jesus, this ideological privilege is overcome in such a way as to abolish the dividing wall between Jew and gentile and thus the exclusion of the nations from the promise and blessing of God.

The practice of Jesus

The narrative texts of the New Testament present us with a wealth of data concerning the way in which the mission and ministry of Jesus were recalled as abolishing this ideological privilege. However, what Jesus does and says in this connection is not without precedent in the self-understanding of Israel. The prophets regularly reminded Israel that God was free in relation to the covenant. This is, for example, the significance of Isaiah's assertion that the temple of God should be a house of prayer for all nations (Isa 56:3-7). As well, the prophet Amos shatters the security of being the chosen people of God through his oracles of judgment on the nations, culminating with the judgment of Israel (Amos 1:3—2:16). In the New Testament, this prophetic tradition is first carried forward by John the Baptist, who is recalled as saying: "And do not presume to say to yourselves, 'We have Abraham for our father'; for I tell you, God is able from these stones to raise up children to Abraham" (Matt 3:9).

Clearly, there is precedent within the traditions of Israel for contesting the exclusive character of Israel's privilege. Yet this universalizing perspective remained a distinctly minority voice, seldom succeeding in rupturing the protective seal of exclusive religious and ethnic privilege.[4] In the mission and ministry of Jesus of Nazareth as recalled by the Gospels, this minority tradition finds dramatic expression.

In the Gospel of Luke, this is foreshadowed in the genealogy of Jesus that goes back not only to David but beyond him to Abraham, the father of many nations, and even further to "Adam, the son of God" (Luke 3:23-38). In this way, the identity of Jesus and the scope of his mission are universal from the beginning.

The decisive inauguration of Jesus' mission and ministry, as we recall, occurs, according to Luke, when Jesus returns from his sojourn in the wilderness to deliver a kind of inaugural address in Nazareth. He quotes the passage from Isaiah: "The Spirit of the Lord is upon me, because he has anointed me to bring good news to the poor" (Luke 4:18 NRSV).

This text, together with Jesus' assertion, "Today this scripture has been fulfilled in your hearing" (Luke 4:21 NRSV), is rightly understood as outlining Jesus' messianic program, with the sociopolitical overtones that accompany this mission. The initial reaction of his hearers is positive. This changes, however, when Jesus recalls the example of Elijah and Elisha, whose mission was to the "outsider":

> There were many widows in Israel in the days of Elijah, when the heaven was shut up three years and six months, when there was great famine over all the land; and Elijah was sent to none of them but only to Zar'ephath, to the land of Sidon [Lebanon] to a woman who was a widow. And there were many lepers in Israel in the time of the prophet Elisha; and none of them was cleansed but only Na'aman the Syrian (Luke 4:25-27)

These words undercut the ideological privilege of Israel as the sphere of the messianic activity of God's Chosen One. Hence the text continues: "When they heard this, all in the synagogue were filled with wrath. And they rose up and put him out of the city, and they led him to the brow of the hill on which their city was built, that they might throw him down headlong" (4:28-29).

In this story, which begins Luke's account of Jesus' public mission, we have the sociopolitical identification of the messianic mission with the oppressed and captive, as well as the divine solidarity with those who are outside the sphere of election. It is this last that is represented as the cause of the opposition of the townspeople, and therefore as generating a prefiguring of the execution of Jesus: "put him out of the city . . . to the brow of the hill" (Luke 4:29). This theme is carried forward in Luke with the story (found also in Matthew) of the healing of the centurion's "beloved slave." The story recalls Jesus' words: "I tell you not even in Israel have I found such faith" (7:1-10).

In the Gospel of Matthew, this story, like many in Matthew, has a more violent character.[5] There, the saying of Jesus continues: "I tell you, many will come from east and west and sit at table with Abraham, Isaac and Jacob, while the sons of the kingdom will be thrown into the outer darkness; there men will weep and gnash their teeth" (Matt 8:11-12). This teaching of Jesus points to the gathering of the gentiles with the patriarchs, while those who are the literal descendants of the patriarchs, "the sons of the kingdom," will be left out.

The response of the "outsiders" to Jesus is also the specific theme of Matthew's version of the birth of Jesus. Those who come to do honor to Jesus are the so-called wise men, actually Persian or Parthian wizards who also functioned as advisors to the Parthian Empire (centered in present-day Iran), at that time the main rival to the Roman Empire, and notorious as those who worshipped gods other than the God of Israel.[6] They were the ideological opposites of Israel and its ruling elite. But in Matthew's Gospel, it is they who do homage to Jesus, while the titular representative of Israel (Herod) seeks his death. Thus, in the story of Jesus' birth, Matthew prepares the reader for the overthrow of religious and ideological privilege.

In Mark (and so also in Matthew and Luke to the extent to which they follow Mark's outline), the ministry of Jesus is depicted as having a double character: a mission to the house of Israel and a mission to the gentile areas of Jordan, Lebanon, and Syria. This double character is represented at regular intervals by Jesus' crossing of the Sea of Galilee. This is why, for example, we have two feedings of the multitudes—one for each side of the sea.

In Mark, Jesus' mission to the gentiles is represented with special drama in the exorcism of the Gadarene demoniac (Mark 5:1-20). The spectacular features of this story, including the name of the demon (Legion, a specifically Roman military institution) and the pig herders' dilemma, attest to the pagan features of the setting.[7] And for the first time, Jesus permits the one who is healed to launch an independent mission among his own people—that is, among the gentiles.

Another story with a similar theme, and one that has caused nightmares to many a preacher when it comes up in the lectionary cycle, is the story of the Syrophoenician woman, that is, the woman whom Jesus encounters when he is on retreat in Lebanon. In Mark she is identified as a Greek (7:24-29); in Matthew she is identified as a Canaanite (15:21-28). In both cases, her initial request for help is rejected by Jesus, who claims that he is sent only to the people of Israel, and she is dismissed as a "dog," a term of contempt sometimes used for those who engage in cultic "prostitution" in pagan temples. In both cases, the woman turns the tables on Jesus with a phrase about even dogs eating the children's crumbs—and in each case, she is given her wish.

It seems an odd and disturbing story until we place it in the context of the question of the exclusive privilege of Israel. Viewed in this way, the story enables us to see a debate within early Christianity—a debate that we encounter also in Paul's letter to the Galatians. There were those who quoted the remembered words and/or deeds of Jesus to insist on the priority of Israel and to attempt to disqualify or severely limit the gentile mission. But we are also confronted with the inescapable fact of gentile adherence to Jesus—of pagan faith. In this case, the conservative proponents of a version of the Jesus tradition simply must give way before the facts, as Jesus also does here in an exemplary fashion.

The "conservatives" who refuse to go beyond the scope of Jesus' original mission may be literally right. Jesus may have at some point said that his mission was only to the lost sheep of Israel—that is, to the Jews of the Diaspora. Indeed, there is other evidence that he was remembered as having made this restriction. In the Gospel of Luke, the disciples speak to the risen Christ of their hope that Jesus would have been the one to redeem Israel (Luke 24:21), and in Acts, as Jesus prepares to ascend into the heavens, the mission of Jesus is still interpreted by his followers as the restoration of Israel (Acts 1:6-7).

But even if Jesus really said that he had been sent to the house of Israel and did in fact so restrict his ministry, then the conservative interpreters are still theologically wrong. For in fact, faith in Jesus is a pagan phenomenon, and this fact cannot be refused without making of Jesus a figure of the past irrelevant to the present reality. If he really is the living Son of God and not only a figure of the past who can be sealed away in tradition, then we have to acknowledge that he himself is at work among the pagans and that he has been won over to this mission. The story of the impertinent pagan, then, may serve to show us how a conflict between the Jesus tradition and the evident reality of pagan faith is overcome.

It should be noted that there is a very different version of this sort of encounter in the Gospel of John, in Jesus' encounter with the Samaritan woman at the well. Like the Syrophoenician woman, she is an outsider, although here a Samaritan rather than a Greek or a Canaanite. And she, like the Gadarene demoniac, becomes an apostle to the outsiders (the Samaritan villagers) who come to know Jesus without the mediation of any of Jesus' Galilean disciples. In the Gospel of John, this leads to the charge that Jesus is himself a Samaritan and so an outsider to the true people of Israel (John 8:48).

We see that in each of the Gospels, the mission to the outsider is presented as a feature of Jesus' own mission and ministry. In this way Jesus is presented as having already called into question the exclusive privilege of God's chosen people. In the case of Luke, this already prefigures Jesus' execution on the cross; in the case of John, this results in Jesus' being identified as an outsider himself: "Are you not a Samaritan?" (John 8:48).

Handed over to the gentiles

These anticipations in the mission and ministry of Jesus are brought to a head in the account of Jesus' trial and execution. Key here is the fact that Jesus is delivered up or "handed over to the gentiles" for execution (Mark 10:31). This means that Jesus, as the Messiah, is renounced by his own people and turned over to those outside the covenant promises.

This fate is anticipated in the prologue to John's Gospel: "He came to his own people but his own did not welcome him. But those who did welcome him received from him grace and truth" (John 1:11-12). What this text anticipates is that the rejection of Jesus by his own people, or rather by the leadership elite of his own people, results in his being welcomed or received by those who were also excluded by these same elite. The exclusion of Jesus makes him one with the excluded, who are then included in what the author calls "grace and truth." This is what the accounts of Jesus' being handed over to the gentiles in his trial and execution will narrate.

In the account of Jesus' trial, it transpires that those who are entrusted with the interpretation of the traditions of Israel and the law of God determine that Jesus is to be handed over to the gentile authorities. As we have seen, the result of this process is that Jesus is crucified by Roman law, and so the cross becomes the sign of the divine solidarity with all who are judged by the political and imperial authorities as subversive—and therefore of the divine solidarity with all who protest against these structures in the name of the oppressed and the humiliated.

But the trial of Jesus before the Sanhedrin could have resulted in a different outcome, for Jesus was considered guilty of blasphemy, or at least of being a false prophet.[8] In such a case, the appropriate sentence was that of stoning, a sentence that was well within the competence of Jewish law, as the example of Stephen's stoning in Acts 7:54—8:1 shows.

This did not happen, of course, and it does not happen because Jesus is handed over, delivered up. This means that he is turned over to the gentiles as if he were himself a gentile. In his execution, he becomes once and for all one who is "outside the gate" (Heb 13:12-13), that is, one who is repudiated by the people who are chosen as God's own, the people who are the insiders.

Now if God's insiders reject him, either this means that they are right to do this and Jesus is excluded from the promise, the covenant, the blessing of God; or, if Jesus is indeed the emissary, the Messiah, or the Son of God, then the understanding of election as entailing the exclusion of others comes to an end.[9] What ends, therefore, is the separation between the included and the excluded, between the chosen and the rejected people, between those with religious privilege and those without. This happens because the one who represents God is placed alongside the excluded gentile. Ironically, this comes to mean that the execution of Jesus by the gentiles signals that the gospel comes to the gentiles.

This is expressed with enormous power in the scene in the Gospels of Mark and Matthew that portrays the actual death of Jesus. After Jesus' final agonized cry of godforsakenness, the veil of the temple is torn in half and the centurion who executed him says, "Truly this was the Son of God."

The rending of the veil of the temple means that the separation between that which pertains to God (the Holy of Holies) and that which pertains to the outside world is abolished. There is not, and can no longer be, a separation between that which pertains to God and that which does not, between the sacred and the profane, the holy and the secular.[10] This also finds expression in the acclamation of faith on the lips of Jesus' executioner. Jesus now "belongs" to the nations, to those who were on the outside of the divine covenant, to those who are decidedly pagan, secular, the outsider and the excluded.

Seen in this way, it is precisely the death of Jesus on the cross that decisively undoes the opposition between Jew and gentile, that effectively abolishes the separation between God's people and "not-my-people" (and thus inverts the sense of Hosea 1:8-10). The anticipations of this decisive siding of the representative of God with those who are outside the covenant now become final and irrevocable in the cross.

Gentile mission

In the accounts of Jesus' mission and ministry in the Gospels, we have already seen a number of episodes that suggest not only that Jesus himself responded to the outsiders (the centurion, the Syrophoenician woman, and so on), but that these gentiles also seem to have been commissioned by Jesus to launch independent missions among those outside of Israel's covenant with God (the Samaritan woman, the Gadarene demoniac). In these last examples, we have indications of the emergence of a pagan proclamation of the gospel independent of the work of the Jewish disciples of Jesus.

This picture seems to be verified by a number of indications in the Acts of the Apostles. One of the most striking indications is found in the various accounts of the conversion of Cornelius. The story is told three times in Acts (10:1-8; 10:30-33; 11:1-18), where the emphasis is placed on the question of the appropriateness of administering baptism to this centurion who appears to have received the gospel altogether apart from the proclamation of the designated disciples of Jesus. However, for our purposes the more important element is that Cornelius appears to have been brought to something like faith prior to the official explication of the gospel by Peter. This occasions astonishment among the circle of Jesus' followers: "The circumcised believers who had come with Peter were astounded that the gift of the Holy Spirit had been poured out even on the Gentiles" (Acts 10:45 NRSV), and "They praised God, saying, 'Then God has given even to the Gentiles the repentance that leads to life'" (11:18 NRSV). These accounts agree that the insiders were astonished, that is, that they had had no idea that the message concerning Jesus was intended for those outside the house of Israel.

There is a strong suggestion in the account of the founding of the community of faith in Antioch that the gospel had first been proclaimed by "Hellenists," and that the subsequent role of Barnabas and Paul was to strengthen a congregation (the first to be called "Christians") that had been inaugurated independently of them or of those associated with the early followers of Jesus (Acts 11:19-26). There are indications as well that Apollos had received and proclaimed the gospel independently (18:24), and when Paul arrives in Ephesus, he finds a group who are loyal to Jesus but who have not been instructed about the Holy Spirit, for example (19:1-6). The impression one gains from reading Acts is that gentiles or pagans seem to have been drawn spontaneously to the one who had been crucified "outside the gates" and to have acclaimed him as their lord or leader.

In the face of this emergence of pagan Christianity, unmediated either by Judaism or even by Jesus' initial group of followers, it became impossible to deny that the gospel was in fact intended for the pagans. And this made it possible to see the cross of Jesus as entailing the abolition of the distinction between the chosen people and all others.

We know from both Acts and Paul that the recognition of this implication of the cross took time and was quite controversial in the early community. There is no appeal made by either Paul or Acts to the teaching or action of Jesus to resolve this issue. This indicates that, for some at least, the memory of the historical Jesus was ambiguous in this regard. What is clear, certainly for Paul, is the implication of the cross. For Paul, the cross decisively demonstrates that God has abandoned the division between those who are and those who are not God's people, and therefore the mission to the gentiles is based in the cross. Of course, in one sense a mission to the gentiles had a precedent in first-century Judaism. Paul's Pharisee compatriots may also have been engaged in a mission to the gentiles predicated on the gentiles' becoming adherents of the Pharisaic version of Judaism. This mission would have been controversial within Judaism, since the Sadducees emphasized the ethnic and cultic identity of Israel. For them, there could be no mission to those outside the ethnic and cultic bounds of Israel. But the Pharisees seem to have maintained that even a gentile could become an inheritor of the divine promise, provided that the gentile adhered to the law. In Acts we hear of a number of "believers who belonged to the sect of the Pharisees" and who maintained that it was necessary for gentile converts to Jesus "to be circumcised and to keep the law of Moses" (Acts 15:5).

It appears from the Gospels that many of Jesus' followers had already broken with the Pharisaic interpretation of the requirements of the law. But many still supposed either that the gospel was directed to those already a part of international Hellenistic Judaism, or that it could be extended to those gentiles who in one way or another became at least token Jews, whether through circumcision or through some minimal acceptance of Mosaic law. What was controversial was the view, espoused by Paul, that pagans could be followers of Jesus as pagans, that is, without coming into the sphere of Jewish tradition and custom at all.

This finds concrete expression in Galatians, where Paul recounts his argument with Peter. It becomes clear that what is at issue is that although Paul is a Jew, he renounces the special characteristics of this identity (the signs of the divine favor) in order to live as though he were a pagan. Thus, he abandons his own scruples about eating with those who knew nothing of what is now called kosher and so comes into direct contradiction to the law of Moses. Paul risks his special standing with God as one of the chosen people, or rather abandons this entirely in order to express solidarity with those who are not God's chosen people. Paul acts as a traitor to his own ethnic, cultural, and religious privilege in order to be in solidarity with the outsiders, just as Christ, especially the crucified Christ, was in solidarity with the outsider, the despised, the excluded, the profane, and the godforsaken.

The point of all this is to be in solidarity with Messiah Jesus, the Crucified One, and so to be in solidarity with those who are excluded by religious, social, and cultural structures of division and exclusion. It is precisely within the context of this argument that Paul refers to being crucified with Christ: "For through the law I died to the law, so that I might live to God. I have been crucified with Christ; and it is no longer I who live, but it is Christ who lives in me" (Gal 2:19-20 NRSV). To be crucified with Christ here means to be one who is excluded or who excludes oneself from the sphere of privilege.[11]

Paul returns to this same theme at the end of Galatians:

But God forbid that I should glory, save in the cross of our Lord Jesus Christ, by whom the world is crucified unto me and I unto the world. For in Christ Jesus neither circumcision counts for anything nor uncircumcision, but a new creature. (Gal 6:14-15)

Here again it is clear that the recollection of the cross of Jesus serves to abolish the ideological privilege of one group (the circumcision) over against the other (the uncircumcision). The cross abolishes the very principle of division since it makes it possible to "glory" only in that which abolishes this privilege by turning in final solidarity with the excluded.

Just as in Galatians Paul can speak of renouncing the privileges of his own belonging to the chosen people of God, so also in Philippians:

> If anyone has reason to be confident in the flesh I have more: circumcised on the eighth day, a member of the house of Israel, of the tribe of Benjamin; as to the law a Pharisee; as to zeal, a persecutor of the church; as to righteousness under the law, blameless. Yet whatever gains I had, these I have come to regard as trash because of Christ. More than that, I regard everything as loss for the surpassing value of knowing Christ Jesus my Lord. For his sake I suffered the loss of all things, and I regard them as dung, in order that I may gain Christ. (Phil 3:4-7)

That in the cross Jesus stands outside and against the system of ideological privilege means that his follower (Paul) also renounces all traces of this same privilege in order to be in solidarity with the Messiah Jesus. Subsequently, we will see that for Paul, this does not mean that God has abandoned his chosen people, or that God's promises to them are in any way revoked by the act of inclusion of all humanity in God's favor or election. That is, the gospel of inclusion of the gentiles must by no means be permitted to become a word of exclusion of Israel in defiance of the very act and promise of God.

Patristic perspectives

In the previous chapter, when we discussed the historical and political significance of the cross, we also saw that later patristic writers seemed to have struggled with some perplexity about how to express this. The church had, in the meantime, become increasingly dominated by gentiles, even if the lines between emerging Christianities and emerging Judaisms were not yet fully clear. But the gentile composition of emerging catholic and orthodox Christianity does mean that the message concerning the significance of the cross as entailing the inclusion of the gentiles remained salient in their minds. Thus, the image of the cross as representing this inclusion remains important. Athanasius can write:

> If the death of the Lord is a ransom for all and by his death *the wall of partition*" is broken down and the call of the Gentiles is effected, how would he have called us had he not been crucified? For only on the cross does one die with arms stretched out. Therefore the Lord had to endure this and stretch out his hands, that with one he might draw the ancient people and with the other those of the Gentiles and that he might join both in himself.[12]

Although Athanasius does not ground this observation in the historical circumstances of Jesus' being handed over to the gentiles, he does emphasize, however "symbolically," that it is the cross that is determinative for the inclusion of both Jews and gentiles.

This symbolic interpretation of the cross is picked up again by Gregory of Nyssa:

> In shape it is divided into four parts in such a way that the four arms converge in the middle. Now he who was extended upon it at the time God's plan was fulfilled in his death is the one who binds all things to himself and makes them one.[13]

By the time of the fourth century, it is not only the abolition of the barrier between Jew and gentile that seemed to be effected by the cross, but also that between Greek and barbarian (and even Scythian as well, as Colossians 3:11 suggests). That is, the ethnic and cultural ecumenism of those who identified themselves with the message concerning the cross was well established. To be sure, in the first century we already see emerging another wall of division between Jew and Christian, erected this time from the side of those who had so recently been included into the promises and blessing of God. And this wall of division was eventually to be understood to license the most horrifying crimes against humanity, in particular the humanity of the very people to whom God had first promised Godself. Thus, Christianity would come to be associated with the very forms of exclusion and division whose destruction had first been its "good news."

But Paul suggested that other forms of division and exclusion were also broken down in the cross, so that there would be no longer "slave nor free, male nor female." How are the division and exclusion represented by these terms to be understood in the light of the cross?

Neither slave nor free

The question of the relationship of emerging Christianity, especially in the first century, and the institutionalized slavocracy of the Roman Empire has been the subject of much scholarly discussion in recent years. Paul's own affirmation that in the messianic reality there can be neither slave nor free may be taken as a programmatic statement that aims not at the abolition of the slavocracy in an empire that was already viewed as coming to a catastrophic and imminent end, but at the abolition of this distinction insofar as it would impact the relationships among members of those new communities that enact the values of the coming reign of justice and mercy.

Paul's brief letter to Philemon shows how in practice this might be worked out in community. The aim of Paul's letter is that one who had been a slave (and quite likely a runaway slave for whom the penalty of law would have been extremely severe) should be received not as a returned slave, but as a beloved brother by his former owner and by the community that gathered in his "house." The ultimate goal is that this escaped slave be returned to Paul as a beloved son and a coworker in Paul's own mission of establishing new communities. In this letter, Paul makes clear that he could have simply commanded Philemon to renounce possession of Onesimus, but chooses instead to appeal to Philemon as fellow laborer with him, thereby saving Philemon from being ordered about by Paul, just as Philemon may well have ordered Onesimus about in their former arrangement. That Paul believes that he could have commanded Philemon in this respect shows, however, that for Paul, the transformation of the relation of master and slave is a direct implication of the gospel of which he is an apostle.

In 1 Corinthians, Paul admonishes those who are free and those who are slave to deal with one another as if they are not slave or free but brothers, just as he urges the circumcised and the uncircumcised to live together without regard for the cultural divisions signified by that mark. However, he is also quite clear that no one should voluntarily become a slave, since the Messiah had already become the source of freedom for the believer (1 Cor 7:21-24). Thus, on the one hand, the existing situation of the believer within the social system of slavery should not interfere with relationships among members of the community, while on the other hand, one should not participate any more than is absolutely unavoidable in the system itself.

In this regard it is intriguing that Paul refers to himself as a slave of the Messiah (Rom 1:1; Phil 1:1; Gal 1:10) and makes use of slave imagery in order to talk about relationships among believers. The Jesus tradition similarly uses this image to speak of his followers as being mutually slaves of one another (Mark 10:44). The point of this seems to be that the mutuality and solidarity that are critical for the life of the community entail something like "downward social mobility," in which those with more social privilege identify with those who have less. In this way they may mirror the way of the Messiah, who, though as equal to God, nevertheless takes on the form of a slave (Phil 2:7) and indeed meets the same fate as escaped slaves, "even death on the cross" (Phil 2:8).

In post- or deutero-Pauline writings in the New Testament, we get a very different picture, as the writers seem to be concerned to rein in the liberative impulse of a community within which the massive social reality of the slavocracy should in principle be abolished. Thus, we read increasingly vigorous admonitions to slaves to be obedient to their masters so as not to bring the Jesus movement into disrepute in the wider society (Col 3:22-25; Eph 6:5-8; 1 Tim 6:1). What these admonitions also do, however, is suggest that the emerging Christian communities were populated in significant numbers by slaves, that is, that the messianic gospel concerning the Crucified One was especially attractive to slaves. This may be rather clearly indicated in 1 Peter, where there is considerable admonition to slaves about how to live with abusive masters, but no admonition to masters (1 Pet 2:18-24).[14] This suggests that the majority of the community is made up of slaves, but that there are no, or virtually no, masters—just as in the community addressed by James where the majority are rather poor, with only a few (but already too many from the standpoint of the writer) who might be deemed prosperous.

In the centuries that followed, Christianity seems to have been torn between the clear sense that in Christ there could be no division between persons based on social rank and, conversely, the compromise with social realities that had seemed necessary in the first century to escape the opprobrium of the ruthless enforcers of that same social reality. What is deeply tragic is that official Christianity itself becomes the ruthless enforcer of these same social divisions, to the point that arguably the worst forms of chattel slavery practiced in history were reenforced by Protestant evangelical doctrine in the antebellum South of the United States. Accordingly, movements for emancipation were typically the work either of small and radical minorities within Christianity or of more powerful secular movements for which Christendom was simply the dead force of a tradition hostile to the aspirations for human solidarity—for "liberty, equality, and fraternity," as the secular radicals of modern revolution held. Thus, we have the horrible irony that slaveholders in the South could be said to become even more brutal when they became "Christians."[15] Obviously something went terribly wrong. And what went wrong has something to do with the way in which the message of the cross was transformed into a license for oppression, for division and exclusion. This happened because the message of the cross had been separated from any connection to the actual fate of Jesus in such a way that the message concerning the abolition of the walls of separation could be silenced in the churches that held themselves to be the only true heirs and interpreters of that message.

The abolition of slavery did little to erase the underlying ideology of white supremacy based upon racialist doctrine that had served to make slavery seem "natural" to many white Christians. Indeed, it was only against the ferocious opposition of much of institutionalized "Christianity" that strides have been made in the United States and in South Africa against legally enforced racial segregation and white domination. Only toward the end of that struggle was it possible for many Christians in South Africa to come to the correct conclusion that systems of racial division, exclusion, and domination were in direct opposition to the meaning of the cross of Christ.[16] In the United States, there are still those who call themselves Christians yet who burn crosses in an attempt to intimidate those who sense the direct opposition between any racialist theory or practice and the cross that breaks down the dividing wall of separation. But the many forms of everyday petty racial "profiling" that are the unvarying background radiation of life in this society are no less outward and visible signs of contempt for the cross of Christ.

Neither male nor female

The overcoming of the division between male and female, and thus of the long history of masculine domination of women, is even more ambiguous in the experience of Christianity. To be sure, there is a growing body of evidence that the Jesus movement itself both embodied and inspired mutuality, solidarity, and equality between male and female adherents. In terms of the central events of the Christian story, there can be no question that women were those who understood the cross as the culmination of Jesus' mission (Mark 14:3-9), who were the witnesses to his execution (15:40-41), who tended the body, and who first were commissioned to announce the resurrection (16:5). The letters of Paul suggest that a number of women acted as coworkers in the inauguration and nurture of the earliest communities and were regarded as apostles.

At the same time, we also can detect rather clear signs that women were progressively (or regressively) edited out of the story of Christian beginnings as the pressures to conform to the expectations of a highly gendered imperial social order made themselves felt and gained the upper hand.[17] Only the repudiation of "marriage and family values" in the Gospels[18] and the stories of Jesus' female companions preserved in minority literature of, for example, the *Gospel of Thomas* continue to bear witness to the significant role of women in the movement, and thus to the actual overcoming of the division and disparity between male and female. Even the authentic letters of Paul (especially segments of 1 Corinthians) have been made to authorize the silencing of women in the community of faith. Admonitions to wives found in deutero-Pauline, Pastoral, and other epistles show the tendency of major segments of Christianity to embrace the gender norms of the Greco-Roman world.

Subsequent history is similarly ambivalent. On the one hand, the place of women martyrs, the accounts of women missionaries such as Thecla, and the long history of remarkable women spiritual guides and theologians bear witness to the emancipatory effects of the message concerning the crucified Messiah.[19] At the same time, we witness the determination of male leadership to solidify their grip on the reins of power and authority within Christianity.

Today the largest institutionalized forms of Christianity (Catholic and Orthodox) continue to insist on the exclusion of women from roles of authority within the churches that claim to speak for the messianic movement that abolished the division between male and female. It is only in the last century that significant numbers of Christians have become advocates of the full participation of women, both in the communities of faith and in the wider social orders that otherwise claim their "Christian" lineage. However, it remains the case that the movements for women's emancipation are far more often secular in character, and the most vociferous opponents are those who claim to speak for one or another version of Christian tradition.

Once again we are confronted with the irony that some secular movements seem to be the concrete effects of the message concerning the cross, while much of Christendom appears to constitute itself as a betrayal of that same message.

The cross and division today

That Jesus was handed over to the gentiles means that he is placed outside the sphere of special privilege and made to be one of the excluded within the world of institutionalized division. It is for this reason that the message concerning the cross is one that abolishes all such forms of division, exclusion, and privilege. The effect of Jesus' being "handed over" is that God is on the side of those who are deprived of this ideological standing; God is on the side of the excluded, the despised, the outsider. And this means that in the cross, we may see the abolition in principle of the walls of division that rupture human community. Hence the saying about God's being no respecter of persons (Acts 10:34; Rom 2:11; Gal 2:6; Eph 6:9; Col 3:25). In each of these passages, what is at stake is the perception that the divine grace articulated in the gospel concerning the cross does not accept the barriers of privilege and prestige erected by human groups. God does not respect these divisions, these classifications, these oppositions, but rather chooses to side with what seems least respectable, least valuable, in order to establish the fully inclusive new humanity whose foundation is the cross of Jesus.

It is this perception that lies at the base of the supposition that in Christ, God was reconciling the world, overcoming all barriers to unity and peace, putting an end to hostility and enmity. The end result of the cross in this sense is the logical conclusion that God will be all in all (1 Cor 15:28), that no separation will withstand the power of that which finds expression in the cross.

Fortunately, there are, throughout history and all the more today, signs of the effects of the gospel in overcoming the divisions that haunt humanity. Christians of many sorts surrender their class and race privileges to live among the destitute and marginalized, whether in the slums of South America or the United States, carrying forward the renunciation of class privilege embodied in a Francis of Assisi or a Catherine of Genoa, even while other Christians maintain that the growing gap between the impoverished and the prosperous is the immutable will of a God they somehow associate with Jesus.

But if we are to follow through on the logic of the cross in breaking down walls of division, we may also have to question the supposition that Christian identity itself represents a certain privilege before God. If the cross means the end of division, then what happens when Christianity itself becomes the principle of division? This is precisely what begins to happen in the first century, in spite of the efforts of the earliest Christian writers.

Who can doubt that today Christianity is widely viewed by its adherents as a position of ideological privilege? If one is baptized, if one shares certain beliefs, if one follows certain practices, these assure one's place among the favored people of God. And those who are outside this sphere of the divine promise and blessing are regarded as pagans, heathens, secular humanists, atheists, and so on.

This has happened over and over again with respect to the Jews. We Christians assert that we are the chosen people, which positions them as the rejected people. That is, we have simply changed places in the same old system of religious privilege. The murderous consequences of this exchange have become especially evident in our own century, with Christianity, especially Protestant Christianity, becoming the source of the Shoah.

Certainly this assertion of ideological privilege is used to maintain the "superiority" of Christianity over other religions, especially those that are regarded as "primitive." And standard missionary theory and practice have resulted in the opposition to the development of indigenous forms of Christianity in Africa and in Asia. Instead, persons are encouraged to adopt our own pagan customs that we pass off as Christianity. Their assimilation to Western forms of pagan religion is made the condition of their becoming Christians, Protestants, evangelicals.

All of this is possible only on the basis of oblivion concerning the cross as the act of reconciliation that abolishes ideological privilege. Here we recall what Paul says in Galatians 6:15: "For neither circumcision nor uncircumcision is anything; but a new creation is everything." But are we willing to transpose this in such a way as also to say: neither baptism nor unbaptism, neither church membership nor non–church membership?

If the cross is to become again a determinative feature of the gospel, then it will be necessary to overcome the ways in which the message concerning solidarity with the excluded, concerning the abolition of barriers and divisions, has been silenced within the very heart of Christianity. Today as in the beginning, the cross of Christ brings the world, including the religious and pious and respectable world, into question. The cross remains the crisis of history that turns everything upside down.

Writing at the conclusion of his autobiography in 1845, Frederick Douglass explains his contempt for the religion that calls itself Christianity while affirming, nonetheless, the truth of the gospel. He writes, "Between the Christianity of this land, and the Christianity of Christ, I recognize the widest possible difference—so wide, that to receive the one as good, pure, and holy is of necessity to reject the other as bad, corrupt, and wicked. To be the friend of the one is of necessity to be the enemy of the other."[20] What Douglas wrote then of what he called "slave-holding religion" is, I believe, just as true of racist, sexist, and homophobic Christianity today.

Excursus: the election of Israel

Does the emphasis on the cross as that which breaks down walls of exclusion entail the rejection of the election of Israel? I have earlier referred to the work of Judith Plaskow, who makes the case from a feminist perspective that election must be replaced with distinctiveness. As a Christian theologian in the aftermath of the Holocaust or Shoah, however, I am reluctant to adopt the view that Israel is no longer the elect people of God, even when I wish to deny that election to Christians also. I remain attracted to the paradox of Israel's nontransferable and nonforfeitable election even, or perhaps especially, in the light of the breaking down of walls of hostility that may be attributable to the cross. Apart from the election of Israel, there would be no sense to the assertion that Jesus is the Messiah of Israel, in spite of the irony of his designation as "King of the Jews." Nothing so clearly marks Israel as God's elect as does the history of Christian anti-Semitism and anti-Judaism. This hostility toward Israel itself testifies to the Christian sense of Israel's priority in divine affection and favor. It displays the marks of a Cain-like jealousy that bears grudging witness to the reality of that which it seeks to eradicate.

I remain persuaded by what I understand to be Paul's argument in Romans 9–11, that "the gifts and the calling of God are irrevocable" (Rom 11:29 NRSV). It is the irrevocability of Israel's election that stands as the bedrock of confidence in the grace of God extended also to the nations. That is, it is the reliability of the particular favor of God with respect to Israel that makes it possible to be confident in the general or universal favor of God.

Forgetting this has made it possible to turn a theology of the cross against Judaism. That the cross of the Jew Jesus should have become a weapon against his fellow Jews is something that must stand as an indictment of Christian theologies. Thus, while I have great respect for those Jews who wrestle with the meaning of election, whether as Reconstructionists or as feminists, I think that the history of Christian anti-Semitism precludes Christian theologians from following the path of questioning the election of the Jewish people. What is questionable is neither particular identity nor election, but the exclusion of others, any others, from the divine promise and blessing.

CHAPTER FOUR

The Cross and Accusation

n the history of theology and of liturgy, especially in the West, the cross of Jesus is most often understood in terms of the problem of sin. By beginning with the concrete historical reality of Jesus' cross, however, which anchors it in the conflict with structures of domination and division, we will be able to give a more adequate account of the connection between the cross and sin. Just as we have seen that the overcoming of division in order to include the outsider is an effect of the cross that grows out of its historical and political concreteness, so also we will see that the cross may be understood to overcome the accusation and condemnation of "sinners" as an extension of the subversion of structures of domination and division. Accordingly, we will be able to give an account of how the cross saves sinners without simply rehabilitating the language of cultic sacrifice that was available to first-century Christian thinkers but, as we have seen, no longer works well for a world in which, thanks to the gospel, the cultic language of sacrifice no longer makes sense.

In what way does the cross of Jesus deal with the condition of sin? If the language of, for example, a "full, perfect, and sufficient sacrifice" is no longer transparent for us, is there then any way to clarify the significance of the cross for sin? And what, in this connection, is sin after all? Rather than plunging immediately into the Pauline and deutero-Pauline terminology, I will begin with what may be somewhat clearer: the narratives that we find in the Gospels. I will try to show that, according to these narratives, Jesus has the deliberate policy of associating himself with people who were regarded by the respectable and religious as being sinners, that is, as being excluded from the realm of God's favor. By paying attention to the behavior of Jesus in this regard, we will get a more concrete sense of what is involved here. It will then be possible to see in what way Jesus' death on the cross could be understood as the culmination of Jesus' policy, as taking this solidarity with "sinners" to its extreme. Then I will try to show how these narratives can help us understand the way in which the first letter of John can say that Jesus "came into the world to save sinners," and how it is that Paul could suppose that the word of the cross is a word of welcome for sinners.

This will not mean that we simply accept the language about sacrifice and welcome. Rather, we will try to do in our context what that language did in its context but cannot do in ours: clarify the way in which the mission and ministry of Jesus, his cross and resurrection, are good news for those who are despised by the religious and respectable—that is, for sinners.[1]

The practice of Jesus

One of the principal features of the Gospel narratives is deliberate association with sinners on the part of Jesus. Actually, as we shall see, this association has several aspects. The first one is that Jesus seems to deliberately scandalize his contemporaries by associating with the "accused." The second is that Jesus launches a counterattack against the accusers. The third is that Jesus refuses to defend himself against accusation. All of this comes to a head in the cross.

Companionship with "sinners"

We begin with Jesus' custom of associating with those who were regarded as sinners. Jesus is recalled in the Gospel narratives as one who indiscriminately "hung out" with the most disreputable people. The catchphrase used in the Gospels is "tax collectors and sinners." This phrase is often set in the context of the call of Levi (Matthew) the tax collector, a member of a class proverbial for its corruption and extortion. Their only associates would be the most disreputable types in Galilean society: gentiles, pimps, whores, and so on, people thrown together by the disdain of respectable people. Jesus is remembered as "eating and drinking" with them and therefore, by this practice, as one of them. "Birds of a feather flock together" (wrote Aristotle); one is known by the company one keeps. This practice of "hanging out" and thereby forging alliances and friendships with the disreputable is the focus of these stories in the Gospels (Mark 2:13-17; Matt 9:9-13; Luke 5:27-32).

The stories not only emphasize Jesus' solidarity and friendship with the most disreputable elements of society, but also show that this caused the outrage of his opponents, the scribes and Pharisees. Jesus' hanging out with the bad elements of society is itself a provocative action. It certainly contrasts with the attitude that was characteristic not only of the scribes and Pharisees (on the basis of their understanding of the law), but perhaps also of John the Baptist (on the basis of ascetic practices).

When the guardians of law give vent to their outrage at Jesus' companionship with those they regard as sinners, each of the three Synoptic Gospels gives us a slightly different version of Jesus' reply (Mark 2:13-17; Matt 9:9-13; Luke 5:27-32). In Mark, Jesus says, "Who needs a doctor, the sick or the well? I call (to me) not the righteous but sinners." Of course many will suppose that here Jesus might be understood as saying that the Pharisees and the scribes are healthy and righteous, but they will soon be disabused of this notion (if they keep reading). For now, it is enough to notice that Jesus is by no means seeking to recruit new members for the group of the scribes and Pharisees by entering into friendship with "sinners." Actually, his making friends with them is changing their condition from those who are abandoned and despised to those who are welcomed and honored, from those who are excluded by the representatives of God to those who are embraced by one who represents God. Perhaps it is this transformation that is meant when Luke adds that Jesus calls sinners to repentance. Of course, what Jesus in fact does is to call the Pharisees to repentance, as we shall see. The repentance of "sinners," then, is not a change in terms of conformity with the rules promulgated by the respectable, but something like reconciliation with the one who does not accuse but welcomes them.

Matthew adds a different saying: that God requires "not sacrifice but mercy." In this way Jesus suggests that those who scrupulously observe religious rules, and who insist that others do the same, are not in fact heeding the most basic claim and call of the divine: to show mercy and thus friendship, rather than to mercilessly accuse and condemn.

In a subsequent explanation of Jesus' comportment with "sinners" (when the Pharisees and scribes complain that he "welcomes" them), Luke then adds a number of parables found only in this Gospel: the parable of the lost sheep (15:35), the parable of the lost coin (15:8-9), and the parable of the lost son/brother. (15:11-32). All deal with ways that the one who is lost is of more concern than all the others, in order that all may be included.

The last parable opens the question (and leaves it open) of the attitude of those who think they are not lost toward the divine extravagance that places a priority on those who appear to be lost, or outside, or disreputable. Will we regard this welcome as a cause for rejoicing or for resentment and bitterness? All too often the response of religious and righteous people has been resentment or, more often, the revocation of this welcome altogether.

That these lost ones are regarded by the respectable as sinners does not mean that Jesus regards them in this way. Jesus regards them as friends and companions, and by his word and deed suggests that God does as well. Jesus goes so far as to push this policy to its provocative extreme when he tells the Pharisees that "tax-collectors and prostitutes are entering the reign of God" before them (Matt 21:31-32).

One of the stories in which this practice finds dramatic expression is the one told by John concerning Jesus and the Samaritan woman. Attention to this story will help us to see important aspects of the theme.

The story begins with Jesus' remarkable solidarity with the woman and ends with the villagers' solidarity with Jesus—a solidarity of which the woman (and not Jesus' official disciples) has been the instrument. Who is this woman?

From the standpoint of official Judaism, she is a sinner simply by virtue of being a Samaritan. This exclusion of the woman from the sphere of God's favor is clearly marked in the text by the woman's surprise that Jesus would ask her for a drink of water. For by doing so, Jesus places himself in a position to be contaminated by her impurity. The notion of sin as contaminating was self-evident in priestly religion and is a crucial feature in many stories about Jesus. We will return below to this notion of sin as contamination.

But the other characteristic of sin also present in this and other stories is that it may refer to an objective social condition that has nothing to do with what we might conceive of as individual or subjective guilt. In this case she is a sinner, simply because she is a Samaritan. The same would be true of being a gentile. Paul uses this term in his argument with Peter when he says to him, "We ourselves are Jews by birth and not Gentile sinners" (Gal 2:15 NRSV). Simply by virtue of birth or of membership in one's social group, one could be thought of as outside the sphere of the divine favor, and so as a "sinner." This is the basis for the surprise that God's grace reaches out to include gentiles and so breaks down the "dividing wall," thereby making peace, as we saw in the previous chapter. So also the Samaritan woman expresses astonishment that one who is a member of a privileged group (and so in that sense not a sinner) would have anything to do with her.

In this story, Jesus responds to the objective distinction between Judean and Samaritan by saying that God will be worshipped "neither in this mountain nor in Jerusalem." The objective condition of the woman as a Samaritan is no barrier to the favor or welcome of God, nor is the objective condition of the Judean (having access to the temple in Jerusalem) an advantage. Thus, by associating with this woman, Jesus abolishes the barrier that had been thought to restrict the divine favor and so constitute her as a "sinner."

But this is not the only barrier, as we soon learn that the woman is also an adulteress. She has had five men, and the man she has now is "not her own." Nothing is said here about whether the woman has been married and divorced or has simply had a series of relationships with men. If the first is the case, then according to Jesus' teaching in the other Gospels, she is in any case an adulteress (Mark 10:11-12; Matt 5:32; 19:9; Luke 16:18). But the current affair is even more clearly adulterous, since the man she has now isn't hers—that is, he belongs to another, or is already in a relationship (marriage) with someone else.

The woman is quite remarkable as an example of what was once called a "loose woman." She is a flagrant "sinner" as far as the sexual mores and the actual religious law are concerned.

All of this is indicated quite clearly by the text, but the astonishing thing is that nothing more is made of it. It is surely remarkable that Jesus knows "all about her." That he has nonetheless asked for a drink, promised that she will become a source of life for herself and others, even caused her to be or become the first apostle to the Samaritans—this is what is astonishing about Jesus' unconditional association with one who was in what the Vatican might call an objective condition of sin. That is, Jesus has unreservedly associated himself and his mission with one who is a sinner. Here is no call for the woman to rectify her situation (find a man of her own, become celibate, or otherwise), nor even a call for repentance; nor does the woman repent of her conduct or, indeed, give any sign that she intends to change her behavior. She is simply the adulterous Samaritan who is accepted and encouraged by Jesus. The fact that she is an adulteress is no more limiting than the fact that she is a Samaritan. She is the one, as adulteress and as Samaritan, who goes to the villagers, who summons them to a direct encounter with Jesus. And the disciples of Jesus here play the role only of somewhat bewildered onlookers.

This story may serve as helpful background for an understanding of a number of other episodes recounted by the other Gospel writers. A motif that runs through the Gospels is Jesus' refusal to worry about contaminating himself with the impurity of others. This behavior is quite scandalous, for according to the law of Scripture, there are certain conditions that are objectively contaminating. We meet with one such instance in the case of the woman with the bleeding womb (Mark 5:25ff.). Her condition was so serious that if she polluted others, they could pollute the land, even the temple of God, causing God to abandon Israel (Lev 15:31). Now she reaches out to touch Jesus. By any reading of the Levitical law, the result of this touch would be that Jesus is contaminated. But the result reported in the Gospel of Mark is that she is healed of her affliction. Jesus is more interested in the healing than in the contamination. Objectively, Jesus is made a sinner by her touch, according to God's own law, but perhaps the God whose coming Jesus announces has something different in mind.

A similar judgment applied to contamination by lepers. One who was so contaminated could not worship God without undertaking certain ritual cleansings and sacrifices. The same was true of touching corpses, which Jesus does, for example, in the case of the raising of Jairus's daughter (Mark 5:21-24, 35-43).

Objectively, Jesus is made to be a sinner (that is, one outside the sphere of God's favor) by touching and being touched by these persons. But to that objective condition corresponds another occurrence: those who are touched in this way are rehabilitated. They find favor with God. The world is turned upside down.[2]

One thing that the religious leaders seem to have found alarming about Jesus and his disciples is that they ignored even the most elementary precautions about contamination (Mark 7:1-5). Thus, they refused to engage in any of the ritual cleansings prescribed to rid oneself of the accidental or incidental contaminations of daily life, despite the fact that they seemed deliberately to go out of their way to be contaminated in the ways I have indicated. In this very dramatic sense, then, Jesus (and his followers) entered into solidarity with those who were regarded as sinners.

This is also expressed in Jesus' refusal to practice fasting, a refusal characteristic of his disciples as well (Mark 2:18-22). This also goes to such an extreme that Jesus himself reports that he is generally regarded as a drunk and a glutton (Luke 7:34). He hangs out with prostitutes, tax collectors, drunks, and assorted other disreputable types. He goes to their parties and seems quite happy to be taken for their friend, even for one of them.

Another story helps to illustrate the point (Luke 7:36-50). In the Gospel of Luke, a woman who is "a notorious sinner" gets into the house of a respectable man who has invited Jesus to dinner. She comes in with the crowd. When the opportunity presents itself, she washes Jesus' feet with her tears and hair. Now, the respectable householder is quite put off by this display. He thinks to himself, if Jesus knew about her, he would be outraged as well. Jesus then says that he knows perfectly well what a notorious sinner she is—but see how much she loves.

Notice that Jesus does not call the woman to repentance. He accepts her love without condition, even though he knows perfectly well that she is a notorious sinner. No particular sort of notoriety is specified here, so we can fill in the blank with whatever seems most outrageous—and perhaps that is why no specific sin is mentioned. Since in our society, sin is regularly linked with sexuality, we may think of her as a famous prostitute or a wanton adulteress. (Odd how unlikely we would be to think of her as an exploiter of the poor or as one engaged in unfair trade.) The point is that it doesn't matter. She is simply accepted by Jesus—and defended by Jesus. We are not told what, if any, moral or lifestyle change was the result of this encounter. The point isn't in her change, but in Jesus' acceptance of and solidarity with her.

The behavior of Jesus is quite astonishing. He seems to go out of his way to associate himself with those who are called sinners, that is, with those whom religious and respectable people accuse of being outside the sphere of God's favor. In whatever situation, Jesus is on the side of the accused, without reserve, without condition, even without demand or expectation.

Despite the moralistic tendency of common reading, there is no indication that the prostitutes who followed Jesus changed their trade or that anybody turned to abstinence or even moderation in drinking. The narratives are not interested in reporting such changes because they want to make a quite different point—namely, that Jesus is unreservedly on the side of the accused and welcomes them into his friendship.

There is one story that may seem to be an exception to this. It is the story of the woman who is found in the very act of adultery. This is a story not found in early New Testament manuscripts, but in some later manuscripts of John and, in some cases, in Luke. It is normally found now in John (8:1-11). The woman has been caught, we are told, in the act of adultery, most likely in the act of having sex with another man, although she is already married. As seems to be generally the case under conditions of patriarchy, it is the woman rather than the man who is punished. She is dragged into the public street, but before the people stone her—as the law of God unambiguously requires (Deut 22:22; Lev 20:10)—they ask Jesus what he thinks. The upshot is that, in spite of what the law requires, Jesus somehow persuades them that they are not in a position to condemn her. It is as if they have been persuaded somehow, perhaps by what Jesus writes in the sand, of the teaching that he gave to his disciples about not judging (Matt 7:1-5; Luke 6:36-38), not condemning, but rather forgiving. In any case, the accusers are somehow persuaded not to accuse. This is quite astonishing. She is an adulteress. There is no indication that she has repented of this. But Jesus not only prevents others from condemning her, but also quite straightforwardly says that he doesn't condemn her either.

Somehow, much Christian preaching has managed to ignore this in favor of Jesus' parting call to her to sin no more. The main thing to notice about this is that it is not a condition of Jesus' refusal to condemn her. That has already happened. Rather, it is that Jesus' refusal to condemn her somehow opens up the possibility that she may actually not sin again. This is a possibility. It is not a condition of his welcome and protection. One might even suppose that the encouragement not to sin in this way again has something to do with the reality that Jesus may not be there next time to prevent the righteous men from carrying out the law against her.

There is one story (and only one) in the Gospel of Luke where we are actually told of the change in behavior of one who has been befriended by Jesus. It is the story of Zacchaeus (Luke 19:1-10). The story is one of mutual welcome, in that Jesus invites himself to the home of a rich tax collector, one who made his living exploiting the poor. As a consequence, rather than as a condition, of this friendship with Jesus, Zacchaeus announces that he will pay back all that he has defrauded (at 400 percent interest!), after giving half of all that he owns to the poor. By any reasonable calculation, this will leave Zacchaeus destitute and so in the position refused by the rich young ruler who had been advised by Jesus to sell all he had and give to the poor in order to follow him. What Zacchaeus does is to act first on mercy (give to the poor) and then on justice (restore what had been defrauded).

As we have seen, when it is a question of what we might call personal ethics, the Gospels do not tell us about a change of behavior. Only when it is a question of social ethics, or rather of justice and mercy, are we told of a transformation in the sinner. In this case again, Jesus announces, "The Human One came to seek and to save the lost." The generosity of the Human One results not in Zacchaeus becoming a law-abiding citizen, but in his acting out the same spirit of mercy and justice exhibited by Jesus' unconditional friendship.

We thus gain from the Gospels the picture of Jesus' consistent policy of siding and identifying himself with the accused, with those regarded by religious and respectable people as "sinners" outside the sphere of the divine favor. Jesus is on the side of the accused and condemned—he welcomes them into his friendship and companionship.

Warning to accusers

This leads to the second major feature of Jesus' practice: that he is always against the accusers. Always. This is something that is particularly stressed in the Gospel of Matthew. In that Gospel, Jesus is quite scathing in his attack on the religious and respectable who accuse and condemn sinners. It is particularly the Pharisees who are singled out as the opponents of Jesus. (In the Gospel of Mark, it is not the Pharisees but the scribes—that is, the interpreters of the law generally.)

This attack on the accusers reaches its greatest intensity in Matthew 23:1-36 (see also Luke 11:37-53), the so-called "woes." Let us consider some of the points of Jesus' denunciation of the accusers:

> "They bind heavy burdens, hard to bear, and lay them on people's shoulders; but they themselves will not move them with their finger." (Matt 23:4)

> "But woe to you, scribes and Pharisees, hypocrites! because you shut the kingdom of heaven against men; for you neither enter yourselves, nor allow those who would to go in." (23:13)

> "Woe to you, scribes and Pharisees, hypocrites! for you traverse sea and land to make a single convert, and when he becomes a convert, you make him twice as much a child of hell as yourselves." (23:15)

> "Woe to you, scribes and Pharisees, hypocrites! for you tithe mint and dill and cumin, and have neglected the weightier matters of the law: justice and mercy and loyalty . . . you blind guides, straining out a gnat and swallowing a camel." (23:23-24)

What is the meaning of these curses hurled at the religious and respectable? It seems that the basic problem of the religious is that they concentrate on the adherence to appearances rather than focusing on the imitation of the divine mercy and justice. This becomes evident in the way they use the law to impose impossible conditions upon people, so as to accuse those others of standing outside the sphere of divine blessing. They accuse in order to excuse themselves. But their own lack of justice prevents their entry into the reign of God, while their accusations against others seem to exclude these others from God's favor. Thus, they shut against others the door that they also refuse to enter. In contrast, Jesus' opening of the door to include the excluded serves to make the reign of the divine mercy and justice available to all.

Jesus' policy of siding with the accused leads him to attack their accusers. Jesus does not pronounce woes against the drunks and prostitutes and the disreputable. He stands with them. But he does pronounce curses on the religious and respectable, on those, that is, who accuse their sister or brother, who use the law as a weapon against the "sinners."

Jesus does not really try to persuade the Pharisees that he is right. It is as if he were intent on picking a fight. He wants it to be clear that God sides with the accused and against the accusers. In this, God is not "evenhanded" or neutral. God resolutely takes sides—for this one and against that one; for the oppressed and against the oppressor; for the poor and against the rich; for the accused sinner and against the accusing righteous.

Solidarity with the accused

A third aspect of Jesus' practice is his refusal to defend himself or his followers against the accusations of the pious. We encounter this curious phenomenon in the early part of the Gospel of Mark, with Jesus' response to the charge that he is possessed by a demon (3:22). This charge is repeated in all four Gospels, so it looks likely that Jesus was accused by the religious establishment of his day of being a madman and in league with Satan (Matt 9:34; 12:22-26; Mark 3:22; Luke 11:14-18; John 8:48). This accusation would serve to indicate how it was that one who acted in defiance of God (for example, with respect to purity and the sabbath) could nevertheless overthrow demons in others. His power was supernatural, to be sure, but it was from what we might call the "dark side of the force."

Jesus' reply in the Synoptics to this charge is a verbal shrug. He explains this with the analogy of the kingdom divided against itself. The analogy goes like this: If I overthrow evil by using the power of evil, then the reign of evil is a kingdom divided—at war with itself. So it is on the verge of collapse. And if the kingdom of evil is collapsing, then what I have been saying about the coming of God's reign is true: it is demonstrated in the overthrow of evil. Thus, it doesn't matter whether Jesus is in league with Satan or not. In either case the reign of evil is collapsing and the reign of God is coming.

The blindness of Jesus' opponents is that, in the name of God, they oppose the overthrow of evil. They are the ones who thus make God to be the defender of evil. It is as if God would prefer that people be possessed by demons. This is the true blasphemy against God.

In the Gospel of John, when this same charge is made against Jesus, he does appear to defend himself by saying that he does the works that are characteristically "divine": healing, exorcizing, and so on. Of course, this straightforward, even simplistic test of whether something is of God amounts to much the same thing as the Synoptic response: in any case, things are happening that reflect the divine act.

But there are other charges in the Gospel of John that are allowed to stand: that Jesus is a "sinner" and that he is a Samaritan (John 8:48). Objectively these come to the same thing. Jesus is excluded from the sphere of the divine favor either because he does not obey the law (sabbath observance, for example), or because of his solidarity with sinners, even Samaritan sinners, in the earlier encounter with the woman at the well.

The condemnation of Jesus

Jesus' practice of not defending himself against the charges of the accusers is one of the most remarkable features of the passion narratives, especially as these narrate Jesus' various trials before bodies of accusers. In the trial before the Sanhedrin, when the various witnesses charge Jesus with a series of unspecified crimes, we find the following: "And the High Priest stood up in the midst and asked Jesus, 'Have you no answer to make? What about what these men testify against you?' But he was silent and made no answer" (Mark 14:60-61; Matt 26:62-63).

The very multiplicity of these "sins" and the way in which the narrative leaves them unspecified makes it possible to include virtually any "sin" in the list of charges. The narrator may intentionally leave this open-ended so that it will be clear that Jesus does not intend to defend himself against any accusation. He does not at any point separate himself from the accused.

It is important to note that the Sanhedrin could in fact make a pretty good case against Jesus. The critique of "family values" that is attributed to him in every Gospel could plausibly provoke a charge that he not only refused filial obedience to parents, but also taught others to break these ties. This is an offense punishable by stoning (Deut 21:20; 27:16). He also seems quite regularly to run afoul of sabbath law and even to affirm that the human is lord of the sabbath. This also could be construed as worthy of stoning (Exod 31:14). His apparent blasphemy in affirming that the human would be seen alongside God would seem a clear violation of the divine transcendence. It is for this that Stephen will be stoned to death in Acts 7:56-58. In general, Jesus is regarded as a false prophet, as one who leads people to believe differently, or even to believe in a different God. The punishment for all these crimes is clearly death by stoning. Jesus may be plausibly understood to merit the death penalty. This seems already to have been recognized by those who, in John, heard him say, "Before Abraham was, I am"; for then we are told, "They picked up stones to stone him" (John 8:59). The point is that for those who were biblical literalists or traditionalists, Jesus was indeed a sinner, and a sinner of the sort that was worthy of the death penalty.

It is often said that the Judeans couldn't impose the death penalty. That would have astonished both the woman taken in adultery and Stephen in Acts (or Paul, who held the coats of those who stoned Stephen to death). It is simply not true that the death penalty could not be imposed. What they could not do was impose the death penalty for political crimes. Only the Romans could crucify subversives.

In the trial before Pilate, Jesus is again charged with various crimes. In the Gospel of Luke, these are summarized thus: "We found this man perverting our nation and forbidding us to pay taxes to Caesar and saying that he himself is Christ the King" (Luke 23:2). These crimes are fairly inclusive ("perverting the nation," for example, may include a multitude of evils). They also make clear that Jesus is, in every sense, a political criminal: a sinner against Rome. The Gospels then tell us: "And Pilate again asked him, 'Have you no answer to make? See how many charges they bring against you?' But Jesus made no further answer" (Mark 15:4-5; Matt 27:12-14). In Matthew the refusal to answer is even more insistent: "He gave him no answer, not even to a single charge" (27:14 NRSV). Only in the Gospel of Luke do we have a trial before Herod. But the same occurs: "So [Herod] questioned [Jesus] at length but he made no answer" (Luke 23:9).

The Synoptic Gospels thus make clear that Jesus resolutely refuses to distance himself from any accusation. The variety of charges against him makes his solidarity with the accused totally open-ended and so universal. Jesus is, in a comprehensive sense, at one with all who are accused by the representatives of the law.

The cross is the consequence of this policy of siding with the accused against the accuser, and Jesus' refusing to separate himself from the accused. His fate is the fate of one who is accused by the law and its authorized representatives and enforcers (the Sanhedrin, Pilate, even Herod). He is abandoned by his friends (even denied and betrayed). He is denounced by his own people. He is executed with criminals and is the subject of derision and revilement, of humiliation and torture. His fate appears to be that of one who is utterly excluded from divine favor. There is no last-minute rescue. Both Mark and Matthew record his final cry of godforsakenness. He dies abandoned, even by God—perhaps especially by God.

This is represented as the outcome of a policy of deliberate solidarity with all those who are accused, with all those whom the law-abiding regard as criminals, with all those whom the respectable regard as sinners. Yet Jesus pursues this policy as a way of demonstrating what it means to affirm that God is drawing near, what it means to assert that God accepts, affirms, and welcomes those who are rejected, scorned, and reviled by those who otherwise pretend to speak for God and to represent the divine will as mediated through the law.

Christ and sinners (Paul)

In this light, we can begin to see the point of certain Pauline assertions that otherwise would appear to be simply mythological in character. Here we may recall two basic assertions. The first is from Galatians: "Christ redeemed us from the curse of the law having become a curse for us, for it is written, 'Cursed be everyone who hangs on a tree'" (Gal 3:13; see Deut 21:22-23). The other is from 2 Corinthians: "For our sake [God] made [Christ] to be sin who knew no sin so that we might become the justice of God" (5:21).

In these and similar statements, the situation of extreme solidarity between Christ and "sinners" is expressed. Christ is in radical solidarity with those who are excluded from the sphere of divine favor. In this sense he becomes identical with those who are cursed by the law (Galatians) and is therefore "sin" as such. Yet at the same time, the one who is thus identified with sinners, whose solidarity with them is sealed by his blood, by his manner of death—this one also is seen to be acting in obedience to the divine will, as in conformity with the divine desire and intention. In this sense, he "knew no sin."

It is critical that we notice that Jesus is *not* said to be "without sin" because he complied with each and every commandment and prohibition in the various legal codes of Israel. These legal codes are not a sort of checklist that can be used to determine whether Jesus was or was not without sin. What makes him "without sin" is that he fully and radically enacted God's mercy and justice, the mercy and justice that include or welcome "sinners." We know in a very simple and direct way that Jesus was right to do this: the one who was accused, condemned, and executed in accordance with the law (of God) was raised from the dead by (the same) God.

If it is true that Jesus' radical solidarity with "sinners" corresponds to the divine will, then a number of startling conclusions follow that can first simply be summarized, prior to examining some of the more important theological points.

First, the curse of the law is broken. That is, the power of the law to accuse and condemn is shattered upon the cross of Jesus. If the law condemns Jesus even though Jesus is the one who represents the divine will, then this accusation and condemnation is fundamentally false—however literally correct it may seem to be. Paul will have to nuance this to show that the law in certain respects is "holy, just, and good" insofar as it represents the divine intention that human beings be just and that they establish a community of justice and mercy. But the negative character of the law as the power of accusation and condemnation is broken. It no longer can have legitimacy.

We should also note that this is true not only of the Jewish law but also of pagan law. For Jesus is condemned by both laws, the Jewish and the Roman. Thus, both legal systems as powers of condemnation and accusation are rendered obsolete. This is why Paul can claim that "there is therefore now no condemnation for those who are [included] in Christ Jesus" (Rom 8:1 NRSV).

Second, it becomes clear that the divine will is not the accusation, condemnation, rejection, and exclusion of "sinners," but is their acceptance, affirmation, inclusion, and adoption as children and heirs of the divine favor. If the end of condemnation is the negative consequence of the cross of Jesus, then the inclusion and adoption of sinners are the positive significance of this same cross. In general, this is what Paul means by "grace." It is the astonishing and clearly unmerited favor of God, who reaches out to the excluded and the condemned in order to claim them as God's own children and heirs, and therefore as the designated recipients of the divine favor.

Third, to say that the policy of Jesus is also the divine policy with respect to those who are accused and condemned is to say that what Jesus does is "from God." This is expressed in 1 Timothy as follows: "This word is certain and trustworthy: Christ Jesus entered the world in order to save sinners" (1:15). Here it is only necessary to recall that sinners are "saved" precisely from accusation and condemnation. That is, they are delivered from the condemnatory force of the law. The solidarity of Jesus with sinners as narrated in the Gospels is generalized to become the deliverance of sinners from the accusation and condemnation by the law.

Finally, the deliverance of sinners from condemnation by the law is something that is regarded as universal in application, as having to do with all. This is expressed in 1 John as follows: "He is the expiation for our sins and not for ours only but for the sins of *the whole world*" (2:2, emphasis added). The universal scope of the significance of Jesus' solidarity with sinners as the policy of God is also a regular feature of Paul's view. For Paul, Jesus is the new humanity, the second Adam in whom all humanity acquires a new starting point, a new beginning. This is largely entailed in the recognition that Jesus' policy is not an aberration, but is the policy of God.

Welcome one another (Paul)

While the language of the forgiveness and pardon offered to sinners through the cross has a strong tradition in Western theology, and has precedent in the New Testament texts that we have considered, it has also been subjected to a number of misunderstandings. It may then be more helpful to make use of the sort of language that is both more Pauline and more consistent with what appears to be the practice of Jesus as attested in the Gospels. This is the language of welcome or hospitality.

Great advances in biblical theology are often the result of attending to the obvious. Some years ago, Krister Stendahl, the Lutheran bishop and New Testament scholar, noted that Paul almost never uses the language of the forgiveness of sins.[3] Since biblical theologians had managed to interpret Paul's talk of justification almost entirely in terms of the forgiveness of sins (in part because this had been the most important existential problem that Martin Luther had struggled with and to which he found Paul providing the answer), this came as a bit of a shock. And to those who simply read the English translations of the letters of Paul, this may seem quite odd. But the truth is that in the Pauline literature, the only time the normal word for "forgiveness" is ever used is in a quotation from the Psalms, which Paul uses simply to emphasize the blessings that come from faith. Otherwise, Paul uses a term that is normally translated as "welcome," or "receive," or "give hospitality to."[4]

One place where Paul seems to be speaking of forgiveness comes in 2 Corinthians, where he is referring to the case of one who has been disciplined by the community. It is possible that this is a reference to the person who had been excluded for apparent incest with his (step-)mother in 1 Corinthians 5:1-5. In the passage in 2 Corinthians, the New Revised Standard Version has Paul writing: "This punishment by the majority is enough for such a person; so now instead you should forgive and console him, so that he may not be overwhelmed by excessive sorrow" (2:6-7). The term used here is not one that is typically translated as "forgive" (*apheien*), but is a form of the term for "grace" (*charizomai*), which means to show oneself favorably disposed to, or to welcome. Since that which caused sorrow was the person's exclusion, the admonition to "welcome" makes more sense than to "forgive"; it is the welcome that enables the consolation. Paul continues: "So I urge you to reaffirm your love for him" (2:8 NRSV). Again, the sense of welcome rather than forgiveness is what is at stake here. This is all the clearer since there is no reference in the passage to confession, repentance, or any of the other actions typically associated with what is called forgiveness. The change of heart, if there is one, is one that characterizes the community; it is the community that welcomes back into the fold one who had been excluded. Paul continues: "Anyone you forgive [welcome], I also forgive [welcome]" (2:10). The point that the passage underscores is the gracious welcome extended to the other, including the other who is or has been regarded as in some way "outside." Thus, the welcome is at the same time grace, and thus does not seem to be conditional at all.

In the deutero-Pauline literature, there are two other cases where the English translation seems to have Paul speak of forgiveness. In Colossians, one reads: "Bear with one another and, if anyone has a complaint against another, forgive each other; just as the Lord has forgiven you" (3:13 NRSV). And in Ephesians: "Be kind to one another, tenderhearted, forgiving one another, as God in Messiah has forgiven you" (4:32). Once again the word that is translated "forgive" is one normally translated as being favorable to or gracious. It is translated in just this way in Romans 15:7, where Paul says, "Welcome one another as Messiah has welcomed you." This is virtually the identical construction as we find in Colossians and in Ephesians: welcome as the Lord has welcomed you, as God in Messiah has welcomed you. Moreover, this comports far better with what the texts are saying: being kind and tenderhearted (Ephesians), bearing with one another (Colossians).

The point here is that the forgiveness of sins has no place in the Pauline theology, including the theology of the cross. This stands in the starkest possible contrast to the theological tradition of the West, whether Protestant or Catholic, that interprets Paul as emphasizing almost nothing else! In its place, Paul talks about being gracious to one another, kind to one another, welcoming of one another—and doing so in imitation of the way God acts in God's own Messiah.

Now this is precisely what we also find in many of the New Testament accounts concerning the practice of Jesus. As we have seen, Jesus simply welcomes those who are regarded by the scrupulous and respectable as sinners. He makes no judgment when he speaks of the lifestyle of the Samaritan woman; he says to the adulterous woman, "Neither do I condemn you"; he goes to dinner at the home of Zacchaeus without condition, just as he also accepts the invitation of a Pharisee (Luke 7:36). None of the barriers to companionship that are often assumed on the basis of talk of the forgiveness of sin are to be found: no confession, no prior repentance, no prior determination to lead a different life. Transformation may occasionally be the result (as in the case of Zacchaeus), and there may even be a word of prudential advice (as to the woman taken in adultery), but it is never something that stands between Jesus and his welcome of the other person.

In the case of Paul, this "extravagant welcome" even goes so far as to provide hospitality to those who unjustly persecute the community: "If your enemies are hungry, feed them; if they are thirsty, give them something to drink" (Rom 12:20 NRSV). In this way Paul anticipates and gives concrete meaning to the saying that Matthew will attribute to Jesus in the Sermon on the Mount: "Love your enemies" (Matt 5:44). For love here has the meaning not of a vague sentimentality but of concrete acts of hospitality and welcome.

Moreover, it is precisely in these terms that Paul describes the action of God in Christ: while we are yet sinners, while we are enemies of God, nevertheless God comes to us in the Messiah and offers us communion with him. And this is accomplished, we recall, through the cross. Thus, we are to "welcome one another as Messiah has welcomed" (Rom 15:7).

The cross against accusation today

In spite of the practice of Jesus in welcoming those who were regarded as sinners, and in spite of the Pauline supposition that the power of the law to accuse and condemn is shattered upon the cross of Jesus, there can be little doubt that Christianity, especially in its Western varieties, has regularly constituted itself as a system of accusation and condemnation of "sinners." It has done this by doing whatever it can to make the sense of sinfulness as acute as possible so that those who are "convicted of sin" will have recourse to the forgiveness of sins that can be dispensed only by ecclesiastical means, whether through the sacraments or through "conversion" and conformity to certain lifestyle requirements of church membership. Accordingly, most who come into contact with Christianity receive the message of a God who is angry at sin and who must be appeased in some way or another.

One of the ways this consciousness of sin comes forward as the basic problem (for which the sacraments or church adherence is the solution) is through a strong emphasis on sexuality as the privileged domain of sinfulness. So pervasive has this become in the late modern era that Paul's references to flesh or to desire, as well as to wickedness or unrighteousness (actually mistranslations of "injustice"), are self-evidently connected to sexuality in spite of the impossibility of this emphasis.

The emphasis on sexual desire and practice has the advantage of indicting virtually everyone, while at the same time upholding the traditional views of marriage and family values. This then makes it possible to scapegoat unconventional sexualities as the most flagrant domain of "sinfulness" while allowing the rest to receive a sort of absolution for more conventional desires. Accordingly, we have the remarkable scapegoating of homosexuality, which allows others to feel that at least they are not "that bad."

Of course, this is only a particularly egregious example of the way in which followers of one who welcomed "sinners," and adherents of a gospel that announces the end of the law of accusation and condemnation, become the chief instruments of accusation and condemnation of other people's forms of life. And all this happens under the safety of not questioning the sorts of things that the biblical authors *do* actually condemn: the violation of the poor, the marginalized, and the vulnerable. This is the practice of the bully: try to intimidate the vulnerable while being essentially cowardly in the face of the more powerful.

A recovery of anything like the message of the cross will mean that this moralizing hypocrisy is simply and completely renounced. And this may well have the same consequence today as it did in the time of Jesus, that the self-appointed arbiters of respectability and religiosity will turn their accusation and condemnation against those who demonstrate the same welcome to sinners exhibited by the Messiah.

At the same time, it will mean that those who have borne the brunt of accusation and condemnation will hear the astonishing word that they are welcome without condition, that there is now no condemnation, that God is on the side of the accused and not the accusers.

CHAPTER FIVE

The Cross and Suffering

W e have seen that the basic form of suffering indicated by the cross is incurred by those who resist or confront powers of domination, particularly in the military-political sphere. Thus, martyrdom in this sense is the basic feature of the cross.

However, the question then arises concerning the generalization of this mode of suffering to include others. How is the suffering that is brought on by confrontation with unjust principalities and powers connected to other forms of suffering? In this chapter, we will explore this question first in terms of the relation between the suffering of those who oppose unjust structures and the suffering of those who seem to be merely the passive victims of those systems. We will then consider the connection between this suffering at the hands of unjust systems and what is sometimes called "natural suffering," that which is the fate of bodies exposed to pain and sickness. In this connection, we will be helped by returning to an examination of the characteristic activity of Jesus' ministry: the healing of broken bodies and minds. We will also have to consider the connection between the body exposed to sickness and suffering, and the general fate of mortality itself. To what extent is our mortality taken up into and transformed by the cross? As we shall see, the incorporation of mortality in general into the cross also entails the incorporation of the earth, and so of creation generally, into the redemptive significance of the cross. The problem with this emphasis upon suffering and sickness, however, is that we may lose sight of the goal of this redemptive work: the enlivening of mortal bodies, and so the bodily affirmation and celebration of life as the gift of God.

Unjust suffering

When Jesus called upon his understudies to "take up their cross," he was calling on them not to be passive victims of the systems and structures of oppression, exclusion, and condemnation, but to become agents who confronted those structures in such a way that their own lives would be placed in jeopardy. That is, the most obvious sense of bearing the cross is that of joining with Christ in the exposure to martyrdom. At the same time, we often hear of the "cross" of those who seem simply to be the passive victims of such structures, of those who, without taking any initiative, are simply made into the objects of suffering at the hands of systems of domination and division. What is the relation between the suffering that is a consequence of confrontation and resistance on the one hand, and the rather more routine effect of these powers in their infliction of human suffering on those who are simply the objects of imperial or political power on the other hand?

The difference has to do with the presence or absence of "agency," of opposition, of resistance, or even of provocation. In modern terms, this would be the difference between the suffering experienced by those who directly opposed segregation or apartheid, and the suffering of those who were the more or less passive victims of this system. Clearly these are very different in important respects. But equally clearly, they have an intimate connection. It is the suffering of the victims of oppression that provokes the determination to resist or oppose such structures on behalf of the victims. Thus, the suffering of the victims most clearly produces the revelation of the injustice of the system and the determination to oppose or resist, even if the ones opposing are sometimes quite distinct from those who are the victims.

Moreover, it is the intention of those who take on the role of resistance and of opposition (confrontation, provocation, and so on) to enter into solidarity with the victims and to act for the sake of the victims, in order to effect their deliverance from the oppression that produces their suffering.

We should note at this point that it may be the case that, as in the nonviolent strategy of Martin Luther King Jr., the intention is also to deliver the "oppressors" from systems that are seen (though not usually by the oppressors themselves) to dehumanize them in the process. That is, the action of the martyrs aims not only at the liberation of the victims from those systems, but also at the deliverance of the oppressors. This universal intention of redemption is not directed at victims and oppressors in the same way, however. Its relation to the victims is direct, both in the sense that their redemption is the immediate goal of action and in the sense that in martyrdom the martyr suffers the same fate as the victim. The relation to those who benefit from, or enforce, such structures is indirect. It aims to convict them of complicity in unjust suffering so that they may renounce that complicity and so renounce their active or passive support of such systems.

The example of the early church martyrs may be helpful. They acted in ways that the guardians of empire often found provocative. Their fearlessness in the face of death strengthened the resolve of their companions, as well. But it is also the case that this fearlessness in the face of death was a means of awakening those who were complicit in these structures to their injustice. Thus, many who were more or less conscious agents of imperial rule become themselves adherents of the persecuted minority. Examples of this abound in stories of martyrdom and, indeed, are already present in the Gospels in the case of the centurion at the cross or of Joseph of Arimathea. Subsequently, we hear of those such as Justin Martyr in the second century, who was converted to the side of the persecuted Christians by the martyrdom of others in such a way that he himself (a privileged philosopher) not only became an adherent of this sect, but suffered ultimately the same fate as the martyrs (hence the name by which he is known to the history of the church). We will return subsequently to this more universal aim of redemption.

At this point, however, what is primarily in view is the relation between the suffering of those who confront unjust systems and the suffering of those who, while not confronting or provoking these systems, are nevertheless the victims of its ferocity or heedlessness. The act of confrontation brings the martyr into deep solidarity with those who are the victims of those systems or structures.

However, it will remain important to maintain some clear distinctions here. For while in certain ways the work of resistance that leads to martyrdom may effect deliverance from the passive suffering of those who are the objects of cruel and unjust structures (that is its aim), the passive suffering itself does not do so directly, even if it may have an indirect effect in provoking resistance. Thus, the suffering of "martyrdom" may have a liberative or redemptive character, while the suffering of victims does not stand in the same direct relation to redemption. It is redeemed but not redemptive, we might say. It is important to keep this distinction in view if we are to prevent the legitimation of unjust suffering itself. Redemption must not become a license for resignation to, still less for the glorification of, unjust suffering.

Thus, while passive suffering may provoke liberative action, the liberative action intends not to "justify" that suffering, but to abolish it. The plight of the sick and demon-possessed may provoke the healing that occurs in the stories concerning Jesus, but that does not mean that it is the sickness rather than the healing that is redemptive or liberative.

Here we may consider the striking story in John 9 concerning a man blind from birth. "His disciples asked him, 'Rabbi, who sinned? This man or his parents, that he was born blind?' Jesus answered, 'It was not that this man sinned, or his parents, but that the works of God might be manifested in him'" (John 9:2-3). At one level, Jesus opposes himself to a theodical justification of the suffering of this man (or his parents). At another level, this suffering is taken up into significance in the ensuing action that abolishes the cause of the suffering. It is the healing, rather than the disease or suffering itself, that has redemptive significance. But when thus taken up into the working of God, it becomes a part of redemptive history. There is much that rewards close scrutiny in this text, but it is noteworthy that it takes up the whole of chapter 9 and much of the following chapter. It is thus decisive for the narrator of the text. As we shall see, the incident combines a concern for healing with the condemnation of Jesus as a "sinner," and so it integrates into this incident the abolition of law as well as the abolition of deformity and disease. But what is most important is to note again that it is not the blindness that is redemptive but the healing—it is the healing that lifts the blindness into the narrative of redemption.

While this distinction is critical, it must not become a disjunction. First, the act of provocation or resistance seeks to identify itself with the suffering of the victim, not to disparage it or distance itself from it, but to transform it. Second, the work of provocation itself at the crucial juncture also becomes passive in the face of suffering so that it may be distinguished from an uprising in the same register as the violence it opposes. The very passivity in which the resistance of the martyr or "witness" culminates is what binds it indissolubly to the suffering of the victims it seeks to "liberate" or redeem. This again underlines the significance of the ultimate passivity of the cross. Finally, it is the work of redemption to confer a certain dignity upon those who are victims and who are thereby integrated into the redemptive act. This is true of them in ways that it is not of their oppressors. That is, the suffering of the victims is transposed into something meaningful in the process of transformation. The suffering of those who died on the Middle Passage of slavery, for example, is "redeemed" insofar as it is incorporated into a history of struggle and resistance, of anamnesis and hope. But by itself, apart from this movement, the suffering is senseless, meaningless, absurd.

There is, however, one sense in which it is possible to say that senseless or absurd suffering is already participating in or inaugurating the redemptive activity of God. In the primal history of Genesis, with the first murder we see something of a hint in this direction. The innocent blood of Abel cries from the ground and in this way provokes the intervention of God (Gen 4:10). That is, unjust suffering is itself a kind of appeal to God, a call to God, an awakening of God. In the case of Abel, this call does not yet result in his deliverance, but instead in the punishment of Cain. Much later, in the Exodus story, when God appears to Moses, God says that the cry of the oppressed slaves has come to God and that this is the basis of the divine redemptive action (Exod 3:7, 9, 16-17). Thus, as a mute appeal to heaven, as that which provokes or summons the divine into action, this suffering is incorporated into the redemptive intention and action of God.[1]

We may also ask to what extent the cross of the Crucified One itself solicits compassionate identification with the victim of unjust suffering.

Adherence to the broken body of the one executed by state-sanctioned violence may be seen to break the spell of the unanimity of the scapegoat mechanism.[2] That is, it is no longer the case that the sufferer is simply assumed to be guilty. Of course, this is not always true; we may recall the astonishing cruelty of persons at public executions. When I was in Latin America, I often heard church leaders say that if people were rounded up (for example, in Argentina, Brazil, or even Mexico), it must be because they were guilty. It is this presumption that the cross undermines. If the body of this one epitomizes "unjust suffering," then wherever unjust suffering is encountered, one encounters an image or mirror of this suffering.

It is on this basis that the title of C. S. Song's book, *Jesus, the Crucified People*, is justified. Even where the suffering is not the result of confrontation with the powers, it is still a suffering that is assumed or taken up into the execution of the Crucified. The cross thus provides us with a clarifying lens with which to see what is before our eyes, the unjust suffering of the other, in an entirely different light. It is this vision, then, that provokes the identification with these victims on the part of those who stand in their place and engage in the struggle for which the victims themselves often lack the resources.

Unjust and "natural" suffering

It is possible to assimilate a considerable degree of human suffering into the model of unjust suffering. For example, the death of millions from sickness and disease is no mere fate or natural condition, but often explicable directly in terms of economic and political forces of oppression. Thus, for example, one of my students in Mexico, Cervando, died of cerebral tubercular meningitis. This disease was caused by microbes to be sure, but microbes that millions carry and only some, weakened by extremes of poverty and deprivation, die from. He was an "indio" raised under conditions of impoverishment, weakened constitutionally by them. Was his death due to natural causes or to systems of deprivation?

When I was teaching in Mexico City in 1985, many thousands perished in a major earthquake. Was this an act of nature? To be sure. But the buildings that collapsed on their occupants were for the most part buildings constructed under government contract in ways that utterly failed to meet the minimum standards of construction (no ancient buildings fell, for example). Was this a natural act, or one that involved human mendacity, corruption, and contempt for life?

We should also think of the deaths of thirty million children a year from preventable starvation, malnutrition, and diseases. Is this a natural calamity, or one in which sheer greed, racism, and culpable indifference play the largest part? Is their suffering and death not also comprehended in the meaning of the cross? Are they not also to be understood as the "crucified people"?[3] The more clearly we see these connections, the more confidently we can suppose that a strategy that aims at the abolition of "unjust suffering" is one that at the same time addresses much of the "natural" suffering of humanity.

However, this is not all that may be said here. The cross, as the infliction of humiliation, damage, pain, and ultimately death and visible decay upon the body, represents in an especially gruesome way the bodiliness of the Christian theme of redemption. The cross aims to reduce its victim to body in the most egregious way. Torture and nakedness expose the rawness of the flesh, its permeability to suffering. Melito of Sardis, in what seems to be the earliest preserved homily on the passion (around 170 C.E.), underscores the naked vulnerability of the Crucified:

> The sovereign has been made unrecognizable by his naked body,
> And is not even allowed a garment to keep him from view.
> That is why the luminaries turned away,
> And the day was darkened, so that he might hide the one stripped
>   bare upon the tree,
> Darkening not the body of the Lord
> But the eyes of men.[4]

The cross displays the body of the presumed malefactor to the deriding gaze, the wounding spear, the elements. It is intended to reduce its victim to body, to corruptibility, to shame and utter vulnerability, to pain and suffering. And beyond that, it serves to display the carcass, the being subject to death and decay that is the common but often disguised lot of all living, embodied creatures.

To the extent that the Crucified is made the site of redemption, the vulnerable body is also made the site or locus of redemption. This has been the bedrock of Christian perspectives on atonement. However watered down or mitigated, however much we are tempted both in antiquity and today to substitute a gnostic escape from the body for this horror of bodily vulnerability as the means of redemption, we are prevented from finally succeeding by the fact of the cross. Insofar as the cross of the Crucified draws us to the vulnerable, the wounded, the shamed and damaged, the dying body, it draws us into compassion with the bodiliness of each and of all.[5]

It is for this reason that patristic Christology so emphasized corruption of the body and mortality as that which is addressed by the "atonement." It is for this reason that incarnation was taken to be the all-encompassing fact that included, but was not reducible to, the cross. For it was becoming flesh that is the presupposition of this sharing in the suffering that is the lot of the bodily.

Accordingly, Athanasius can maintain:

> And thus taking a body like ours, since all were liable to the corruption of death, and surrendering it to death on behalf of all, he offered it to the Father. And this he did in his loving kindness in order that, as all die in him, the law concerning corruption in men might be abolished.[6]

Athanasius further maintains: "The death of all was fulfilled in the Lord's body, and also death and corruption were destroyed because of the Word who was in it."[7]

The point for Athanasius—as well as for earlier theologians such as Irenaeus and later ones such as Gregory of Nyssa—is that the incarnation, which culminates in the cross, is to be understood as addressing the subjection of human being to vulnerability and mortality. However much we may have to lament the forgetfulness of the historical concreteness of the cross in much of this thinking, it is possible, I believe, to affirm with these authors that the cross of Jesus does indeed address the universal human predicament of suffering and death. In order to see how this is so, we may turn to the grounding of this theme in the ministry of Jesus.

The ministry of Jesus

The attachment to the body, and especially to the suffering body, is not something that suddenly appears out of nowhere in the cross of Jesus, but is something that already characterizes his ministry among the poor as a ministry of healing.

The very fact of Jesus' ministry as engaged in healing already signals quite strongly that bodily infirmity, sickness, and death are not "the will of God." To the extent to which the suffering of bodily infirmity had been understood as punishment for sin, the ministry of healing that enacts the coming of the divine reign decisively breaks with that view. Thus, in Luke, Jesus rebukes the supposition that those killed by Pilate or those killed by the fall of the tower of Siloam were especially guilty of sin (Luke 13:2-4), and in the Gospel of John, he denies that it is because of either the blind man's sin or that of his parents that the man has been blind since birth (John 9:3). On the contrary, that God comes means that bodies are made whole, vigorous, alive. God is not on the side of affliction but on the side of healing.

All too often, it is the case that in theological and homiletical emphasis upon salvation, including salvation through the cross, the connection to the healing of bodies, and thus to the sheer bodiliness of the mission of Jesus, becomes forgotten or marginalized. Attention to the Gospels themselves may prevent such a misunderstanding.

The most consistent and normative act of Jesus relative to his ministry is that of healing the sick. If there is anything else beyond the cross itself that may be affirmed with confidence concerning the "historical Jesus," it would be this activity of healing.

The Gospel of Mark, for example, immediately begins to demonstrate what it means to say that the reign of God is come upon us through Jesus' healing, first of a man with an unclean spirit (Mark 1:23), and then of Peter's wife's mother (1:30-31). The immediate result of this is that "they would bring all the sick and demon-possessed to him. And the whole city would crowd about the door. On such occasions he cured many people afflicted with various diseases and drove out many demons" (1:32-34). From this point on, the characteristic sign of Jesus' ministry is the work of healing. Among the most important of these, we may recall the case of the lepers (1:40ff.), a paralytic (2:1-12), a man with a crippled hand (3:1-6), a demoniac (5:1-19), a woman bleeding from her womb (5:24-34), the daughter of Jairus (5:21-24; 35-43), the Syrophoenician woman's daughter (7:24-30), a deaf-mute (7:32-37), a blind man (8:22-25), another mute lad (9:14-29), and blind Bartimaus

(10:46-52). The other Gospels present us with a number of additional stories of the healing of leprosy, of blindness, and of all manner of infirmity. The point of this brief summary is simply to remind ourselves that the mission of the one who will be executed is a ministry to the broken bodies and burdened minds of others.

The resuscitations constitute an especially striking instance of healing. Here the damage to the body is most severe, and what becomes clear is that sickness and injury presage mortality. Thus, the resuscitations of the dead—Jairus's daughter (Mark 5:21-24, 35-43), the son of the widow at Nain (Luke 7:11-16), as well as the lengthy narrative of the raising of Lazarus (John 11:1-53)—all stand in a certain continuity with the healings. This is already clear in the case of Jairus's daughter. When Jairus first comes to Jesus, the girl is said to be desperately ill and Jesus agrees to accompany him to his home (5:21-24). However, as Jesus continues on his way to the official's home, the news arrives that the girl has already died (5:35). In this way all illness, all human infirmity, may be understood as but the anticipation of death, or rather as the invasion of death into the living body. Nor is it simply the body of the afflicted that is thus invaded. As the plight of the widow at Nain makes clear (Luke 7:11-17), the death of her son brings her also closer to death, not only in the sense of heartrending grief, but also in the sense of the loss of her only means of economic survival. This is also clear in the case of the resuscitation of Lazarus. We are first told of his illness (John 11:1-5), then, with the passage of time, of his death (11:7-16), a death that we may suppose also menaces his sisters with economic ruin. The intervention of Jesus not only on behalf of the sick and infirm, but also on behalf of those whose loss has brought the survivors within the power of death, makes clear that what is at stake in the healings is an overcoming of the power of death.

We note also that in many cases, bodily contact is involved. This is true of the hemorrhaging woman, of the lepers, of the dead. This is especially striking where the decay or corruption, including "uncleanness," is regarded as contagious. This means that the ministry of healing involves intimate association with or contamination by the degradations of bodily corruption. We may recall that the menstruating woman, the leper, and the corpse are all regarded as loci of contamination or pollution that is contagious, thus rendering any who come into contact "unclean." The healing ministry of Jesus already involves him in the ritual uncleanness that will be part of the significance of his cross.

We may also note that no clear demarcation appears to be possible between demonic possession (madness) and bodily damage. This appears in the case of the Gadarene (Mark 5:1-20), of the centurion's boyfriend (Matt 8:5-13), and of the lad who was deaf-mute (Mark 7:31-37). Thus, the texts suggest a very strong unity of body and mind, as well as a very strong sense that whatever damages human bodily being is diabolical. This will serve as the connecting link, I believe, to patristic suggestions of the cross as the defeat of the devil.

Healings and the cross

Jesus' mission and ministry of healing is connected at every point in these narratives to his fate, to his being handed over to be executed. It is important that we give attention to this relationship if we are to keep close to our theme of the theology of the cross.

The connection between healing and the cross is most obviously implicated in the idea of the conflict with sabbath regulation. That is, the work of healing and exorcism is set up in a mode of confrontation with religious authorities. Thus, the confrontation and provocation that lead to Jesus' execution are already deeply implicated in Jesus' assault upon sickness. It is imperative to attend to this connection if we are not to separate the reflection on the relation of the cross to suffering from our discussion of other aspects of the cross's significance.

We will have to note how both are regularly related to his conflict with the law, as well as the way in which the stories of healings bring Jesus into relation to those who are "outside" the bounds of Israel, and so "outside" the people of God. And finally, we must indicate that there is even a way in which the healings anticipate Jesus' conflict with the political or imperial authorities and their surrogates.

The most easily recognized feature of Jesus' healings in this connection is the conflict with the law as understood by those who had responsibility to administer or apply the law of Israel, thereby making Jesus out to be a sinner, or a religious "outlaw."

This feature is evident in one story that we have already referenced, namely, the story of the man born blind (John 9). There, Jesus is explicitly called a sinner precisely because his healings are in collision with the law of Moses concerning the sabbath. The conflict comes out into the open when John announces that the healing that has just been recounted occurred on the sabbath (John 9:14). In the debate among the Pharisees that is subsequently recounted, some say that he "is not from God because he does not keep the sabbath," to which others reply, "How could a sinner do such wonders?" (9:16). It is thereby clear that the assertion that Jesus does not keep the sabbath is equated with the characterization of Jesus as a sinner. This characterization is then repeated later in this passage (9:24). In this Gospel, the conflict had already broken out when Jesus healed a man who had been crippled for thirty-eight years (5:5). That story concludes with the notice, "This is the reason that the Judeans continued to hound Jesus: he would do things like this on the sabbath day" (5:16). Thus, in the Gospel of John, the activity of healing is quite strongly connected to the determination of the religious or legal authorities to oppose and even kill Jesus: "So this is the reason the Judeans then tried even harder to kill him" (5:18).

This theme is also found in the Synoptic Gospels. The healing of the man with a withered hand in Matthew has a result quite like the one we encountered in the Gospel of John: "The Pharisees went out and hatched a plot to get rid of him" (Matt 12:14).

In the Gospel of Luke, the theme of conflict with the law is somewhat more muted. On several occasions, the reader is let in on the conflict. In chapter 13, we encounter the woman who had been bent over for eighteen years (Luke 13:11).[8] We are not told of a plot as the aftermath, but somewhat dryly told by the narrator that "his opponents were put to shame" (13:17). Almost immediately afterward, at dinner with a Pharisee, Jesus encounters a man with dropsy. After Jesus has healed him, he again speaks of the appropriateness of healing on the sabbath, and we are simply told that "they had no response to this" (14:6).

The first indication of a plot to get rid of Jesus, and indeed the first attempt on his life, is related to Jesus' inaugural sermon in Nazareth, when he referred to the work of Elijah and Elisha in healing those outside of Israel (Luke 4:14-30). That Jesus' activity of healing will regularly bring him into contact with those who are outside the house of Israel, and so those who seem to be excluded from the covenant, is similarly a regular feature of healing narratives. In Luke, when only one of ten lepers who have been healed returns to thank Jesus, we are told that he was a Samaritan (17:11-19). Both Matthew and Luke report Jesus as responding to the request of a centurion to heal the affliction of one who was dear to him (Matt 8:5-13; Luke 7:2-10). Both Mark and Matthew have Jesus respond to the request of the woman of Tyre for the healing of her daughter (Mark 7:24-30; Matt 15:21-28). This is simply to say that Jesus' ministry of healing leads him outside the bounds of Israel, thereby anticipating what we have seen to be an important aspect of the significance of the cross.

In the Gospel of Mark, we also have a glimpse of the way in which the healing activity of Jesus anticipates his conflict with the political authorities, and so is connected to what we have called the political (and most obvious) meaning of the cross. According to Mark, one of Jesus' first healings exhibits this connection quite clearly. In this instance Jesus is met by a person with a withered hand in the synagogue. Jesus asks the man to hold out his hand. The man complies and therewith his hand is restored. We then hear: "Then the Pharisees went right out with the Herodians and hatched a plot against him, to get rid of him" (Mark 3:6; cf. Matt 12:9-14 and Luke 6:6-11). What is especially remarkable in Mark's telling of this episode is the presence of the Herodians with the Pharisees. This is eliminated from the retelling that we encounter in Matthew and Luke. Indeed, comparing these accounts only serves to further highlight this feature. But what is the meaning of this? It is that both Jesus' religious and political opponents are here united in the determination to get rid of Jesus by their joint suspicion of his healing activity that appears to be in contravention of the law. Later, it will be this same pairing of opponents who will inquire of Jesus whether one should pay taxes to Caesar or not (Mark 12:13-17). The author of the Gospel of Mark, therefore, is setting up a direct relation between Jesus' activity of healing (in the synagogue, on the sabbath, and so in contravention with the law) and the ultimate conflict in which Jesus will actually be executed by the authorities responsible to Caesar.[9]

In the long narrative of the resuscitation of Lazarus, this connection is made in a somewhat different way. There we are told that wonders and signs performed by Jesus will provoke the wrath of the Romans, who "will come and destroy both our holy place and our nation" (John 11:48 NRSV). The only way to prevent this, according to Caiaphas, is to remove the source of Roman ire: "It is better for you to have one man die for the people than to have the whole nation destroyed" (11:50 NRSV). Again it is Jesus' intervention against death on behalf of life that is represented as the cause of his execution.

Martyrdom and mortality

It is important to connect the experience of persecution and martyrdom that was assimilated to the public or political character of the cross with the realization of mortality. In order to do this, we must attend to the way in which systems of division and domination ensure their rule through the threat to the body, the threat, above all, of torture, humiliation, and death. If the body were not vulnerable to suffering and death, then the threat of violence to enforce systems of domination would have no function. Such systems depend upon the violation of the vulnerable body as their ultimate means of enforcement.

This means, conversely, that vulnerability of bodiliness is a precondition of the cross. The cross as the humiliation, torture, and execution of a human being depends upon the general condition of vulnerability and mortality.

In this way, the early church theologians appear to have been led to identify a connection between cross and incarnation. Even if this recognition increasingly pointed to a substitution of mortality for oppression as the basic "problem" addressed by the atonement, and so led to the loss of the cross's concrete meaning, it is still the case that the cross as torture and execution depends upon the bodiliness, the vulnerability and mortality, of the human body.

In this way, the theme of God's becoming flesh in the death of the Messiah is an appropriate way to indicate the significance of the cross. Accordingly, these theologians concerned themselves with mortality as the problem, to which incarnation is the basis of the solution, and the resurrection of the body is the goal, where the resurrected body is conceived of in some way as no longer subjected to violation. Thus,

for Paul, death is the "last enemy" whose power is overcome in the resurrection body that is no longer subject to corruption (1 Cor 15).[10]

The ongoing experience of martyrdom, then, was connected to
the question of mortality, since the fate of the martyrs drove home in
a graphic way the mortality of the flesh that was tortured and shamed
and cruelly assaulted. To be a martyr means taking on the vulnerability and mortality of the body in a particularly profound way, thus
bringing the Christian into solidarity with the suffering or vulnerable
or mortal body in extremis. Rather than escaping the body in this
sense, the body as this vulnerability is itself assumed, asserted, even
brandished.

If holiness was not incompatible with all the disgusting things that
befell the body, then there was and could be no reason to abandon the
bodies of others who were similarly vulnerable to suffering and decay.
This keeps the Christian community riveted upon the bodies of those
who suffer. It also means that the care of the sick and dying becomes
an essential part of Christian communal practice, for every broken and
suffering body is a recognizable mirror of the body of the Crucified.[11]
This means, further, that those who become Jesus' understudies will
abide with the unclean. This breaks the back of pollution taboos in
early Christianity, for which neither lepers nor menstrual blood nor
corpses were regarded as either unclean or contaminating. This is a
quite remarkable development.

In his remarkably suggestive study entitled *The Rise of Christianity*, Roy Stark points to the importance of the Christian determination
to stay with the bodies of the sick and dying as part of an explanation of Christianity's growth in the second and third centuries.[12] It was
during this time that the empire was depopulated by a succession of
plagues. Christian communities stayed with the victims, rather than
fleeing the cities. This had the effect of enabling many victims to survive, owing to simple nursing care. And while it meant that Christians
were exposed to the plague, this also meant that those who survived
developed immunity that seemed to their neighbors to be a sure sign
of divine protection. Encouraged by the example of the martyrs to be
unafraid of death, these communities actually overcame the onslaught
of plague-borne death in statistically significant ways.

The bodies of women and slaves

The unjust social order inscribes itself upon bodies and distributes bodiliness differentially: women are regarded as more bodily than men, slaves than masters, and so on. That is, some reserve for themselves a certain distance from the body, and thus from vulnerability, suffering, passivity, and mortality.

The identification with bodiliness on the part of the one who becomes body and becomes contaminated with impure (leprous, bleeding, or dead) bodies, and the submergence in body that is the implication of torture and execution, makes of Jesus one who is body as such. We have noted that women are more bodily (in the ideological sense) than males, slaves more than free, and so on. It is the immersion in the vulnerability and passivity of the body that makes Jesus one with slaves (as the hymn in Philippians insists) and with women.

That Jesus is one with the female in his death is expressed quite dramatically in the preparation of Jesus for death by the anonymous woman in Bethany, as well as in the accompaniment by women of Jesus' execution, death, and burial. These stories underline the "feminization" of the body of the Messiah such that it becomes the object of feminine accompaniment.

Here we see the beginning of an answer to Rosemary Radford Ruether's famous question: How can a male messiah save women?[13] Whether as babe in arms or as exposed to shame and reduction to body, Jesus shares the fate of women. He becomes one who shares the attributes traditionally ascribed to women.

Body and earth

Solidarity with the violated body of those who suffer is the gateway to solidarity with the earth itself. Earth and body, the bodies committed to the earth, becoming earth, body as earth (the earthling), body as that which human shares with the earth as a creature of the earth—all this is implicated in the image of the relation between the resurrection of the body of the Crucified, the resurrection of the dead, the restoration of all things, the new earth and heaven of patristic imagination.

It was the inescapability of the earth as the site of redemption that was fixed upon by the cross.[14] Conversely, when the bodiliness and earthiness of redemption are lost sight of, it becomes all too easy to sever Christian hope from the fate of the earth.[15] Thus, the patristic anticipation of a restoration of all things has become largely unintelligible for us.[16] At the same time, Christian imagination seems all too ready to abandon the earth to its fate. A considerable part of our tradition views the earth as simply the object of exploitation, while, at war with that perspective, we also encounter an ecologically oriented care for the earth and its creatures. It is the latter that seems to be the heir, even if unconsciously, of the patristic sense of the earth as the site of redemption.

Thus, Paul fixes upon the image of the suffering and groaning of the earth as the point at which it is possible to see in redemption a future for the earth, or the resurrection of the body as the claim also of redemption for the earth, for creation. In Romans 8, Paul links together the groaning of creation and the groaning of the human yearning for deliverance from the body of death. The creation itself, he suggests, is under the same weight of futility and suffering that we too experience as "mortal bodies." Thus, the cosmos as creation undergoes the same futility that is mortality. To this, Paul adds the divine Spirit who also "intercedes with sighs too deep for words" (Rom 8:26). All of this has been anticipated in his reference to the coming of the Messiah "in the likeness of sinful flesh" (8:3). Thus, Paul presents us with a certain homology in suffering: the Messiah, the earthling, the earth itself, and the Spirit of God. In this way he points to an extraordinary solidarity in suffering that thus overcomes the divisions between the human and the earth, and between the earth and the divine.[17]

This solidarity is itself the concrete sign, here and now, of the hoped-for redemption. This redemption is anticipated in the resurrection of the Messiah that brings in its train the resurrection of all the dead, and so the groaning of the earth is refigured not as futility, but as "labor pains." The deliverance of the earth is thus tied to the deliverance of the human, which in turn is tied to the deliverance of the Messiah from the futility of death. The suffering of the mortal body is what brings it into relation to the death of the Messiah on the one hand, and to the yearning of the whole creation on the other. This compassion of fellow suffering is the sign of the love that overcomes all separation. Thus, suffering, so far from suggesting separation from the divine, brings us into unshakeable solidarity with the divine, from which, then, nothing whatever can separate us (Rom 8:38-39). This then may serve as the basis for the hope, as Paul indicates, of the divine aim at something like a new creation, or a new heaven and earth, one that ultimately aims at the divine becoming or being "all in all" (Col 3:11).

What is most important here is to notice how all this depends upon taking with absolute seriousness the suffering and death of the Messiah. It is this that brings the divine into solidarity with the suffering of the mortal body. Because of this solidarity, there can be no flight from the body, since the body is precisely where that solidarity is realized. In the same way, there can be no flight from the earth, whose agony is simply the longing for that deliverance that is anticipated in the resurrection of the one in whom God already becomes one with the body and the earth. Resurrection and redemption, then, will mean not escape from earth and the body, but the transformation of these. The answer to the mortality of the body is not escape from the body, but the "redemption of our mortal bodies," and this can only mean deliverance for the earth as earth.[18]

When these connections are severed, then the body that suffers, our own or another's, must simply be escaped. The same is true of the earth.

The festival of life released from death

In this chapter, we have focused attention on the body as the site of suffering and death, of sickness and deprivation. But this is not the most fundamental meaning of the body. The accounts of healing point us to the body delivered from pain and suffering as the true destiny of bodiliness. Suffering and death then appear not as the truth of the body, but as the falsification of the body, the perversion of the body. The body is made not for suffering but for enjoyment, not for the separation that is meant by death but for the relationality that is meant by love. The scandal of the cross, by which the divine enters into the vicissitudes and vulnerability of the mortal body, is met by the no less scandalous resurrection of the body. For redemption means not deliverance *from* the body but the deliverance *of* the body, from death and all its cognates and anticipations. This is already signaled in the healing narratives, when those who are healed rise up to eat and drink and enter into the companionship of others. Similarly, the Eucharistic participation in the broken body is also an anticipation of the banquet of shared bread and wine, the feast of the body made for love.

Calamitously, the spell of a body- and world-denying "spirituality" has been cast, almost from the beginning, over the essential affirmation of the body as the site of redemption. And this body-denying spell has been nowhere more efficacious than in casting suspicion upon the body as the site of the erotic. This suspicion, I believe, has served to make possible a gradual erosion of the care of and for the body, and for the earth of which the body is our portion.

Conclusion

We began with the question of the relation of the cross to human suffering. We have seen that this must not be articulated in such a way as to lose contact with the historical significance of the cross as the unjust suffering inflicted upon the body by the powers of domination and division.

Yet it is precisely the effect of this suffering of the body that brings into the open the vulnerability of the body as the site of redemption, and the fact that it is this "weakness" in which is displayed the strange power of God—the power, above all, to assume vulnerable flesh for the sake of the transformation of that vulnerable flesh.

The woundedness of this flesh and its evident mortality thus incorporate the woundable and mortal flesh of humanity. It is this vulnerability and mortality that is the common plight of all flesh, of all humanity. This is also made evident to us in experiences of sickness, injury, dying, and death.

Accordingly, when we and those we love are subjected to bodily suffering in these ways, we can see in this suffering the suffering that is adopted by the Crucified. The afflicted body is incorporated in the afflicted body of Jesus as the Messiah of God. The effect of this incorporation is that those who adhere to the cross are also those who are in solidarity with the suffering and afflicted body of vulnerable and wounded humanity.

This is by no means obvious even today, as much conspires to lead us toward a shunning of the afflicted body. We professionalize health care and mortuary services in ways that close off ordinary and tender contact with the afflicted body. Indeed, we are even inclined to "blame the victim" as we seek the cause of sickness and of death in "lifestyle choices," as if it were not the case that all mortal flesh inevitably dies of something.

Indeed, we may even speak of a persecution of the sick and dying: their being blamed, shut away, disregarded, devalued. The same is largely true of the wounded earth as well. But the cross demonstrates divine solidarity with the suffering body of humanity and the earth, and through the resurrection of the Crucified, it summons us to hope for the redemption of the mortal body of both the earth and the earthling.

CHAPTER SIX

Reconciliation with God

The Western, or Latin, Christian tradition has been characterized by an emphasis upon the sinfulness of human being as the problem addressed by the event of the cross. (This is in contrast to the Eastern or Orthodox tradition, in which the focus has been far more upon the mortality and infirmity of human being.) Because of the emphasis upon sin in the West, the cross came to be seen increasingly as the event in which the wrath of God was to be somehow placated. As a consequence, the theme of reconciliation or atonement has been quite generally construed as indicating the way in which the anger or judgment of God is placated, in which God is somehow reconciled to sinful humanity. Yet, as we shall see, this rather commonsense view of the meaning of reconciliation is almost exactly the reverse of what appears in New Testament perspectives. In order to grasp the magnitude of the transformation in Western tradition that may be at stake here, we will first need to review in summary form the character of that tradition.

Appeasing divine wrath

From the time of Augustine, the doctrine of human sin was elaborated into a doctrine of universal or original sin that was correlated with the idea of eternal punishment or damnation as the proper effect of divine justice, and finding expression in final judgment. The notion of damnation as the balancing of the scales required by divine justice in the face of human sin was mitigated only by the supposition that the effect of redemption was somehow to cancel the punishment and thus admit some (those claimed by the redemptive event) into salvation. Salvation here is understood as salvation from damnation.

It was the genius of Anselm to provide a rationalized version of this view in his "Why God Became Man." In summary, Anselm's view was that God willed the salvation of humanity. In this, he agreed with the patristic supposition that it would be unseemly for the divine to be defeated by sin and evil in the creative intent to generate a human image and likeness. Thus, the starting point for Anselm is not the wrath but the benevolence of God. However, the divine intention to save appears to be blocked by the divine justice that cannot simply overlook sin as damage to the honor of God, and so also as damage to the balance of justice. Therefore, a way must be found to satisfy the divine justice and restore the divine honor while permitting to go forward the divine intention/will to save humanity. This was the function of the "God/human," who makes reparations to the divine honor in such a way as to permit salvation without surrendering the norm of justice.[1]

In this development, Anselm generally keeps the focus upon the divine intent to save, and thus the divine determination to do so in a way that effects divine mercy without compromising divine justice. However, following the time of Anselm, the perspective of Western theology grew progressively more dire. Certainly from the late Middle Ages well into the early modern period, the character of the divine seems to have been increasingly depicted in terms of rage, wrath, fury, and anger, which in turn were linked to human sin. Thus, there is a tendency to emphasize the divine wrath and its corollary, human depravity. The more the one is underlined, the more the other is emphasized, so that they become mutually reinforcing ideas, each side inciting the other to greater and greater extremes.

The fixation upon the wrath or rage of God toward humanity and creation may have seemed quite plausible in a time of extraordinary calamity. For this period was inaugurated under the shadow of the "Black Death" (a version of the bubonic plague) in the fourteenth century that visited unimaginable death upon Europe, verging on bio-logically induced genocide. And it was perpetuated during the period of the religious wars of the sixteenth and seventeenth centuries that subsequently decimated the European population. Thus, from the time of the fiery preachers of the fourteenth century (Savonarola) to the time of Jonathan Edwards in the eighteenth century, the sense of humanity as sinners in the hands of an angry God predominated in the Western tradition.

Notably, the Reformation comes in the midst of this period. As is well known, Luther was deeply affected by the sense of an angry and wrathful God, and by the urgent quest to discover some way by which it might be possible to escape that wrath, finding instead a merciful or gracious God. Luther did eventually discover a way to speak of such a gracious God, and the image of the cross played no small part in his transformation of the understanding of Christian faith.

Nevertheless, the image of divine wrath that had in some way to be appeased if sinners were to have any hope of redemption remained strongly in the background of Reformation notions of atonement and reconciliation. It has thus come to seem self-evident that the aim of atonement has to do with the appeasement of this anger directed at humanity, and that the death of the Messiah or Son is what effects this transformation in the attitude of the divine toward that humanity that had incurred this wrath. Reconciliation, then, means that somehow God's anger is assuaged and God is "reconciled" to us, or at least to that group of us who are included in the messianic event that comes to a head in the execution of the Messiah.

This is the background for the plausibility of the substitutionary and satisfaction theories of atonement that emphasize the price that had to be paid in order for us (or for some) to escape this wrath.

Who is reconciled?

It appears rather difficult for contemporary readers of the New Testa-ment to notice that the texts that speak of reconciliation in relation to God do not speak of reconciling a wrathful God to a sinful humanity, of overcoming God's enmity toward us, but speak rather of our being reconciled to God. That is, these texts seem to presuppose that it is humanity that is alienated from God, humanity that has an enmity toward God, humanity that is, or thinks it is, the offended party, and that what has happened in the cross is such that it is our enmity or anger that is somehow appeased or overcome so that we might turn back to God. It's as if we are the ones who have a "beef" with God, a complaint against God, and as if this lies at the base of our alienation from God. But God has done something that takes away our anger, our enmity, or our complaint, so that there is now no obstacle to our reconciling ourselves with and to God. In order to see how this is so, we must attend in particular to a few of the salient passages of Paul's letters to see how this is stated.

Perhaps the most important text in this regard is the following passage from 2 Corinthians:

> All this is from God, who reconciled us to himself through Christ, and has given us the ministry of reconciliation; that is, in Christ God was reconciling the world to himself, not counting their trespasses against them, and entrusting the message of reconciliation to us. So we are ambassadors for Christ, since God is making his appeal through us; we entreat you on behalf of Christ, be reconciled to God (5:18-20 NRSV).

There are many dimensions of this passage that may call for commentary, but the most startling is the designation of who it is who is to be reconciled. The effect of the divine action is designated precisely as reconciling *us*. That is, it is not that the action of the Messiah or his death somehow reconciles an angry God, but that it has the aim and intention of reconciling us to God. Thus, we find (in the past tense), "God, who reconciled us to himself"—not the other way around (2 Cor 5:18). And this is repeated, but this time to make clear that it is through the Messiah that this occurs: "In Messiah, God was reconciling the world to himself" (5:19). Here, the reconciling deed is one that is associated with the Messiah, who is the medium or means whereby reconciliation is effected. But note: not the reconciliation of an angry God, but the reconciliation of "the world." Then this is further made into an appeal. God has acted in Messiah in such a way as to overcome our enmity, or that of the world, to God, but this must somehow be made known (the message of reconciliation). And thus this message is an appeal; that is, it is God's own continuing attempt to reach out to an offended or angry humanity and say, "Be reconciled."

The reader of this text may indeed recall that Paul has formerly also maintained that the message (here called the message of reconciliation) is, in 1 Corinthians, named the message of the cross. Thus, that which is supposed to overcome our enmity toward God is precisely something to do with the cross. And this is, to an extent, confirmed here by the immediate context in 2 Corinthians, by way of reference to the manner in which the Messiah was made "to be sin who knew no sin" (2 Cor 5:21), and by the reference to "not counting their trespasses against them" (5:19). We have previously seen that these texts illumine the cross event, and we shall return to them in this connection soon. However, it is also easy to see how, in a theological context fraught with the fear of a God filled with wrath toward a sinful humanity, it was possible for the appearance of sin language to cause the very fundamental structure of reconciliation itself to disappear into the presupposed framework of the appeasement of wrath.

This framework, of course, is not peculiar to Christianity. It is rather common among religious traditions to suppose that the work of religion is to appease the wrath of offended deities. The spread of Christianity among populations whose own religious traditions had focused on discovering effective ways of appeasing divine displeasure would have made it natural to overlook the quite opposite structure of the perspective offered by Paul. This also helps to explain the persuasiveness of metaphors of sacrifice in articulating doctrines of atonement. In many religious traditions, one of the principal functions of sacrifice is specifically to placate or appease an angry deity. Thus, populations whose own traditions had made use of sacrifice in this way may have found the talk of the extreme sacrifice of "the Son" as a way of bridging their former religious understandings and practices toward the newly proffered faith in a God whose wrath had been appeased through sacrifice.[2]

Accordingly, the presupposed pattern of reconciliation as involving the appeasement of divine wrath has been able to override what might be termed the "plain meaning" of the text when it points instead to the overcoming of human enmity toward God. Because of this, it is important to notice that the pattern I am suggesting is not confined to a single text, but is exhibited as a regular feature of texts that deal with the theme of reconciliation.

The passage from 2 Corinthians is not the only text where we are confronted by this surprising reversal of what we may have supposed to be the effect of reconciliation. One of the most cited, yet perhaps least understood, is from Romans: "For if while we were enemies, we were reconciled to God through the death of his Son, much more surely, having been reconciled, will we be saved by his life" (5:10 NRSV). Again we notice that it is we who are being reconciled, not God. And here it is explicitly maintained that this has to do with our enmity: "while we were enemies." That is, God has somehow taken the initiative in the Messiah, here designated as the "Son," to overcome our enmity. To be sure, Paul has just mentioned both our sin and "wrath," and this has no doubt made it possible to (mis)understand, or simply pass over, the structure of reconciliation that is exhibited in the text. This is all the more so since the translators generally, as is also the case with the New Revised Standard Version, amplify the Greek, which simply says "the wrath," into "the wrath of God," thereby bringing the passage into conformity with the theological perspective that has governed talk of reconciliation. But the sense of the passage is that the impending world catastrophe, which Paul has made clear is connected to the unjust condition of the world (Rom 2:5), will not overtake us because of the action of God in Christ.

Moreover, this text makes explicit what was only implicit in the 2 Corinthians passage that we have discussed, namely, that it is the death—that is, the cross—of his Son that somehow reconciles us to God by overcoming our enmity toward God. Thus, he concludes, "We even exult in God through our Lord Jesus Messiah, through whom we have now received reconciliation" (Rom 5:11).

It is important to note that reconciliation is something present. That is, if we understand what it is that God has done, then our enmity is itself already overcome.[3] This is not something that awaits some further decision of God. Rather, it is something that presumably is already present. This is far more intelligible if it is simply a statement of the change in our attitude toward God. Thus, the implicit order would be: God has done something dramatic in the Messiah, and this comes to a head in the fate of the Messiah. This act/event has the effect of removing any cause of complaint we might have against God. The message concerning what God has done, to the extent to which it is received, has the effect of reconciling us to God—that is, of leading us to thank God rather than resent God. This, then, gives us reason to suppose that an even greater transformation (salvation) in our condition will be effected through a closely related event: the resurrection of the Messiah. In this way, Paul also suggests that reconciliation is a "foretaste" of what we subsequently hope for, namely, being "saved by his life" (Rom 5:10).

A subsequent text that is sometimes attributed to Paul is found in Colossians. It bears precisely the same structure: "For in him all the fullness of God was pleased to dwell, and through him God was pleased to reconcile to himself all things, whether on earth or in heaven, by making peace through the blood of the cross" (Col 1:19-20 NRSV). Again we have the structure whereby it is not God who is reconciled but "all things." And again we see it clearly maintained that this occurs by way of the cross, or as the text says, the blood of the cross.

We have already attended (in chapter 3) to another related text, Ephesians 2:11-22, especially 2:16. Here what is at stake is the reaching out to the excluded gentiles and, therefore, the joint "reconciliation" of both groups to God.

Our quick survey should have served to demonstrate that the talk of reconciliation in these texts points to our enmity toward God, not God's enmity toward us, as that which is somehow overcome in the cross. Of course, it is not simply a matter of looking at the words of texts. It is also a question of how these texts are to be understood, especially given what our previous examination of the meaning of the cross has brought to light.

Overcoming *han*

One of the ways I have found most helpful in coming to understand these texts, and the surprising structure of reconciliation that they exhibit, is to take into account the Korean notion of *han*, especially as it has been developed by Andrew Sung Park.[4] He writes:

The victims of various types of wrongdoing express the ineffable experience of deep bitterness and helplessness. Such an experience of pain is called *han* in the Far East. Han can be defined as the critical wound of the heart generated by unjust psychosomatic repression as well as by the social, political, economic, and cultural oppression. It is entrenched in the hearts of the victims of sin and violence. And is expressed through such diverse reactions as sadness, helplessness, hopelessness, resentment, hatred and the will to revenge.[5]

Park uses this notion to reflect on the effects of interhuman violation, and so as a supplement to the doctrine of sin. But the sense of a kind of deep bitterness and resentment also characterizes the enmity toward God that seems to be presupposed by Pauline talk about reconciliation. It is this sense of enmity and bitterness toward God that is overcome in the cross.

The sense of bitterness and enmity directed toward God is one that is already deeply rooted in the literature of ancient Israel, as is the sense that God acts in such a way as to overcome this hostility and resentment. The prophet Jeremiah regularly gives passionate expression to his complaints against the ways in which God deals with him and, by extension, with his people. "Why is my pain unceasing, my wound incurable, refusing to be healed? Truly, you are to me like a deceitful brook, like waters that fail" (Jer 15:18 NRSV). And he can even complain of his very birth: "Why did I come out of the womb, to see trouble and sorrow?" (20:18). Indeed, Jeremiah may even complain that God has violated him (20:7).

The book of Job is an attempt to grapple with the sense that God is the ultimate source of the evils that are experienced in life, and it is indeed this that has made it an unavoidable and frequently restaged classic of literature.

But above all it is in the psalms of lament that Israel has given voice to the *han* that is produced by God's apparent mistreatment of humanity: "Why, O LORD, do you stand far off? Why do you hide yourself in times of trouble?" (Ps 10:1 NRSV). Or again: "How long, O LORD? Will you forget me forever? How long will you hide your face from me? How long must I bear pain in my soul, and have sorrow in my heart all day long? How long shall my enemy be exalted over me?" (13:1-2

NRSV). Or in the words that come to play so important a part in the narrative of the cross: "My God, my God, why have you forsaken me? Why are you so far from helping me, from the words of my groaning? O my God, I cry by day, but you do not answer; and by night, but find no rest" (22:1-2 NRSV). The expressions of a sense of God's absence, or of God's injustice when God does act, are a deep and strong chord in the life and lament of Israel. Moreover, it is to the yearning for God to act in such a way as to decisively overcome this separation, this helplessness and near hopelessness, that the poetry and prayer of prophet and psalmist give voice.

It is also here, I believe, that the voice of Israel comes nearest to being the voice of humanity as such. And so it is here that we enter into that reality to which the message of the cross is a response. This, of course, will mean that this message is not a break with the faith of Israel, but rather something like its intensification, in such a way as to make it available to humanity as a whole.

But how, if we use this notion of *han*, are we to understand concretely the resentment toward God and the overcoming of this resentment and bitterness in the cross? In order to understand, we may briefly review the themes that we have already seen to be connected to the meaning of the cross. In what follows, we will simply show how the themes to which we have already given attention may be seen as coming to a head in the idea that what God has done in and through the Messiah, and especially in his fate, may be represented as overcoming resentment toward God.

God of oppression

In our discussion of the public or political cross, we noted that the most evident reference of the cross was to the execution of Jesus at the hands of state authority of the dominant imperial slavocracy, ruling through the force of military "justice." Moreover, we saw that the cross in this sense is something that does not befall Jesus by accident, but is the result of his policy of siding with the oppressed and of provoking these same imperial forces. Thus, the cross exposes the powers of division and domination as the enemies of God, stripping them of their presumed legitimacy and thereby causing them to crumble.

If we think of the vast majority of peoples in the course of history in relation to structures and powers of oppression and domination, we will be in a position to see how the message of the cross could constitute an appeal to them to be reconciled to God. Nothing is more common than for structures of oppression and domination to legitimate themselves as the representatives of divine will and might. In the political realm, this is the most typical function of what might be termed "God-talk." The divine is invoked as the authorizing and legitimating power behind the forces of domination.

Thus, Roman imperial might was legitimated as the will of the gods, and this came to be concentrated in many parts of the empire through the elaboration of an imperial cult, whether focused upon "Roma" or upon the emperor and the imperial family.[6] Accordingly, the message that God was on the side not of that imperial rule but of one executed by the empire would have had a rather startling effect.

It is not the case that Rome was in any way unusual in providing religious legitimacy for itself and its dominion. Indeed, many of the trappings of an imperial cult had been borrowed from earlier Greek or Hellenistic practices, and these in turn had been borrowed from imperial paradigms familiar to the Persian Empire and the antecedent Babylonian Empire.

Nor is this pattern restricted to antiquity. The notion, for example, of the divine right of kings that issued in the aftermath of feudalism suggests that the king rules in the stead of, and as the representative of, divine power. The imperial adventures of nineteenth-century nation-states were also regularly legitimated as an expression of divine right. Even today it is often the case that hegemony of the United States is implied to be a consequence of the (no doubt benevolent) will of divine power.

For those who benefit, or who believe that they benefit, from such structures and forces of domination, the appeal to divine legitimation may seem self-evident. And for those who suffer at the hands of such structures and forces, it may also seem that they express the sovereign power of an inescapable fate. Thus, it is often the case that those who are ruled accept the claim that their rulers are the concrete expression of divine will and power. But this does not mean that they therefore cease to suffer from these structures. What it instead means is that their bitterness and resentment can only be directed at the God whose regents are so ruthless, whose vicars are so violent.

Whether we think of ancient or of more modern systems of domination, we can be assured that the large majority of the planet's population will have reason to suppose that the powers that afflict them are sanctioned by God and that, therefore, God is their implacable enemy. Thus, the announcement of or message of the cross, which shows that God is on the side not of the ruthless powers that oppress, but rather of those who have been the victims of state-sponsored violence, would make it quite possible to say, paraphrasing Paul (2 Cor 5:9), that "God was in Christ, reconciling the oppressed, us, the world, to Godself."

God of exclusion

Another theme that we have found to be closely connected to the cross is that of the overcoming of an exclusionary religious privilege. In the time and cultural location of the emergence of Christianity, the most obvious form taken by such an exclusionary privilege was the assertion of religious privilege on the part of Israel. It is this privilege that both Paul and the traditions ascribed to Jesus are at pains to contest, as we have seen. The exclusionary character of this privilege was exacerbated by the supposition that being a member of the elect people was at least sometimes taken to be hereditary, and thus irremediable through conversion.

The author of Ephesians makes this the focus of reflection on the theme of reconciliation. Speaking to the gentiles, the writer maintains that through the Messiah, both groups, Jews and gentiles, have been made one (Eph 2:13-14). This is because Messiah "has broken down the dividing wall, that is, the hostility between us." But what is the ground of this hostility? First, it is being excluded from "the covenants of promise," which means that the excluded are those "without hope and without God" (2:12). And the instrument of this exclusion is precisely "the law with its commandments and ordinances" (2:15). However, the instrument that abolishes this division is "the blood of Messiah" (2:13) or, as the writer specifies, "the cross" (2:16). The result of the abolition of exclusionary privilege is that enmity and hostility, first of all between the two peoples, are abolished. In consequence, both groups are "reconciled" (2:16) to one another but also, and therefore, to God, for it was

God, through both the covenant of promise and the commandments and ordinances, who had seemed to be the basis of exclusion. But insofar as the cross abolishes this exclusionary privilege, it means that the excluded are no longer without hope or God in the world. Thus, where before there had been enmity, there now can be thanksgiving.

Moreover, Paul, it seems certain, is concerned that this not result in a mere reversal of privilege, so that it would now be gentiles rather than Jews who enjoy exclusionary religious privilege. The argument of Romans 11 seems carefully designed to contest the view that now it is gentile "Christians" who may "rest on their laurels" as the privileged people of God. Paul warns them that just as they have been grafted onto the promises of God, they can be taken out, so they must not exult over the former (and, as it turns out, future) people of God.

To the extent to which persons believed that God had indeed chosen another and quite different people as the object of benevolence, and consigned others to abandonment, the announcement that through the cross this exclusion had been abrogated by God, and that God, instead of excluding, had determined to include the formerly excluded, could plausibly have addressed a bitter complaint against God and thus have resulted in the formerly excluded being reconciled to God—precisely, as we have seen, through the cross.

Is this only a circumstance that would apply to the distinction between "Jews and gentiles"? Certainly the application of racist ideology from the time of the early modern period could be the occasion of a similar complaint against God. Has God chosen only or especially "white people" as the privileged recipients of divine favor? Certainly white supremacist propaganda then and now seems to make this claim.

Similarly, as we have seen, the overcoming of the division between male and female, and the resultant exclusion of women from full participation in society, is in principle overcome in the new messianic reality attested to by Paul. The exclusions that are engrained into structures and institutions of masculine domination and patriarchy have generally been legitimated through appeal to a divinely sanctioned order, and the submission of women to these structures and their inherent violence has been said to reflect the divine will, thereby producing incalculable *han* in women directed toward God. The message concerning the over-turning of such structures of division and exclusion in the cross may then be or become a beginning point of glad reconciliation to the one who was in Christ reconciling the world to God.

Some may also see a certain analogy in the way in which homosexual orientation is regarded by heterosexist propaganda. Certainly many persons who are gay or lesbian have been led to believe that they are abandoned by the God who favors heterosexuals. Would they then have reason to feel resentment and bitterness toward God? And if they were shown that God had in fact not abandoned them, but looked upon them with the same favor (and at great cost), would it make sense to say that they who were once resentful and bitter toward God may now be reconciled to God? This may be clearer if we connect it to the question of condemnation, to which we next turn.

God of condemnation

We have seen that the Western tradition has focused upon sin as the basic human problem that alienates humanity from God. This has been intensified through the sense of a wrathful God whose implacable ire is directed against sinners. But the mechanism for identifying sin is the law. That is, it is the "commandments and ordinances" that serve as an index of human failure, a failure that can be understood as "total depravity." The threats that accompany the law serve to make clear the penalty for sin. In human law, this is generally expressed through the death penalty, which makes clear the severity of the law. When this is raised to the "theological power," the death penalty gets transposed into damnation.

But the essential thing here is that it is the law as an accusatory and condemning force that serves to underline the desperate character of sin, and to make clear that all stand accused and under the sentence of death or, as the theologians have said, damnation. This sense of God as implacable judge may produce bitterness and resentment toward God. This is especially true, of course, in religious traditions like Judaism, Christianity, and Islam that give expression to the "moral" claim of the divine.

In our consideration of the cross, however, we have seen that the effect of the cross is to abolish the accusatory and condemnatory function of the law. That is, those who understood themselves to be condemned by the law now hear that the power of the law to condemn has been shattered upon the cross. This happens because the Messiah of God is himself one who is accused and condemned by the law, rather than one who imposes or reinforces the law. It is because the law, whether as Roman or Israelite law, has condemned God in the Messiah that the law's power to condemn is broken.

However, if this is true, it means that those who had believed themselves to be condemned through the law now hear that on account of the Messiah there is no condemnation. Those who had reason to resent the harshness of God, who, it seemed, condemned any infraction of the law as worthy of death and even of damnation, now hear that the cause of their complaint, of their bitterness and resentment, has been taken away. Thus, it is now possible to "be reconciled" to God. Again, bitterness is replaced by thanksgiving.

This is precisely the sense of Paul's exhortation: "Be reconciled to God" (2 Cor 5:20 NRSV). It is rooted in the reference to the cross where "for our sake he made him to be sin who knew no sin" (5:21 NRSV). By being condemned by the law, and most especially by that law that is "of God," the Messiah becomes sin itself. But as the one who is vindicated by God, through the resurrection, he is without sin. In this way, it is the case that "in Messiah God was reconciling the world to himself, not counting their trespasses against them" (5:19).

The action of God in Christ then takes away the *han* of resentment on the part of those who had been condemned by the law as the representation of the judgment of God. They may now be joyfully reconciled to God.

God of indifference and affliction

While the accusatory power of the law may be most keenly felt in religious traditions like the so-called "ethical monotheisms," the supposition that the divine is either indifferent to, or the agent of, human suffering appears in a variety of religious traditions and is certainly not absent even from contemporary Christianity.

Thus, even today it is quite common to hear people in the throes of grief over the death of a loved one cry out against God: Why did she have to die? Why did you not protect him? What did I, or he, or she, do wrong such that this has happened? These cries have in common the supposition that God is the cause of calamity. Indeed, the oldest use for God-talk may be something like the supposition that God or the gods are the cause of what happens. And the particular tendency to see divine causality in the occurrence of tragic events is enshrined even in insurance policies that speak of an "act of God" in connection with natural calamities. While this use of God-talk focuses upon "natural disaster," it is regularly generalized to embrace all disaster, including the more personal disasters associated with bodily pain, suffering, sickness, and death. Certainly for all who understand the divine in this way, there is ample occasion in the course of life to protest against the indifference, the silence, perhaps even the malevolent agency of the divine: It's not fair! It's not just! Why her? Why him? Why me? The sorrows with which life afflicts us provide ample fuel for the buildup of resentment and bitterness, of *han*, directed against God.

In our discussion of the relation of the cross to suffering and death, we emphasized that the suffering and death of the Messiah place him in solidarity with the vulnerability and mortality of creaturely being. The recognition that God is fully present in the suffering and death of this one means that God has taken on the suffering and dying of creaturely existence.

This is consistent with the messianic action of Jesus. The near approach of God, or of the reign of God, means that sickness and suffering are overcome. Hence the prominence given to episodes of healing and exorcism in the Gospels. And this even goes so far as the resuscitation of those who have perished. In these narratives, we see dramatically enacted the good news that God does not will sickness and suffering, but rather health and wholeness—that paralysis, infirmity, even death, are not attributable to the divine, but rather, healing and life are.

That the Messiah or Son of God suffers and dies, yet is raised on the third day, then, means that the afflictions of creaturely being are being overcome through the coming of God. The divine solidarity with human vulnerability and mortality aims at the transformation of creaturely being beyond suffering and death. As the Western tradition had emphasized sin as the negative dimension of the human condition for which the cross provided the remedy, the Eastern tradition has emphasized corruptibility (fragility, vulnerability) and mortality as that which the incarnation and cross overcome.

For all humanity that has wrongly supposed that God is indifferent to human suffering, for all who have feared that God is the arbitrary agent of their suffering, for all who have thus had reason to curse God, the message of the cross as the message of divine solidarity with the depths of human suffering is the message of reconciliation. Be reconciled to God, for God was present in the suffering and death of his Son in such a way as to overcome suffering and death for all.

God of abandonment

In order to clarify how it could be possible that the New Testament speaks of our being reconciled to God, rather than of God's being reconciled to us, we have looked at four basic contexts in which we had previously seen the cross to be the decisive event of God's act in history. In each case, we have seen the way in which humanity may be understood as having a complaint against God, at least God as generally understood. Those who suffer oppression may understandably resent the God who is said to be the sanctification of forces of violence and violation. Those who suffer exclusion or denigration may understandably feel resentment toward the God who has sanctioned systems of division, exclusion, and privilege. Those who suffer accusation and condemnation by laws that are said to represent the divine will may understandably feel bitterness and resentment against one who seems to be petty and harsh as judge. And all who suffer the grief and pain of vulnerability and mortality may understandably feel outrage at the God who is depicted as indifferent to their suffering, or even as the agent of that suffering. For these people, the message of the cross is that God is not on the side of oppressors but on the side of the oppressed, not on the side of the privileged who exclude others but on the side of the marginalized and despised, not on the side of those who accuse but who is one of the condemned, not the cause of suffering but the wounded healer. Thus, they may find their tears of lament turned to songs of praise. For them the message of the cross is indeed the message of reconciliation—to God.

Perhaps the most dramatic way in which this reversal of the human situation relative to God finds expression in the New Testament is through images of abandonment and adoption. The image of abandonment finds expression most dramatically in the death cry of Jesus in the narratives of Mark and Matthew, while the image of adoption is most impressively expressed in Paul's letters to the Galatians and Romans.

In Mark's depiction of the death of Jesus, the culmination of Jesus' passion is the cry of protest against abandonment by the God whom he had addressed as Abba. Thus, his being subjected to execution at the hands of imperial and military rule, his having been rejected and excluded from the people of God, his condemnation as sinner and as blasphemer, his torture, humiliation, and inevitable death, all come to a head in this cry of protest against abandonment. The one who had been claimed by the divine voice as the beloved Son is now abandoned to silence, to the emptiness of the heavens, the absence of God.

With this cry of abandonment, Jesus enters into profound solidarity with the human condition. His cry is not his alone; it is the cry of a wounded, humiliated, aggrieved humanity. All who suffer under the oppression of the arrogant and violent, all who are despised as outsiders, all who are condemned by moralistic guardians of the divine law, all who suffer the agonies of their loved ones and their own lonely deaths, utter the same cry, a cry that rises up to a silent heaven from millions of throats every hour of every day. "My God, my God, why have you abandoned me?"

Yet this cry is itself the cry of God. It is the cry of God made flesh, who has come among us and who takes up the cry of vulnerable and violated humanity as God's own cry. Immanuel, God with us. In our abandonment. In our godforsakenness.

However, the one who is thus abandoned is not finally abandoned and forsaken. While the narrative does not rush away from this scene of desolation, but allows us space and time for the desolation to sink in—the removal from the cross, the burial, the waiting, the grieving vigil—the narrative does not end without the announcement of an astonishing reversal: the one abandoned by God has been raised by God.

Paul seems to have understood the resurrection as in some way like the adoption of Jesus as Son of God. In Romans, he is the one who "was declared to be Son of God with power according to the spirit of holiness by resurrection from the dead" (Rom 1:4 NRSV). That is, it is the resurrection from among the dead that declares Jesus to be Son of God, that effectively adopts him as God's own.

Certainly this notion of adoption is one that Paul uses to significant effect in his preaching. In Galatia, the consequence of his proclamation of the cross is that his hearers acclaim God as "Abba, the Father," and this is the same result he supposes to be true for those to whom he writes in Rome (Rom 8:15-17; Gal 4:6-7). A humanity that had once understood itself to be the enemy of God or the helpless slave of an arbitrary and despotic deity now knows itself to be adopted by a loving parent.

From abandonment to adoption is the movement that seems to be traced by the proclamation of the cross. It is thus quite clear how those who had felt themselves to be abandoned by an inscrutable and implacable deity, and who now find that they have been claimed by a relentless and infallible love, might well find themselves, as Paul has said, reconciled to God.

It is precisely as the effect of the message concerning the cross that Paul reaches the conclusion in Romans 8 that nothing can possibly separate us from the love of God that is enacted and announced in Messiah Jesus.

> For I am convinced that neither death, nor life, nor angels, nor rulers, nor things present, nor things to come, nor powers, nor height, nor depth, nor anything else in all creation, will be able to separate us from the love of God in Christ Jesus our Lord. (Rom 8:38-39 NRSV)

Excursus: *God of religion*

But if the cross is the end of any possible separation between humanity and God, does this also mean the end of religion? It certainly will insofar as religion is predicated on this separation, even if it is a separation that claims the prerogative of mediating.

Religion is often constituted, as Eliade has maintained, by the disjuncture between the sacred and the profane. It is the task of religion, whether as institution or as "feeling," to guard this disjuncture, to maintain this distance.

Yet it is precisely this separation, and thus this distance, that seems to be abolished in and through the cross. This is dramatically enacted in the ripping of the temple veil that immediately follows Jesus' cry of protest against abandonment. The curtain's function is to protect the holiness of the divine from even priestly eyes. Thus, it guards the Holy of Holies. The cry of dereliction seems to rip this separating curtain asunder. That is, it destroys the separation between God and all that is profane.

Henceforth, God is not hidden away behind the veil of religion, separated from the profane world in which we live, but is instead dispersed among humanity. Jesus had said that the divine could be encountered only among the vulnerable, the violated, the destitute, for it is in tending to the needs of those who are destitute and despised that we respond to the one who comes to judge, the one who is in person the cry and claim of justice (Matt 25:31-46).

The message of the cross is, at the same time, the message of the end of religion, of all the ways of hiding God and of hiding from God—of all the ways of substituting religious games and trappings for the simple claim of justice and mercy. That this abolition of religion as the institutionalization of the separation between God and humanity, the sacred and the profane, should be the consequence of Jesus' fate should itself not be surprising, since the structure of religion is so often in question in his ministry as recorded in the Gospels.

Perhaps the most contentious of Jesus' interventions in the sphere of religion is his abolition of the distinction between the sabbath and other days when it comes to responding to human welfare needs. We have already seen that this is a radical siding with the claim of suffering, which makes human health and wholeness the sign of the in-breaking of the divine reign. But it also means that the separation of holy time from secular time is abolished. If secular time means the time that is dedicated to the doing of justice and compassion among humans, then all times are secular. If holy time means the time that is "set aside" for doing the divine will, then all times are holy. In any case, the distinction is abolished, and with it the religious institutionalization of the separation of time.

Similarly, the separation of holy space from secular space is abolished. It is not just that all holy places are equal: the mountain of

Samaria and that of Zion, for example. It is, rather, that the adoration of God takes place neither in this place nor in that, neither on this mountain nor in Jerusalem, but wherever the image of God is encountered.

A decisive way in which religion perpetuates itself is in the designation of specific practices and personnel that mediate the favor of the divine. In the Gospels, this is dramatically expressed with respect to the question of the forgiveness of sins. The whole array of priestly personnel and practices was dedicated to this subject. Yet Jesus intervenes in such a way as to make clear that all have the authority to forgive sins. This, at least, is the conclusion drawn by the author of Matthew's Gospel, who has the crowds, after Jesus has healed the paralytic (and so demonstrated the power to forgive sins), "glorify God, who had given such authority to human beings" (Matt 9:8). If mere human beings are enabled to represent the divine in this way without the mediation of sacrifice or of specially conferred authority, then the institutions of religion are rendered useless.

This ruin of religion finds expression in the sayings concerning the temple that seemed to cause such consternation among the religious elite of Jerusalem. For when the disciples draw Jesus' attention to the magnificence of the temple (and thus all that it represents), he claims that it will be reduced to rubble (Mark 13:1-2). This episode culminates in Jesus' encounter with the chief priest, in which Jesus asserts that humanity (the Human One) and the divine are to be seen alongside one another (Mark 14:62). It is the abolition of this distinction between God and humanity that brings upon him the charge of blasphemy.

This abolition of religion as the principle of separation is something that becomes important in Paul's teaching as well. As we have seen, in Romans 14 and 15, Paul deals with a number of ways in which members of the new messianic community may be divided. These include disputes about the holiness of specific times, days, or seasons, as well as disputes about what is proper to eat or drink. These are precisely "religious disputes," or disputes about religion, because they are disputes about what is to be separated, made holy, or used to mark the difference between the holy and the profane. In this case, Paul is not maintaining that religious differences are inconsequential, only that the messianic life that he is promoting should not regard them as ultimate, as a cause of separation. The overcoming of the distinction between God and humanity results in the overcoming of the separation among persons based on religion.

Although the controversies in which Jesus is engaged concerning religion are controversies with and within Judaism, those with which Paul is concerned seem to deal equally as much with pagan as with Jewish religious perspectives. It is therefore a mistake to suppose that only in Judaism is there a problem of erecting religious distinctions concerning days or places or practices. Nor is the assault upon such divisions an attack on something like a particular religion (Judaism, for example) rather than others. This is clear, above all, in the way that Jesus (and Paul) maintains this connection as a continuation of the prophetic stance that insists that justice and mercy are always more important than any religious practices whatsoever, and that religious practices and places are often no more than an attempt to evade the call and claim of God to enact justice and mercy.[7]

If religion is an evasion of God's act in the Messiah Jesus, then in what way are we to understand the constitution of assemblies through the message concerning the cross? If these are not called to be religious communities, then how are they to be understood? What forms of life, corporate and personal, follow from the message concerning the cross, and if they are not religious, then what are they? It is to questions such as these that we must turn in the next chapters.

In chapter 9, "The Cross of God," I will consider whether we may think of an even more dramatic and fundamental sense in which the cross anticipates God's becoming one with us, and so the death or end of what has been traditionally understood to be the God of command and control, of transcendental distance and demand.

PART TWO

Implications of the Cross

CHAPTER SEVEN

The Community of the Crucified

I f we look closely at the way in which Paul deploys talk of cross and crucifixion, we come across two surprising and interrelated situations. On the one hand, when Paul makes a good deal of the cross of Christ, it is typically in the context of admonishing his communities against the tendency to break apart into factions (1 Cor 1–3), or encouraging them into attitudes and behaviors that make living together possible (Phil 2:1-18). On the other hand, much of Paul's use of the theme of the cross is deployed in what seems to be an exhortation to understand oneself as having "died to the world" or to the flesh in ways that make possible a new form or style of life, one that can be understood as embodying concern for the other. The surprise is that Paul does not actually provide us with something like an exposition of a "theology of the cross," but rather seems to presuppose his (prior) proclamation in order to apply it to life, perhaps especially corporate life or life together.

In this chapter, we will focus attention on the way in which the theme of the cross is deployed in contexts that have the life of the community of faith (or faithfulness) in view. In chapter 8, we will attend more directly to uses of the theme of the cross that seem to have the individual in view as one who has already died with Christ, or as one who is being exhorted to live out the significance of the cross.

In this discussion, we will try to demonstrate the use of the motif of the cross to combat factionalism and the attitudes that make it difficult to relate positively to others. We will have to ask why factionalism is the issue, why this is the meaning of the cross as determined by its use. We will also have to ask whether this may be discerned as relating to what we have previously discussed as the significance of the cross of Christ, and whether it also may be seen as rooted in the traditions concerning the mission and ministry of Jesus.[1]

The centrality of the cross (1 Corinthians 1–3)

It is often maintained that the cross of Christ is at the center of Pauline theology. Perhaps the most direct evidence for this centrality comes in the opening argument of 1 Corinthians, in which Paul himself "thematizes" this centrality. We will first seek to trace the main outline of the argument within which Paul emphasizes the centrality of the cross, or rather, of the *message* concerning the cross, and then see how Paul himself places this squarely within the context of an exhortation to the community to correspond to the cross in its own life together.

In 1 Corinthians 2:2, Paul writes, "I decided to know nothing among you except Jesus Christ and him crucified." In this statement, Paul gives us an indication of the theme or content of his initial proclamation to the people in Corinth. Here he maintains that the crucifixion of the Messiah was the whole content of his message and mission to them. He will not give his readers a rehearsal or repetition of that message; rather, he will presuppose it as something they already know or will recall. This makes it especially important for us to attend to the clues that he gives us about this message by writing about the effects this message is supposed to have upon the members of this community.

He has previously said that the message about the cross is "foolishness to those who are perishing, but to us who are being saved it is the power of God" (1 Cor 1:18 NRSV). Here we note the emphasis on the message—that is, somehow the theme or content of Pauline proclamation, at least in Corinth, has had to do with the cross. This is something that we may also gather from the quite different situation of Galatia, for Paul reminds his readers there that his own message to them and ministry among them can be represented as having placarded the cross of the Messiah (Gal 3:1).

To be sure, there is much about this assertion that remains mysterious to us. We do not know in what terms Paul actually spoke to the apparently gentile hearers in Galatia and in Corinth about the execution of the Messiah of God. Rather, Paul presupposes that his readers will recall that this was in fact somehow the center, indeed the whole content, of his message to them. What we get in the letters is not a repetition nor even a summary of that initial proclamation, but an attempt on Paul's part to address subsequent issues in the life of these communities in a way that is, he will maintain, consistent with his earlier proclamation to them, a proclamation whose entire content, he maintains, was the execution of the divine Messiah. It is by attending to the effects that Paul supposes should follow the reception of his message concerning the cross that we begin to see what was at stake in this proclamation.

In the extended discussion in the first chapters of 1 Corinthians, we see that Paul deploys talk of the execution of the Messiah in prominent relation to the terms of weakness as opposed to power, and folly as opposed to wisdom. Thus, to get at the meaning of the cross for him, we should first pursue these contrasts, both to see how they are treated and to discern whether they line up with additional contrasts.

The rulers of the age

Before pursuing these contrasts, however, it is important to notice that the discussion of the significance of the cross has an immediate connection with what we have maintained is the most basic meaning of the cross, namely, the conflict between Jesus as Messiah and the public powers of oppression, arrogance, and violence.

On the only occasion on which Paul will speak of his own message as a kind of wisdom, he hastens to make clear how it is that this wisdom is not what the world would regard as wisdom: "It is not a wisdom of this age or of the rulers of this age" (1 Cor 2:6 NRSV). He adds concerning this age, and especially its rulers, that they "are doomed to perish." Readers of this in Corinth, a city that had first been razed to the ground by Roman forces, its population murdered or enslaved, and then subsequently founded as a colony by the Roman military,[2] would have been in no doubt concerning the identity of "the rulers of this age." Those who had power to utterly destroy and then recreate in their own image certainly resembled the awful deities of old, and indeed had taken their place in the Corinthian pantheon of divinities in the honor paid to the emperors and the imperial family.[3]

What would have been astonishing is the news that these uncontested rulers of the age, at the zenith of their military power, ruling a slavocracy as a police state—these ruthless rulers of the age were doomed to perish. Eternal Rome was on the point of utter ruin.[4]

On what grounds could such an assertion be made? For Paul, the ground of this assertion seems to be the way in which this imperial plan had come into opposition to the plan of God. The wisdom by which they had conquered and ruled was as nothing compared with the wisdom whose counsels they had violated: the wisdom of God. And what is that wisdom? It is the cross. Or rather, it is the message of divine solidarity and goodwill, brought by the Messiah but rejected by the powerful who seek to crush it with the extreme penalty of crucifixion, and in that way demonstrate their utter incompatibility with the will and wisdom of God: "None of the rulers of this age understood this; for if they had, they would not have crucified the Lord of glory" (1 Cor 2:8 NRSV).

What the rulers of this age sought to crush, just as they had crushed the former city-state of Corinth, was the will of God. In bringing themselves into utter opposition to God, they had made their own final ruin inevitable.[5] In developing the contrast between human wisdom and the wisdom of God, as well as between human power and that of God, this public meaning of the cross provides the indispensable template.

The foolishness of God

The contrast of foolishness and wisdom is introduced almost immediately in Paul's discussion. This contrast appears first as having to do with the proclamation of the gospel. Paul is referring to his own practice as a proclaimer of the good news concerning human well-being brought by God through the Messiah. But this proclamation is one that is, first of all, not eloquent, and so one that lacks the appearance of wisdom. This strategy of avoiding the appearance of wisdom is related immediately to the imperative to conform the message, its manner of presentation, to its subject matter: "not with eloquent wisdom, so that the cross of Christ might not be emptied of its power" (1 Cor 1:17 NRSV). The message concerns the cross and thus cannot have the appearance of conforming to, or exemplifying, worldly wisdom. Indeed, this message is "foolishness to those who are perishing" (1:18). This relates directly to what Paul will have said concerning those who are perishing, namely, that they are "the rulers of this age" (2:6). It is precisely this connection between those who are perishing in 1:18 and the rulers of this age in 2:6 that is so often ignored in conventional exegesis of this passage. The result is a depoliticizing of Paul's message concerning a messiah who was executed by the state apparatus of Roman rule. The wisdom that is at stake here is the wisdom of statecraft. Thus, we should first understand wisdom, or rather the appearance of wisdom, as that which enables rule, the rulership of the present age.

The combination of wisdom and eloquence in Paul's assertion that he did not avail himself of the eloquence associated with worldly wisdom (1 Cor 1:17) suggests how this connection may be made. The very point of eloquence is to rule, to exercise some sort of dominion over the affairs of society, to persuade concerning matters of state policy. Thus, training in rhetoric was indispensable for those who hoped to intervene successfully in the affairs of city and state, whether in questions of trial or in decision making concerning policy.

The contrast, then, is between the message concerning the cross and the politics of worldly rule (eloquent wisdom). That contrast is itself grounded in the contrast between the cross as the strategically "wise" application of force to maintain empire on the one hand, and, on the other hand, the cross as that which brings empire into fatal contradiction to the "decree" of God, and so brings about the ruin of the social (dis)order it was designed to protect.

But here, Paul wants to suggest that his own practice as announcer of the message concerning the cross itself conforms to the content of that message, and so is devoid of the stratagems of rhetorical rule, that is, of (worldly) wisdom.

This contrast is then linked to the spirit. What is spirited is contrasted with human wisdom: "not with plausible words of wisdom but with a demonstration of spirit" (1 Cor 2:4). Precisely insofar as it is spirited, to that extent it must appear as "foolishness." Here, as often in Paul, spirit designates that which exceeds the order of knowledge. Insofar as one comes to think or speak in accordance with the way of God in the cross, to that extent one is empowered or spirited. The difficulty is that whatever "exceeds" knowledge will always appear, from the standpoint of knowledge, to be foolish or absurd. This is true because particularly in defying the conventions of what may be supposed to be common sense or the received opinion (about God, about humanity, and so on), that which is excessive relative to knowledge may also seem to be the same as that which is defective with respect to knowledge. How is the suprarational to be distinguished from the subrational, that which simply lacks knowledge (*gnosis*) or wisdom (*sophia*)? One way, of course, to insist that something that doesn't appear to make sense is nonetheless true is to appeal to revelation, or to one's own special authority. It is important to notice that this is precisely what Paul does not do. Here it is not a question of an appeal to authority, or even to a sort of "take it or leave it" revelation. Instead, Paul will write about what it would mean for the community to live out the truth of the message concerning the cross. It is as if the lifestyle of the community of the Crucified One is to become the most persuasive evidence of the truth of that message. For this reason, Paul will be seeking to clarify what he believes should be the effect of the message concerning the cross in the community that has been formed through the proclamation concerning the cross.

Of course, Paul's arguments in this text do not settle the matter. Pagan critics of the upstart Christian movement will long argue that its message concerning a crucified messiah, a "Son of God" who suffers and dies, is ludicrous because it maintains completely unseemly and incongruous things about God. Some of the most important documents of the early church contend with this voice of wisdom, of the friends of wisdom—that is to say, of philosophy. From Origen's "Contra Celsum" to Athanasius's "On the Incarnation" and beyond, the challenge for theologians was to demonstrate the "wisdom" of this self-evident "foolishness." In these defenses of the "rationality" of the message concerning the cross, a constant feature will be an appeal to the form of life of those who came to be called Christians. But what is in certain respects distinctive about Paul's invention of this argument is that it is so closely linked not to the lifestyle of individuals, but rather to the lifestyle of communities.

The weakness of God

Along with, and closely intertwined with, the theme of wisdom is the theme of power. It is through the exercise of power or force that the empire establishes its own credentials as divine. For what is the divine if not the locus of overawing power or force?[6] Thus, whether in the awesome and overpowering displays of nature in storm and earthquake, or in the ferocious displays of what contemporary empire calls the tactics of "shock and awe," the power of the mighty is God-like in its overwhelming display of "weapons of mass destruction." When it is a question of conquest, it is the display of invincible military machines (the chariots of Assyria and Babylon, the legions of Rome), and this is accompanied by the tactic of utter devastation unleashed against resistance to imperial might. Rome, as we have seen, displayed just such devastating power in the utter destruction of Corinth. But for maintaining the control thus gained, the most effective tool of Roman power was arguably the instrument of crucifixion, by which the hopelessness and the horrifying cost of resistance were displayed.

Paul's reference to the power of the message concerning the cross (1 Cor 1:17) is thus deeply ironic, for it turns the symbol of Roman power upside down. Precisely as the display of the weakness of the victim, it becomes somehow the demonstration of divine power: the power to suffer, the power to die, the power that is verified through the resurrection of the executed.

It was of course not only to the Romans that such a claim to power in weakness must have seemed risible. In the history of Israel as well, the mighty deeds of God had seemed the best way to verify the divine sanction for the existence of Israel. That God or the Messiah should be the victim, rather than the victor over imperial Roman power, was quite clearly also a "stumbling block," as Paul says (1 Cor 1:23). Yet this is precisely what is affirmed in the message concerning the cross.

Moreover, for Paul, it is essential that his own behavior, and by extension that of others, should mirror not the effects of imperial power but the true power of the cross. Thus, he can point to his own weakness as itself a fitting representation of the cross. In terms that echo the reflections of power and weakness that he has employed here, Paul can write of his own affliction:

> Three times I appealed to the Lord about this, that it would leave me, but he said to me, "My grace is sufficient for you, for power is made perfect in weakness." So, I will boast all the more gladly of my weakness, so that the power of Christ may dwell in me. (2 Cor 12:8-9 NRSV)

This messianic power is precisely the power that he maintains is manifest in the message concerning the cross. Here he will redistribute this sense of weakness and power by saying, "For he was crucified in weakness, but lives by the power of God" (2 Cor 13:4 NRSV).[7] Later we will see that this is taken quite far in his own imitation of the cross.

As in the question of wisdom, so also in the question of divine power, the early church theologians continued to wrestle with finding ways to insist on the compatibility of divine power with the fate of the cross. One of the most beautiful early expressions of this is found in the second-century Epistle to Diognetes, which maintains that one may imitate God not by lording it over others or by forcing them to do as one wants, but rather by being one who cares for the weak and needy.[8]

In this connection, Paul can turn to those he is addressing with the reminder that "not many of you were wise by human standards, not many were powerful, not many were of noble birth" (1 Cor 1:26 NRSV). That is, God, through the message of the cross, had called not those who had power and prestige, but rather the weak and lowly. But why should this be so? "God chose what is foolish in the world to shame the wise; God chose what is weak in the world to shame the strong" (1:27 NRSV). The whole strategy of God, then, depends upon this turning to what seems weak and foolish in order to overthrow the pretentions of the wise and powerful.

The divided community

While Paul's discussion of the message concerning the execution of the Messiah has been regularly cited by those who argue for the centrality of the cross in the theology of Paul, and its connection to themes of wisdom and power has regularly been noted, what is less often noted is what may be termed the use or function of this talk of the cross, that which occasions this reflection.

What is clear above all is that it is not Paul's concern to develop a doctrine of the cross here as an independent theme of reflection. His recollection of his message has a specific function and purpose. It is not Christology but ecclesiology, not doctrine but the life of the community that is his chief concern.

Immediately following the preliminary greetings, Paul indicates his reason for writing: "I appeal to you . . . that all of you be in agreement and that there be no divisions among you" (1 Cor 1:10 NRSV). The pertinence of this appeal is made immediately clear: "It has been reported to me . . . that there are quarrels among you" (1:11). It is the fact of quarreling, bickering, or contentions among the *adelphoi* that occasions Paul's writing, and he is writing in order to urge them to reconcile their differences. In this connection, he introduces the theme of the cross: "Has Christ been divided, or has Paul been crucified for you?" (1:13). He then recalls the subject matter and manner of his preaching: "Christ [sent me] to proclaim the gospel and not with eloquent wisdom so that the cross of Christ might not be emptied of its power" (1:17). Right at the beginning, the theme of the cross and its connection to wisdom and power are introduced in order to address the issue of contentions and quarrelings.

We may say, then, that at least as far as this letter is concerned, the point of what might be called a "theology of the cross" is not speculative or dogmatic, but rather the apparently somewhat mundane business of addressing the tendencies to divisive quarrels in the community of faith.

This is also quite clear as Paul draws this discussion of the message of the cross (and the related themes of wisdom and power) to a close. In chapter 3, he returns to the specific issue of division: "For as long as there is jealousy and quarreling among you, are you not of the flesh . . . ? For when one says, 'I belong to Paul,' and another, 'I belong to Apollos,' are you not merely human?" (1 Cor 3:3–4 NRSV). These are the very terms in which he had introduced this discussion earlier: "I belong to Paul" or "I belong to Apollos" (1:12).

The theme of the cross, then, and the related themes of wisdom and power, is mobilized precisely in relation to the question of division in the community. Somehow, the cross "means" the end of certain forms of division—though as Paul will also insist in chapters 12–14 of 1 Corinthians, not the end of remarkable diversity.

How might this be so? Here we should give full weight to the questions of "wisdom" and "power." Power in general has the function of distributing more to some and less to others. Wisdom, as it is used here, also has the function of getting others to follow one's own lead, of persuading others to subordinate themselves to one's own position.

The most extreme forms of wisdom and power in this sense are those that are displayed by the imperial domination to which Paul has unmistakably alluded. But there are less egregious, and therefore also quite ubiquitous, ways of deploying power and wisdom so as to increase the prestige of some at the expense of others. What is visible on the grand scale of imperial political history also lodges itself in the dynamics of quite small-scale communities, including those that may seem to be, may think of themselves as, and may even in important respects actually be, "countercultural" in respect to the politics of empire.

What Paul is suggesting is that if the cross of the Messiah brings to ruin the stratagems of imperial power, it also must bring to ruin the stratagems by which, even among the poor and despised, the struggle for power and prestige takes place and so threatens the group with division, jealousy, and envy. Put another way: the community founded through the proclamation of the cross (which reflects the ruin of imperial power) must not be simply a reflection, in its own reduced circumstances, of the same power dynamics that led the empire to execute the divine Messiah.

The genius of Paul, then, is precisely to see the connection—to see that divisive dynamics based upon strivings for influence or control within this countercultural and marginal community are a small-scale replica of the empire that crucified the Messiah. Put yet another way, this means that the community of faith, insofar as it is constituted on the "sure foundation that is Jesus Messiah" (1 Cor 3:11), is one in which diversity is not only tolerated but celebrated. For this is what makes the community distinctive, what demonstrates that it does not belong to the world that is perishing—namely, that it celebrates the diversity that others abhor.

The question of Communion

The next time that the passion of the Messiah is mentioned in 1 Corinthians, it is in connection with the question of the Eucharist, or Communion. Once again, it is the question of the struggle for prestige, and thus a mirroring of the Greco-Roman social order, that will provide the impetus for Paul's discussion. Furthermore, the theme of the cross emerges at the point where Paul must confront quarreling and division within the community that has been constituted through the message concerning the execution of the Messiah.

Although the main discussion of gathering for a common meal in the name of the crucified Messiah does not occur until chapter 11 of 1 Corinthians, it is already prefigured in chapter 10 in the midst of a discussion about appearing to participate in worship of idols or demons through banqueting on meat that had been consecrated in temples. In order to comprehend the significance of this, it is important to note that this sort of public banqueting was the primary source of meat for the lower-class populations of the cities. The "sacrifice" was rather more like a "dedication," and the meat thus sacrificed was then distributed to the public at the temple site. It is also important to recall that the "demons" to whom sacrifice was made (and therefore in whose name the distribution of meat to the public was also made) were the pantheon of deities that prominently included the imperial cult. It should therefore be clear that sacrifice to "the rulers of this age" who "crucified the Lord of glory" is here included in the case of sacrifice to "demons."

This latter connection is all the more evident in the concluding assertion and question: "You cannot drink the cup of the Lord and the cup of demons. You cannot partake of the table of the Lord and the table of demons" (1 Cor 10:21 NRSV). The "cup" here is earlier associated with blood: "The cup of blessing that we bless, is it not a sharing in the blood of Messiah?" (10:16). The connection of blood and cup, and its contrast with "demons," makes eminent sense to the degree that the term *demons* is a code inclusive of the imperial cult—that is, the cult directed to those who "crucified the Lord of glory." The incompatibility of sharing in the table of the one along with the table of the other is thus quite glaring.

It is clear from this discussion that disputes that would be potentially divisive of the community are at stake. Those who participate in these public meat distributions can plausibly claim that the power of idols and demons is broken, and that therefore the rules of eating or drinking are unimportant. And those who are horrified by this practice can plausibly claim that honoring the Messiah and honoring those who executed the Messiah are incompatible activities. Paul, in fact, takes both positions. In addition to maintaining that eating food sacrificed to demons is impossible, he will subsequently agree that the believer should not inquire too closely into the source of the meat that is offered to her or him. Beyond that, Paul also maintains, "For why should my liberty be subject to the judgment of someone else's conscience? If I partake with thankfulness, why should I be denounced because of that for which I give thanks?" (1 Cor 10:29b-30 NRSV), and so is able to conclude, "So, whether you eat or drink, or whatever you do, do everything for the glory of God" (10:31 NRSV).

After an interlude concerning head coverings (1 Cor 11:2-16),[9] Paul returns to the question of the manner of the community's eating and drinking together. At stake here is the sort of practice that will eventually be seen as a precursor to the practice of Eucharist, the Lord's Supper, Communion, or the Mass. While before, Paul had simply drawn attention to this practice to contrast it with the practice of participating in the public banquets and meat distribution organized by temples, here he turns to contrast the incongruity of the internal practices of the community with the meaning or foundation of the practice of sharing meals in honor of the Messiah.

"Now in the following instructions I do not commend you, because when you come together it is not for the better but for the worse" (1 Cor 11:17 NRSV). With these stern words of warning, Paul opens his discussion of the coming together of the community, or assembly (11:18). As we would expect, his concern is that "there are divisions among you" (11:18)—that is, it is precisely the same question that had motivated his discussion of the cross at the beginning of the letter (1:11). This coming together is then further identified as the manner of enacting "the Lord's supper" (11:20).

In order to clarify what is at stake here, Paul will provide us with the earliest depiction of what comes to be called the "institution," or the origin of the custom of celebrating a meal in honor of the Messiah: "For I received from the Lord what I also handed on to you, that the Lord Jesus on the night when he was betrayed took a loaf of bread . . ." (1 Cor 11:23 NRSV).[10] With these words, so familiar to Christians from their repetition at the celebration of the Lord's Supper, Communion, or Eucharist, Paul seeks to place a footing under his argument about how his hearers actually put into practice their way of "proclaim[ing] the Lord's death until he comes [again]" (11:26).

What stands in opposition to this intention of proclaiming the Lord's death, and so the cross, is the way the community or assembly actually eats and drinks together. As we learn, their manner of doing so underlines, rather than overcomes, differences in status and wealth among the members. Some have too much; others go hungry. In order to understand the force of this observation, it is important to recall that the point of banquets or feasts in the Greco-Roman world was precisely to emphasize and display such differences of wealth and power, of prestige and class. The fascinating satire of Juvenal, written a few years after this text of Paul's, shows us clearly the way in which feasts in the home of a "patron" had the deliberate intent of demonstrating the wealth of some and the poverty of the rest, the difference between patrons and clients, and so on.[11] This was the normal function of coming together to eat in such social settings. In those settings, one could say that the whole point was that "one goes hungry and another becomes drunk." The feast displayed, performed, and legitimated social division and class separation.

The point that Paul is making is that what is self-evident social behavior in the Greco-Roman world is manifestly contrary to the recollection of the death of the Messiah. He makes this point in an especially dramatic way when he asserts, "Whoever, therefore, eats the bread or drinks the cup of the Lord in an unworthy manner will be answerable for the body and blood of the Lord" (1 Cor 11:27 NRSV). Quite obviously, what is at stake in this dire warning is not dribbling drops of wine (an excuse used by Christendom for centuries to deny the cup to laity) or spilling crumbs, not even some proto-psychoanalytic examination of interior intention, but the social divisions exhibited and exacerbated by the very manner in which Christians presumably recall the death of Christ.

To see the force of this argument, one need only ask in what ways the manner of assembling as communities of faith serves to demonstrate and exacerbate differences of wealth or prestige, of class, perhaps of gender, or a multitude of other differences, in order to see what is the import of Paul's warning and its pertinence across the centuries of Christian practice. In how many ways does our very manner of coming together reflect the structures of a world that is perishing, and deserves to perish! Too often, our own assemblies tend to be divided by race, by ethnicity, and by class.

For centuries, Christians repeated the self-serving libel about the Jews as "Christ killers." Paul is quite clear about who is accountable for the death of the Messiah: the so-called Christians whose very manner of coming together, as Christians, echoes the divisiveness of the world. And the bitterest division that has been paraded about and exacerbated by the Eucharistic coming together is precisely the most virulent form of anti-Judaism.

For those who make a great deal of the decline of Christianity (by which of course they usually mean the decline of their favorite form of Christianity, their faction as it were, or the faction of which they would like to gain control), it might be well to wonder whether it is precisely this divisiveness that reflects the world of division and domination that is the cause of the decline they lament: "For this reason many of you are weak and ill, and some have died" (1 Cor 11:30 NRSV).

However opaque some elements of Paul's argument may remain, as separated as we are by time and culture, it seems that the main outline at least can be made quite clear. The message concerning the executed Messiah is deployed precisely in order to warn the community against imitating the social order that "crucified the Lord of glory." The divisive competition for influence and power within the community is taken by Paul as reflecting the same antagonism to the Messiah that led the authorities of the wider social order (the rulers of this age) to crucify him. Hence, this sort of divisiveness makes us responsible for the blood of the Messiah, precisely as those who betray him or hand him over to the enemies of the messianic mission (11:27).

This general picture is verified if we look at the passage in Philippians that is also sometimes taken to be indicative of a Pauline "theology of the cross": the so-called kenosis hymn of Philippians 2:6-11. This "hymn" is often cited without attention to its context within Paul's argument. When this happens, it seems simply to be a depiction of a certain theology of the cross of the Messiah Jesus:

> . . . Who, though he was in the form of God, did not regard equality with God as something to be exploited, but emptied himself, taking the form of a slave, being born in human likeness. And being found in human form, he humbled himself and became obedient to the point of death—even death on a cross. (Phil 2:6-8 NRSV).

However, Paul does not produce this semi-creedal statement in order to give information about Christology. Rather, his aim is to call the community of readers away from an ethos of competitiveness and self-promotion. Thus, the hymn is introduced with the admonition: "Do nothing from selfish ambition or conceit, but in humility regard others as better than yourselves. Let each of you look not to your own interests, but to the interests of others. Let the same mind be in you that was in Messiah Jesus" (Phil 2:3-5). Following the citation of the hymn, Paul comes back to the theme of a certain kind of cooperative, rather than competitive, spirit in the community: "Do all things without murmuring and arguing" (2:14 NRSV). Although Paul is here addressing a community with which he is on much better terms than the Corinthians, he is nevertheless concerned about the possibility of the sort of competitiveness and selfishness that would bring this community, unwittingly, into opposition to the cross of Jesus and align the community with the "crooked and perverse generation" (2:15) that rejected and executed God's Messiah. In the next chapter, we will return to this text and this concern when we take up the significance of talk of the cross for the life of the members of this community.

Jesus and quarreling disciples

Does Paul's concern with the meaning of the cross as putting an end to quarreling and divisiveness represent a distinctive Pauline emphasis? Or is it also to be discerned in the message and mission of Jesus as portrayed in the Gospels?

It is quite clear that something very similar is found in the Gospel narratives. The question of dissension among the understudies of Jesus is introduced in Mark 9:33-35, as Jesus and his apprentices arrive in Capernaum, and it serves as an overarching theme through the succeeding narrative of the progress to Jericho (10:46). In other words, it is the thematic unity of the last section of the narrative before the approach to Jerusalem, and therefore anticipates the passion narrative of the rejection and execution of Jesus.

At the beginning of this narrative section, we are told that when they arrived in Capernaum, "he asked them, 'What were you arguing about on the road?'" (Mark 9:33). This is the first time we are told that there was dissension among the disciples. Later we will also hear: "When the ten heard it they were furious with James and John" (10:41).

What is the ground of this dissension and enmity? In response to Jesus' first question, we are told that the disciples were silent. That is, they weren't speaking to one another "because they had been arguing about who was the greatest" (Mark 9:34). Similarly, the outrage of the ten directed at James and John is motivated by the brothers' approach to Jesus with the petition to be the ones chosen to sit at his right and left hand, that is, to be the greatest (after Jesus) in the reign of God.

In response to the first notice of dissension based on a quest for importance or even power over the others, Jesus points the disciples to the vulnerability of children as that which should be their pattern. In response to the second notice of dissension among the disciples, Jesus gives his last instruction to the disciples before entering into Jerusalem:

> "You know that those who are supposed to rule over the nations lord it (impose power) over them; and their great ones exercise authority over them. But it shall not be so among you; but whoever would be great among you must be your server, and whoever would be first must be slave of all. For the human came not to be served but to serve and to surrender his own life as a ransom for many." (Mark 10:42-45)

What the Markan passage (and the parallel in Matt 20:20-28) makes clear is that the problem of dissension is grounded in the sort of jockeying for power and prestige that has also been diagnosed in quite different terms by Paul. Moreover, the episode shows that this jockeying is contrary to the way of solidarity with the one who gives up his own life for the good of many—that is, competition for prestige is opposed to the way of the cross. Instead, it is this sort of power and authority that is part and parcel of the structures of division and domination that will be responsible for the death of the Human One, the execution of God's Messiah. What is at stake here is whether the followers of Jesus will be the understudies of the one who will be executed by those in authority, by the great ones among the nations—or instead will be the understudies of the very powers and authorities who will impose their violent authority through the execution of the Messiah.

The connection of this issue of dissension to that of the cross is also made clear in Jesus' discussion with James and John, who have come seeking prestigious positions in the coming "glory" of the Human One. Jesus asks them if they can drink of the cup of which he will drink, or be washed as he will be washed. Both of these are clear references to his own impending fate: the cup of suffering, the baptism of bloody death. The brothers claim that they are able to live and die in solidarity with the one who will be executed. Of course, we know that they will fail the first test of this solidarity, for they will join the other followers of Jesus who abandon him in his final agony. Jesus, however, does not take this initial failure as the last word. They will somehow still share in this way of the cross (Mark 10:39). But this does not become a means of gaining the prestige they had sought: "But to sit at my left hand or at my right hand is not mine to grant" (10:40). Jesus does not grant privilege or power among his companions. What he does grant is solidarity in the way of martyrdom. If this is what it means to be his understudy, then it is utterly useless to seek advantage or prestige. Instead, it is through service to the other, and the surrender of one's own self-interest for the benefit of the other, that one begins to learn how to give up one's life for the other, and so become an effective part of the new humanity that is being inaugurated among Jesus' followers.[12]

Once again, the question of the internalization of the way of the cross is connected to the abolition of dissension in the community by abolishing the very source of that division: the competition for power and prestige. Moreover, we should also notice that this episode connects this teaching to something like the participation in the "cup that I drink," and so anticipates the community's Eucharistic practice as a decisive site for the embodiment of a noncompetitive ethos that will stand in marked contrast to the way in which the world is presently organized and ruled. This further ties the teaching ascribed to Jesus to that of Paul, which, as we have seen, is also connected to the practices that recall the "cup."

The material at which we have been looking concerns, above all, the internal relations among the disciples, but this question of internal division is connected as well to the relation of the disciples to those who are or seem to be outsiders. Within the same context determined by the theme of dissension, there is a related episode that also sheds light on this theme in the Gospels. The saying, reported in Mark, concerns those who are casting out demons but who are not of the group of the disciples (Mark 9:38-41). As we have seen, Jesus' initial response to divisiveness was to point to the vulnerability of children as a paradigm for the disciples. Immediately following this teaching concerning children, we have the question posed by John (who will subsequently be asking for pride of place in the coming "glory"): "Teacher, we saw someone casting out demons in your name, [who was not following us], and we tried to stop him, because he was not following us" (9:38 NRSV). The bracketed repetition of "who was not following us" is present in many ancient texts and omitted by others. What it brings to the fore, or underlines through repetition, is the exclusion of those who do what the disciples are commissioned to do (cast out demons), yet who do not follow the disciples. Put another way, the action of those who are in question is itself indistinguishable from that which Jesus calls upon his followers to do. They are dramatically enacting the in-breaking or coming of the divine reign, a reign whose concrete expression is the healing of the minds and bodies of the vulnerable and violated. But the disciples forbid them or exclude them "because they are not following us."

The division among the followers of Jesus is here transposed into the division between the followers and others who do not recognize the leadership of the "true" followers. The quest for privilege within the community is transposed into the attempt to secure the privilege of the community vis-à-vis outsiders. This latter quest is certainly recognizable. How often do we hear ourselves claiming that we or our group are the true followers of Jesus and that the others are not? How often do we hear ourselves saying that we at least are "Christians," while those who are not are somehow to be excluded or even condemned, even if their actions of justice and mercy seem to correspond at least as well as our own actions to the command and commission of the Messiah?

The attempt here of the community of followers to secure its own advantage or privilege against those who "do not follow us" means that we think of following Jesus as somehow our own possession, our own privilege, which we may use to boast over others who are not members of our community or whose following is somehow dissimilar to our own.

In this case as well, we are bringing ourselves into contradiction to the way of the cross, and indeed becoming like those who crucify because the one who comes casting out demons "does not follow us." Is this not also the objection of the Judean leaders who are offended by Jesus' innovations?[13] Is this not the objection of the imperial authorities who would be only too glad to have exorcists announce the authority of Rome?

Whether in the case of those who seek to gain prestige within the community, or in the case of those who seek to protect the privilege of the community against those who are or seem to be outsiders, we have the same struggle of division and domination that mirrors not the fate of the Crucified, but the action of those who are the agents of crucifixion. The theme of the cross then serves to call the community of the Crucified into a new way of being community in which the forces of dissension are abolished.[14]

Let love be genuine (Paul)

We should also note the way in which Paul deals in Romans with the theme of the mutual welcome to be extended by members of the community to one another in spite of the serious disagreements about matters of principle within that community (Rom 14:1—15:13).

We should not suppose that these are mere disagreements about matters of no real significance. Among the subjects of disagreement, Paul lists the question of what may or may not be eaten or drunk, and the matter of days set aside for worship. A moment's reflection will help to contextualize this: these are the very issues that typically divide persons of, as we say, different religions. Take the question of food and drink, for example. Hindus will not eat meat, but Jews and Christians and Muslims will. Muslims will not drink wine, but Jews and most Christians will. Jews and Muslims will not eat pork, but most Christians will, and may even make a point of doing so. Indeed, this is one of the most obvious ways of distinguishing religions, and the one difference that would be most directly encountered by those of different religions seeking to live together amicably, that is, to welcome one another. Of course, the same is true of "days." For Jews, it is the sabbath (Saturday in contemporary secular parlance); for Christians, it is Sunday; for Muslims, Friday. If we add questions of holy seasons into this mix, we get an idea of the seriousness of the possible divisions here.[15]

Paul is also quite clear about the gravity of these matters. He understands the importance that "all be convinced in their own minds" (Rom 14:5), and that each person should act with integrity in accordance with deeply held conviction. Even the one for whom none of this makes any difference (the secular humanist, we might say, or the "liberal") has a conviction and is deeply persuaded—namely, that none of this should make a difference. But this is simply another set of convictions and practices alongside the others, another "religion" if you will.

Of course, some might say that we are talking about people of the same religion here, namely, followers of the Messiah of God. That is true. It may be the case, however, that this could also be said of Jews, Muslims, and Christians, and perhaps of others as well.[16] For there is an important sense in which all these "Abrahamic" faiths are in some ways adherents of the messianic mission of Jesus, even if they do not subscribe to certain creedal formulations. Moreover, it is clearly the case that those who understand themselves as belonging to what might be termed "the Christian religion" have been known to make these very issues into differences of religion: think of the abstinence campaigns and associated rhetoric, for example, or of sabbatarian movements.

What I am getting at here is that Paul is pointing to quite volatile differences in terms of religious convictions and practices. And he is saying that these very strongly held views and practices should not be an occasion of division: "Welcome one another, but not for the sake of disputing about opinions" (Rom 14:1).

Of particular interest to us in this connection is the way this instruction is framed and grounded in that messianic event that quite clearly comes to a head in the execution and subsequent resurrection of the Messiah. In other words, what is at stake here is the meaning of the cross as it bears upon the life of community.

The appeal that Paul has been making to the community in Rome about the life of love concludes with words that set up the discussion in which we are interested here. "Let us live honorably as in the day, . . . not in quarreling and jealousy" (Rom 13:13 NRSV). With this theme of the problem of quarreling and jealousy, now familiar to us, we hear another connection to the cross: "Instead put on the Lord Jesus Messiah, and make no provision for the flesh, to gratify its desires" (13:14). These words that seek to oppose quarreling to life in the Messiah are those that serve as the basis for what will follow concerning welcoming instead of quarreling.[17]

After the theme of welcoming has been introduced as an antidote to quarreling, Paul points to the foundation of his argument: "We do not live to ourselves, and we do not die to ourselves. If we live, we live to the Lord, and if we die, we die to the Lord; so then, whether we live or whether we die, we are the Lord's" (Rom 14:7-8 NRSV). But if this distinction between living and dying does not separate us from the Lord, then no other difference should either. Moreover, this is to be based squarely in the fate of the Messiah: "For to this end Messiah died and lived again, so that he might be Lord of both the living and the dead" (14:9).

This refrain is picked up again in respect to the issue of eating as follows: "Do not let what you eat cause the ruin of one for whom Messiah died" (Rom 14:15). Again, it is specifically the death of Messiah that serves as the basis for the end of quarreling, and of the behavior that produces quarreling.

A further allusion to the cross, or rather to the passion of the Messiah, is found toward the end of this discussion. Paul writes, "Each of us must please our neighbor for the good purpose of building up the neighbor. For Messiah did not please himself; but, as it is written, 'The insults of those who insult you have fallen on me'" (Rom 15:2-3). The reference here to "insult" recalls the passion of the Messiah. Paul's point seems to be that the humiliation of the Messiah means that those who identify with the Messiah cannot humiliate one another, but instead must welcome one another, seeking not the degradation or submission of the other, but the good of the other.

What we discover from this quick survey of Paul's admonition to a community that he has not founded is consonant with what we found in his argument to the community in Corinth that he had already founded—namely, that the cross of the Messiah applies to the corporate life of those who respond to the Messiah in such a way as to overcome the causes of division and quarreling. Moreover, it does this not by reducing but by celebrating diversity, including especially diversity as it bears upon matters of conscience or, as we earlier suggested, differences of religion.

The embattled community

Thus far, we have been exploring some of the ways in which the community assembled through the proclamation of the cross is summoned to adopt a form of corporate life through which it is conformed to this message in its internal polity,[18] the form of its internal relationships, in which the competition for prestige and power is abolished in favor of solidarity and mutual welcome. Correlated with this theme of the cruciform community is that of the persecuted community. Paul, in common with other New Testament writers, takes it for granted that the community will be the persecuted community, the community that provokes the same sort of opposition that overtook its Lord, the one it heralds as Messiah.

This theme is, of course, already implicit in the identification of this community with the public fate of its Messiah, as we have seen in the chapter on the public cross. But now I want to ask whether the anticipated persecution of the community at the hands of those in authority is related to what we have been discussing as the ethos of that community in contrast to the polities of religion and empire.

In his earliest letter, Paul assumes that the community in Thessalonica is persecuted (1 Thess 1:6), and in this, he says, they are imitators of Paul "and the Lord." Furthermore, he suggests that the persecution of the gentile community by gentile authorities mirrors the persecution of the prophets and the Messiah (and the apostle) by the Judean authorities (1:14-15). But is this also related to the ethos that Paul foments among his hearers to "be at peace among yourselves" (5:13), or to Paul's prayer, "May the Lord make you increase and abound in love for one another and for all" (3:12 NRSV)?

Similarly in Philippians, Paul assumes that this beloved community is threatened by fierce opposition, "since you are having the same struggle that you saw I had and now hear that I still have" (Phil 1:30 NRSV). But is this connected to the form of life that abolishes the spirit of competition and self-preservation?

Even in Romans, written to a community that Paul has not founded, he still supposes that they are all too familiar with the opposition of authorities, and even exhorts them to "bless those who persecute you" (Rom 12:14), having just exhorted them to "let love be genuine," to "love one another with mutual affection," and so on (12:9-10).

These examples could readily be multiplied, not only from Paul, but also from other letters to beleaguered communities, such as 1 Peter or James or John.

For example, 1 Peter presupposes that the community is undergoing considerable suffering. It begins with the recognition that "you have had to suffer various trials" (1 Pet 1:6), which only demonstrates the genuineness of their faithfulness (1:7). The writer exhorts the communities (for several are identified as recipients of the letter) to bear their suffering in ways that conform to the example of the Messiah: "When he was abused, he did not return abuse" (2:23 NRSV). Moreover, their present sufferings are to be understood as "sharing in Christ's sufferings" (4:13), and thus the writer admonishes, "If any of you suffers as a Christian, do not consider it a disgrace, but glorify God because you bear this name" (4:16 NRSV). In addition, their suffering also places them in solidarity with that of the other communities that honor the name of the Messiah: "Your brothers and sisters in all the world are undergoing the same kinds of suffering" (5:9 NRSV).

In all this, there is intermixed the exhortation to demonstrate daily a profound love for one another: "Above all, maintain constant love for one another" (1 Pet 4:8 NRSV). Thus, in spite of what appear to be quite distinct circumstances and importantly different perspectives on many issues,[19] the Petrine correspondence seems to bear witness to many of the features that we have found in Paul. What is important for our purposes here is to see how the corporate style of life of this community places it in the position of likely persecution.

That the community is under threat of rejection and persecution is clear from the fact that it is constituted through adherence to the Messiah, who had been rejected by the official leadership of his own religio-political community and had been executed as a criminal by the state apparatus of the Roman Empire. Simply the fact of its loyalty to one who had already been rejected and executed by the authorities makes it an object of deep suspicion on the part of these same authorities.

Moreover, this community appears to have been composed to a very significant degree of members of the urban underclass. The emergence, in the overcrowded slums of small cities, of groups of the underclass may always be an object of suspicion and understandable concern on the part of those whose task was to ensure "law and order." This may have been particularly true of groups that included among their members those who were both slave and free, thereby constituting a community that implicitly abolished the most significant division of Greco-Roman social order.

To this we may add that the small groups gathered in any particular urban area were connected to similar groups in other urban areas, spreading both inside and outside any particular city or town, aiding one another in times of persecution and opposition, and thus escaping the control of local and regional bodies of social order. But what may have seemed to be most menacing about these small cells of an expanding movement was the extent to which these communities seemed to embody values and practices that were at odds with the values of Greco-Roman social order. I have already mentioned the coming together in friendship and solidarity of those who were otherwise divided by the wall of separation between slave and free. Of course, there seems at this point to be no movement to abolish slavery as an institution, but the forms of life of this community may already have effectively abolished the very conditions of slavery, in that slave and free could welcome one another as friends and as companions, or as Paul said of Onesimus to Philemon, "as more than a brother" (Philemon 15).

Similarly, the structures of the Greco-Roman family seem to have been threatened by this movement, not only because of the possible valorization of the single state among its members (and thus the refusal to perpetuate the social order through its literal reproduction), but also by the way in which it tended to separate its members from their families of origin and to offer a substitute for the family system. But perhaps the deepest assault upon the social order was precisely that which seems to have so concerned Paul: the refusal of the ethos of competitive self-regard in favor of a deep love for one another that sought the good of the other before one's own, practiced real solidarity and generosity, and so offered a compelling alternative to the existing social order at its very roots.

Seen in this light, persecution must have seemed inevitable, and indeed appears to have been the experience of all the first-century communities of Messiah followers of which we have knowledge. It is precisely this most radical challenge to all systems of authority and rule, of privilege and power, of domination and division, that must make of such communities, always and everywhere, the continually crucified body of the crucified Messiah.

Old community or new?

We have seen that the "theology of the cross" is represented in New Testament documents as having certain implications for the corporate life of followers of the Messiah. While these consequences are most heavily emphasized in the Pauline literature, they are by no means absent from the narrative literature that represents traditions concerning the mission and message of Jesus. What these documents have in common is the clear conviction that the cross of the Messiah entails that the community of the Messiah must not be one that is riven by internal disputes. Rather, it must exemplify a mutuality of service and a celebration of diversity that make division impossible. And it must do and be this because divisiveness is itself the force that has crucified the Messiah. This is especially evident when divisiveness is seen as the jostling for prestige and power that mirrors the politics of empire.

A moment's reflection will suffice to bring home how deeply radical this implication of the cross is for the life of Christian community. For who can doubt that fractiousness is empirically quite evident in communities of faith? Or as well, between communities of faith? How is it possible to form and nurture communities that do not betray, through their fractiousness, the very one identified as Lord and Messiah?

Perhaps even more radically, we may wonder at the disappearance of the cross from the experience of the Christian churches. Of course, the cross is present as a symbol, but very seldom as an experience. The church all too readily makes itself the mirror of and support for social orders based upon the ethos of self-preservation and self-aggrandizement. All too often, the church has become the spiritual handmaiden of social orders of competition for power and prestige, and so mirrors these same values in its own internal life. Insofar as it does this, the church becomes not the community of the Crucified, but the sanctification of the crucifiers.

Of course, it will be maintained that communities of the Crucified cannot exist, or at least not for long, since the human being is always constituted by precisely those needs for self-assertion and competition for advantage that render the aspiration for a different sort of community doomed from the start. The human being would have to be completely transformed in order to be able to constitute such a community.

It is precisely in order to see what is at stake here that we will turn, in the next chapter, to a consideration of the Pauline (and other) language concerning dying with Christ as it applies to the members of such communities.

CHAPTER EIGHT

Dying with/in the Messiah

I n the previous chapter, we have seen that the theme of the cross is deployed in such a way as to create a new form of human society or community. But we have also been led to wonder whether or in what way such a community, society, or form of "being-with"[1] might become actual, since it appears that human self-regard regularly interferes with the sort of corporate relations that are evoked as necessary to this form of sociality. What style or form of life would make possible the atrophy of the self-regard and competitiveness that seem always to doom the sort of being-with that is essential to the community of the Crucified, the cruciform community? It is in this connection that we find a number of passages, above all in the letters of Paul, that speak of the believer as one who has died with, or in, the Messiah, and thus has died to the law, the flesh, and the world.

These texts are often understood as referring to an individualistic form of life that aims at a certain heroism of renunciation, or asceticism. It is in this connection that the image of "dying with Christ" or "crucifying the flesh with its sinful desires" has had enormous influence in the history of Christianity, whether we think of the practices of hermits and monks or of the wandering flagellants who afflict their own bodies so as to bring themselves into some sort of bloody imitation of the fate of the Christ.

I am far from wanting to disparage the remarkable disciplines and sacrifices that these persons of faith have inflicted upon themselves in order to identify with the passion of Christ, or to anticipate (in the case of early ascetic movements) the resurrection body.[2] But in this chapter, I will read these texts differently, and in ways that I believe come closer to the insights that they contain concerning what it is to become a "new creation," as one who has passed from death to life, through an identification with the death of the Messiah.

Many of the references to sharing or participating in the death of the Messiah seem to have the literal sense of facing the violent hostility of structures of power in ways that result in a sort of violence directed against oneself. Of course, this reflects the actual fate of Jesus at the hands of the power structures of Israel and Rome. We have already seen that one's following of Jesus means precisely the acceptance of his confrontation with these structures as the paradigm for a discipleship or apprenticeship that emulates his destiny.[3] And we have seen that Paul and others generally suppose that the community of faithfulness to the executed Messiah will experience this same hostility. Accordingly, we will first attend to some of the ways that sharing in the suffering of the Messiah seems to have this literal significance in the letters attributed to Paul.

But there are a number of other texts that seem to point in the direction of a less literal "martyrdom," and in the direction of a form of life that results from having already in some way been assimilated to the death of the Messiah. I will contend that it is here that we encounter the answer to the exigency that persons be made new in order to be effective "members" of the corporate body that we described in the previous chapter. Death to the flesh or world, I will contend, has to do precisely with death to those values or that ethos that makes the new society impossible.

It will be necessary also to attend to the way that this question is sometimes linked to baptism. One of the ways in which the social effects of the identification with the cross have been reduced or abolished is through a "sacramentalizing" of this concern, a focus upon baptism as a relatively harmless ritual of entrance into community or transfer of oneself into the domain of "salvation" that has no actual effects in terms of fitting us for life in a new sociality or new creation.

A further way in which the theme of dying with Christ has been rendered politically harmless is by absorbing it into the valorization of conventionally ascetic practices. Thus, it will also be necessary to show that this is not what is at stake here. Put positively, the asceticism that is in view here is one that "unplugs" the adherent from the ethos of self-preservation and self-preoccupation in order to make possible a new style of being with others that these texts conceive as love of the neighbor.

We may take the assertion of Paul in 2 Corinthians 5:14 (NRSV) as a point of entry into this discussion: "The love of Christ urges us on, because we are convinced that one has died for all; therefore all have died." This verse may also be translated as "Messianic love sets us in motion, since we are persuaded that one has died for all, and thus that all have died." How is this messianic love derived from a death that all share? How does that death include all death? And how does having died in the death of the Messiah release love as a force that transforms life? These will be questions that we will need to attend to as we proceed with our investigations. But certainly we have an indication already, for Paul continues: "And he [the Messiah] died [for] all, so that those who live might live no longer [for] themselves" (2 Cor 5:15); that is, the participation in the death of the Messiah is "for us" in the sense that it opens us to a way of living outside our own self-interest, and thus in openness to the other. By no means is this death a substitution for us, as Western views of the atonement would have it. It is instead a representation of or inclusion of our death.[4] Only in this way does it make sense to say that it overcomes self-interest and so opens us to the other person. This openness is oriented by the messianic death that opens the way to life: "not [for] ourselves, but [for] him who died and was raised for them."[5] That is, the having died of the Messiah is by no means an end in itself, but rather the beginning of life for us that has death behind it, and is therefore in some way a life that may be characterized as no longer self-interested, but now oriented by and toward love. This, at least, is what we will be exploring as we seek to understand what it might mean to live after death, a death that is taken up into the messianic death.

The way of the cross

The direction in which we will be moving is toward this wider sense of dying with or in the Messiah as the most general sense of dying with, or even being crucified with, the Messiah. We must also recognize that this is grounded in a rather more literal sense of sharing in the fate of the Messiah. It is precisely the analogy between the fate of the adherent of the Messiah and the fate of the Messiah himself that underwrites the extension of the analogy into a more universal, and perhaps also more radical, meaning of sharing in messianic death, and so in the life that is messianic, or resurrection life.

In Romans, Paul writes that we hope to share in his resurrection if we share in a "death like his" (Rom 6:5). Here I want to look first at passages that seem to have in view a rather literal sharing in the sort of violent opposition from the side of religious and imperial authorities that characterized the fate of the Messiah. Paul himself makes this connection quite explicit in 2 Corinthians, in which he repeatedly makes reference to his own imitation of the passion of the Messiah.

"We are afflicted in every way, but not crushed; perplexed, but not driven to despair; persecuted, but not forsaken; struck down, but not destroyed" (2 Cor 4:8-9 NRSV). This fate is expressly linked to an identification with the fate of the Messiah: "Always carrying in the body the death of Jesus, so that the life of Jesus may also be made visible in our bodies. For while we live, we are always being given up to death for Jesus' sake, so that the life of Jesus may be made visible in our mortal flesh" (4:10-11 NRSV). The afflictions that Paul experiences at the hands of the opponents of the messianic mission are understood to be the concrete way in which "the death of Jesus" remains a reality in the ongoing mission. Interestingly, Paul here speaks of Jesus without using the customary designation of him as Lord or Messiah, as if to emphasize the extreme vulnerability in which Jesus was placed. It is precisely by accentuating this vulnerability that Paul makes "the life of Jesus" visible in an ongoing way—a life that was for Jesus, and now also for Paul, a "being given over to death." In the same way, "the life of Jesus may be made visible" even now, in flesh that is just as vulnerable, as mortal, as that of Jesus. This mortality is made evident as one is persecuted by the "same" forces that also persecuted Jesus.

That Paul has in mind rather concrete instances of persecution is made evident as well in the catalog of suffering that he enumerates subsequently in the "same" letter:[6]

> Five times I have received from the Judeans the forty lashes minus one. Three times I was beaten with rods. Once I received a stoning. Three times I was shipwrecked; for a night and a day I was adrift at sea; on frequent journeys, in danger from rivers, danger from bandits, danger from my own people, danger from the gentiles, danger in the city, danger in the wilderness, danger at sea, danger from false brothers; in toil and hardship, through many a sleepless night, hungry and thirsty, often without food, cold and naked. (2 Cor 11:24-27)

And he adds, almost as an afterthought, "In Damascus, the governor under King Aretas guarded the city of Damascus in order to seize me, but I was let down in a basket through a window in the wall, and escaped from his hands" (11:32-33 NRSV).

Although we may cringe at the extremes to which Paul will go to defend his apostolate to the apparently recalcitrant community in Corinth, it is notable that Paul defends the authenticity of his mission specifically in terms of the sorts of sufferings that can be construed as a participation in the sufferings of the Messiah. And as we have seen, when he writes to communities with which he is on better terms (the Thessalonians and Philippians), he supposes that they also experience this same sort of treatment at the hands of the authorities.[7]

In a letter that may well come from one of Paul's companions in the aftermath of Paul's own death, this imitation of the messianic passion on the part of Paul is given a rather striking formulation: "I am now rejoicing in my sufferings for your sake, and in my flesh I am completing what is lacking in Christ's afflictions for the sake of his body, that is, the church" (Col 1:24 NRSV). Perhaps the most remarkable part of this formulation is that the sufferings of the follower "complete what is lacking" in the passion of the Messiah. That is, the messianic suffering that opens the way to redemption is not restricted to the death of the Messiah, but extends as well to the suffering (and possible death) of his emissaries. While this may seem rather shocking to those who maintain that the death of Christ is unique in having salvific effect, it is quite consistent with the picture that we found in the Gospels that insists that the followers are "understudies" in the messianic mission, and thus continue (and in that sense, complete) the mission of the Messiah Jesus. And although the sense of completing what is lacking is remarkable, it is the case that 1 Peter also can comfort a persecuted community with the thought that in their suffering at the hands of the powerful, they also share in Christ's sufferings (1 Pet 5:13).

Crucified to the flesh

In addition to, and building upon, the more literal sense of sharing in the suffering of the Messiah at the hands of religio-political authorities, the image of dying with Christ—or dying to law, flesh, or world—has an extended, or perhaps metaphorical, meaning in the letters of Paul. It is to these meanings that we must now attend if we are to have a fuller sense of the ways in which this image is deployed.

First, we will explore Paul's talk of dying to the law as an indication of the renunciation of (religious) privilege, especially in Galatians. We will then explore dying to the flesh as Paul's way of indicating a renunciation of those attitudes and behaviors that make a genuine "being-with" impossible. Finally, "dying," or being crucified to the world, will be explored in terms of the relativizing of worldly structures that aim at self-preservation. This discussion returns us to the theme of that which makes community possible, which was the focus of the previous chapter.

Dying to the law: renouncing advantage

In our discussion of the cross of Jesus in chapter 3, we noticed that the cross serves to break down the walls of religious privilege that divide humanity into those who are recipients of the divine favor and those who are not. The Gospels suggest that Jesus suffered rejection by the officials of his own people, in significant degree, because he radically undermined the religious privilege of Israel as narrowly conceived, that is, as exclusive.

It is therefore not surprising that one of the ways in which Paul deploys talk of participation in the cross of the Messiah is to speak of his own task of breaking down the exclusive privilege of Israel. Of course, we must recall that for Paul this does not mean the abolition of a certain priority and election of Israel. On the contrary, he goes to great lengths in Romans 9–11 to insist that the divine promise to Israel has never been abrogated. But the *exclusivity* of this privilege is indeed undermined by Paul, typically with respect to the question of circumcision. This finds forceful expression in Galatians.

> But God forbid that I should glory, save in the cross of our Lord Jesus Messiah, by whom the world is crucified unto me and I unto the world. For in Messiah Jesus neither circumcision counts for anything nor uncircumcision, but a new creature. (Gal 6:14-15)

What is most important for our purposes here is that Paul links the question of the cross and of participation in the cross to the elimination of the exclusive privilege signaled by circumcision. To be crucified to the world is precisely to be crucified to the game of religious privilege. It is religion that is "worldly" on this view! This has important similarities to the teachings ascribed to Jesus in the Gospels that make religious observance "merely human," while insisting that openness to the needs of the neighbor, especially the most vulnerable, is what is really "divine" (see chapter 3).

In an earlier passage in which Paul seems to be reflecting on a wider set of religious obligations than circumcision alone, he writes: "For through the law I died to the law, so that I might live to God. I have been crucified with Christ; and it is no longer I who live, but it is Christ who lives in me" (Gal 2:19-20 NRSV). What Paul has in mind here is his own decision to live as if he were a gentile, especially regarding table fellowship, so as to be in solidarity with gentiles. In this way he deliberately comes into contradiction with the law that circumscribes the bounds of the religious privilege of the elect people. To be crucified with Christ here means to be one who is excluded or who excludes oneself from the sphere of (religious) privilege. But what would it mean to live outside the shelter of religious privilege? It is one thing to think of this as simply an escape from certain onerous obligations of the "Mosaic" law. It is quite another if we try to think with Paul of what it would mean to surrender the shelter of religious privilege as such—not to trade it in for a better or more secure shelter, but to live without the protection of any religious privilege. This would mean bringing into question not only a certain Jewish privilege but, even more, Christian privilege as well. For this is precisely the way Christianity is often "sold": as a better or more secure shelter, as a better or higher form of religious privilege. To be crucified with Christ would seem to mean to live utterly without that sort of shelter, that sort of privilege.

And this may indeed be a kind of death, not only because of the potential outrage of those who seek to defend their privilege, but also because it means giving up or renouncing the sense of religious security, the reassurance that is provided by adherence to a religious institution or tradition.

Dying to the flesh: renouncing competitiveness

In Galatians, Paul has spoken of dying to the law, a theme that will recur in Romans, but he also speaks in Galatians of dying to the flesh, or rather, more graphically, as having "crucified the flesh." How is this to be understood? What he writes is that "those who belong to Messiah Jesus have crucified the flesh with its passions and desires" (Gal 5:24). This text has often been taken to be a warrant for the close introspection of passion and desire, an introspection that in the West, following Augustine, focused more and more narrowly on what may be termed sexuality. But is that the sort of "passion and desire" that Paul has in view? It seems not. For he continues: "Let us not become conceited, competing against one another, envying one another" (5:26 NRSV). The passion of the flesh here is taken to be that which sets us into competition with one another, which makes us envy one another. It is born of what the translators call "conceit," which here points to the sort of self-regard or self-preoccupation that makes of the other a competitor for the scarce goods of prestige, power, and influence.

Here, Paul situates his distinction between flesh and spirit. He exhorts his readers to "be guided by the spirit" (Gal 5:25), and in this way to renounce the competition and envy that bring to expression the passions of the flesh—that very flesh that is to have been "crucified" through identification with the cross of the Messiah.

This addresses the question of what must happen if we are to be able to enter into the sort of community that Paul has been emphasizing in his other discussions of the effects of the cross, as we saw in the previous chapter. Being crucified with Christ, then, means renouncing the passion for self-regard, self-assertion, self-aggrandizement that makes the other an object of envy (does he have more than I do?) or an object of competition (I must have more than she does).

The meaning of Paul's speaking of the crucifixion of the flesh is made evident when we look more closely at the contrast that he sets up between the life, or rather pseudo-life, of flesh and the new life or hyper-life of spirit. He writes of this contrast in quite strong terms: "Live by the Spirit, I say, and do not gratify the desires of the flesh. For what the flesh desires is opposed to the Spirit, and what the Spirit desires is opposed to the flesh; for these are opposed to each other" (Gal 5:16-17 NRSV). He then offers a list, perhaps random, of what he has in mind. If we begin with spirit, we will see what is at stake in this contrast: "The fruit of the Spirit is love, joy, peace, patience, kindness, generosity, faithfulness, gentleness, and self-control" (5:22-23 NRSV). Now what is clear from this list is that Paul identifies a number of attitudes or ways of being that make it possible to live with the other without envy and competition. These are precisely the forms of life that make it possible to have what Emmanuel Levinas termed a "non-allergic" relation with the other, with one another.[8]

By contrast, then, we have the passions of the flesh that prominently include things like "enmities, strife, jealousy, anger, quarrels, dissensions, factions, envy" (cf. Gal 5:20-21). These items, taken from the center of Paul's list, clearly correspond to that which makes community or being with one another impossible. And it is these central characteristics of the flesh that Paul highlights when he speaks of having "crucified the flesh with its passions and desires" (5:24).

What has made it difficult to see the centrality of this concern has been the addition of items that are all too conventionally regarded as "vices": "fornication, impurity, licentiousness," as well as "drunkenness, carousing, and things like these." In fact, it is by focusing attention on these "vices" that Paul's true concern has been obscured and that the tradition has substituted new laws or regulations into Christian life in place of the "law of Moses," but with exactly the same effect. If we allow ourselves to be guided by what Paul clearly identifies as his central concern, it is easy to see in what respect these "vices" may be understood as evidences of the same sort of self-preoccupation that tends to express itself as enmity and envy. It would then be not sexuality (fornication and so on), but the use of sexuality for self-promotion, or to ensure for oneself that one has a certain power or prestige.[9] Similarly, it is not a question of drinking (wine, for example), but of the desperate attempt to give oneself more than enough and so to deprive others. It was this sort of drunkenness, we recall, that Paul noted in his discussion of the behavior of the Corinthians at their common meals (1 Cor 11). In this regard, we may say that Augustine was right to regard concupiscence as the basic character of "sin," insofar as concupiscence is the desire for more, the insistence upon one's own benefit at the expense of others, of all others. But what concupiscence as conventionally understood has not done is to place the emphasis where Paul placed it, namely, on the question of what makes it impossible for us to live in community with others. In consequence, the Western tradition following Augustine has developed an emphasis on the individual and on inwardness that makes it impossible to see the significance in Paul of what makes life with others possible.[10]

In summary, then, the contrast between flesh and spirit is a contrast between attitudes and comportments that make oneself the "center of the universe" and attitudes and comportments that allow for life with one another—that enable us to be open and vulnerable to the other instead of seeking our own advantage at the expense of the other.

The danger here is that some will say to others, "You must not seek your own advantage," while continuing to seek their own. This is what has all too often happened when masters have cited these words to slaves, or males to females, or parents to children, or rulers to the dominated, or the privileged to the marginalized. Then what happens is that the same old polity or politics of selfish advantage for some has been sanctified by insisting that others relinquish their own quest for life. But in that case, what has happened is that the social order that "crucified the Lord of glory" ensures its rule by telling others that they must imitate the one this same social order has crucified! In such a case, the only possibility is the path of resistance and confrontation that in truth imitates the path of the Messiah, the crucified Messiah.

What Paul's perspective at its best has in view is an ethos for a genuinely equitable society, one in which all seek to outdo one another in doing good, in which all, especially those who have the most power, surrender privilege for the sake of the other. This would indeed be a truly revolutionary polity or politics.[11]

The perspectives that have been developed in Galatians will be extended and deepened within similar reflections in Romans, where again the theme of dying with Christ, dying to the law, to the flesh, and to the world, will be developed further. Paul's argument in Romans is a very intricate one, and thus it is perilous to extract bits and pieces of his argument from the overarching context in which they operate. Nevertheless, we must make an effort to determine whether his usage of the metaphor of dying with Christ (or to the law, the world, and/or the flesh) agrees with and deepens what we have found in the discussion of the relevant passages from Galatians.

The critical passages are found in a section of the argument in which Paul is insisting that the new life in the Messiah is fundamentally different from the old life that must now be left behind. In this argument, he employs a series of analogies to indicate that the adherent of the Messiah has passed from one state to another, most dramatically from death to life. The images he uses are those of baptismal participation in the death of the Messiah (Rom 6:3ff.), death as an escape from the reach of the law (7:4ff.), the transfer of a slave from one owner to another (6:15-19), and the wife who is liberated by the death of her husband (7:1-3). These are all rather striking metaphors that aim ultimately at the assertion that "there is now no condemnation for those who are in Messiah Jesus" (8:1). This is all developed in complex relation to questions of law, of sin, of flesh, and of death in ways that resist easy summary. Here, we will simply risk pointing to the way Paul is led to refer to dying with the Messiah and thus to the world, the law, sin, and flesh without seeking to unpack all that is going on in these passages.[12]

Paul introduces this discussion by making it clear that, in his view, those who are faithful to the Messiah should not "continue in sin" because they/we have already "died to sin." In connection with this, he makes an allusion to baptism: "All of us who have been baptized into Messiah Jesus were baptized into his death. Therefore we have been buried with him by baptism into death" (Rom 6:4). The end result appears to be something like what we found in Galatians, since the goal is "that we might walk in newness of life." That is, the death or participation in death is not an end in itself, but has in view the new or renewed life that will correspond to the resurrection, that is, to life that has already passed through death. It is here that Paul uses the phrase that we have already noticed: "For if we have been united in a death like his, we will certainly be united with him in a resurrection like his" (Rom 6:5). We have seen that this having a death "like his" is understandable first in a literal sense; that is, as a death that results from the opposition of the powers of the religio-political order. But once the sentence of death has been carried out, then these powers no longer have a hold on the object of their opposition. Death means that their threat of death no longer has any meaning. They can no longer threaten the "sinner" or criminal with the force of law, with the ultimate penalty of death.

Thus, a radically new situation obtains for one who has already died. Now everything that seemed so urgently important (securing one's own life) and so urgently threatening (avoiding the sentence of death) no longer has any force. Paul is suggesting that insofar as we have in some way identified ourselves with the death of Jesus, we too have already died, and thus the force of the prospect of death no longer has any hold on us. This will mean that we are free to live without protecting ourselves from death or its surrogates, and so to live "in newness of life," in a life so new that the old has truly passed away.

What Paul seems to be struggling with is the sense that human injustice has its roots in the competitiveness and enmity that are produced by something like the fear or prospect or threat of death. It is as if what Heidegger called our being-toward-death were the root of our attempts to secure our existence in the world, typically at the expense of others. Moreover, it is as if the fear of death or its surrogates (social ostracism, religious condemnation, legal penalties) forced us to collaborate with structures of injustice, to at least "go along" with them or keep silent about them, even to side with them or identify with them—all in order to preserve our life, or what passes for life in this world. This threat and this desire to save our lives enter us through our vulnerability to death, namely, ourselves as "flesh." For in Hebrew at least, what *basar* or flesh designates is precisely the weakness or vulnerability of our life as mortal life, as life toward death.[13] Mortal life is always life under threat, indeed, under sentence of death, and so this life may seek to ward off death, to defend itself against death. Life does this by seeking its own advantage, even at the expense of others. That is why Paul can take covetousness as the exemplary sin here (Rom 7:7-8), as he does competitiveness and envy in Galatians.

But if that is the problem, what is the solution? What Paul suggests is that we live as if we have already died. In that case, death has no power over us, neither as a menace that incites us to collaborate in injustice, nor as an incentive to seek our own advantage at the expense of others. He in fact says this: now that you have already died, "no longer offer your members as instruments of injustice . . . but offer your members [your ways of engaging the world and your neighbor] as instruments of justice" (Rom 6:13). It is thus the having death in front of us that explains our collaboration with injustice (our members as instruments or, as he also says, slaves of injustice [6:18]). And it is having death behind us, and therefore having nothing left to lose, that frees us to become instruments of justice.

When Paul comes, toward the end of Romans, to indicate what this new life of justice entails, he again deploys some of the themes familiar to us from Galatians and 1 Corinthians. For example, he uses a contrast that we found in Galatians: "Let us live honorably as in the day, not in reveling and drunkenness, not in debauchery and licentiousness, not in quarreling and jealousy" (Rom 13:13 NRSV). He then goes on to relate this to being "in Messiah," and to a renunciation of the passions of the flesh: "Instead put on the Lord Jesus Messiah, and make no provision for the flesh to gratify its desires" (13:14). If we stopped here, we might think that the emphasis falls on drunken parties. But in fact where Paul places the emphasis is on the question of quarreling, for the next chapter or so deals precisely with the question of living together in spite of great differences in opinion and practice (14:1—15:7).

The theme of this discussion is introduced at the beginning: "Welcome those who are weak in faith, but not for the purpose of quarreling over opinions" (Rom 14:1 NRSV). It concludes with the exhortation: "Welcome one another, therefore, just as Messiah has welcomed you" (15:7).

We have already seen in the previous chapter that the differences are actually differences of conscience concerning what is the appropriate way to honor God. Some suppose that this has to do with abstinence from certain foods (Rom 14:2); some suppose that this has to do with setting aside special days (14:5). Others suppose that nothing of

the sort is required of those who seek to honor God. These are fundamental issues of religious difference. Paul supposes both that these differences of opinion and practice should be taken with great seriousness
("Let everyone be convinced in their own mind" [14:5; see also 14:22])
and that these differences should not be the occasion of division, quarreling, condemnation, or judgment.

Indeed, it is here that Paul applies the theme that we saw to be
important in chapter 4 concerning the renunciation of judgment or
condemnation within the community. Since God has "welcomed" those
of quite different opinions and practices, we are not to pass judgment
on, or to despise, one another (Rom 14:4). And this admonition is
repeated several times: "Why do you pass judgment on your brother?"
(14:10). "Let us therefore no longer pass judgment on one another"
(14:13 NRSV).

In the earlier chapters, we saw how the abolition of religious privilege was also connected to the abolition of the power of the law to
judge. It seems quite consistent that Paul should suppose that the sorts
of persons who can constitute the assembly of the Crucified (or body of
the Messiah) would be those who renounce the need to pass judgment
on others. For, after all, it is precisely this passing of judgment, this condemnation of the other, that is implicated in the rejection, condemnation, and execution of the Messiah.

Dying to the world

The question of being "crucified to the world" finds expression in other
ways in the Pauline texts. In general, Paul does not encourage his readers to escape from the world, but rather to deal with the world "as if
not" doing so. Indeed, it is precisely this "as if not" that certain contemporary political philosophers have identified as one of Paul's most
important contributions to an understanding of messianic existence in
a world that has no permanence.[14]

The key passage in this regard comes from Paul's admonitions to
Christ's followers in 1 Corinthians:

> I mean, brothers and sisters, the appointed time has grown short;
> from now on, let even those who have wives be as though they had
> none, and those who mourn as though they were not mourning,

and those who rejoice as though they were not rejoicing, and those who buy as though they had no possessions, and those who deal with the world as though they had no dealings with it. For the present form of this world is passing away. (1 Cor 7:29-31 NRSV)

The Greek is even more dramatic with its fivefold *hos me*: "as if not." Moreover, to this list of ways in which we engage the world as if not engaging it may be added Paul's assertions that the slave is as if free, the free as if slave (1 Cor 7:22), and that neither circumcision nor uncircumcision matters (1 Cor 7:19; Gal 6:14-15). Thus, all that which constitutes one's relation to the world is in a certain way suspended. This does not mean that one does not rejoice or mourn, for example, or that one withdraws from the world of religious difference (circumcision or uncircumcision). This does not appear to be a counsel to completely disengage from the world and its structures, but rather to engage "as if not."

What is involved here is a withdrawal of a certain kind of belief, belief in the ultimacy of these structures, their permanence or self-evidence. Whatever it is that binds us to these structures loses its hold or claim. We engage them, but without being determined by them.[15]

On one level, this may appear to be parallel to certain stoic postures toward the structures of the world, a certain inner detachment from them so as not to be troubled by them, so as to be able to live with a certain peace of mind or tranquility. But that does not seem to be exactly what Paul is after here. For one thing, his perspective is "eschatological": the time is grown short, the structures are passing away. That is, time itself, and with it the structures that bind time and regulate our relation to time (economic, familial, religious), is disrupted.

Why should this be so? One feature of these structures is that they are or may become ways of assuring ourselves against time and its ravages—thus the attempt to secure our existence religiously, economically, or by way of marriage and family. But those who have in a certain sense already passed from life into death have no motive for securing their own existence.

Moreover, taking these structures of family and religion and economy at face value has the inevitable result of putting us at odds with one another. If we take our religious practices with ultimate seriousness, then differences as central as circumcision and sabbath, or as second-ary as days of fasting and feasting, become insurmountable barriers to community. Similarly, if "making a living" has basic importance, then I am placed in a situation of competing with my neighbor for the scarce goods that I desire in order to prosper. Even the ties of marriage can make us anxious to control or possess our partners, or make us jealous and angry at the slightest appearance of a lack of total commitment.

While participation in these structures may be inevitable, and Paul does not dispute that, he urges his readers to view them as temporary expedients that are on the verge of disappearing with the coming of the full messianic daybreak. We may engage in these worldly structures for the moment, but only as if we were not really engaged in them—for the form of this world is passing away.

In this way, Paul is again pointing to essential conditions for the actualization, here and now, of a being with one another that is just and peaceable, that is no longer characterized by hostility, envy, jealousy, anger, and division. The "as if not" will appear to the world as a kind of nihilism, because it is a decided relativizing of what the world regards as ultimately serious.[16] But this is what it means, Paul is saying, to live in this world as those who have already passed from death into life through solidarity with the crucified and risen Messiah.

The question of asceticism

We have already noticed that one of the ways in which talk of par-ticipation in the cross of the Messiah has been (mis)understood is to take this as an exhortation to one or another form of ascetic discipline of the body. Whether we think of the extraordinary efforts of early Christian hermits, or the disciplines of corporate monastic life, or even some Protestant emphases on the importance of not smoking, drinking, dancing, and so on, these have all frequently turned to the metaphor of dying to the world or to the flesh, and its "passions and desires," as warrant for ascetic practices.

But such a view seems to stand in irreconcilable contrast to the tra-ditions concerning Jesus in the Gospels. There, Jesus is presented as one who was a winebibber and a glutton, as he is recalled to have remarked (Matt 11:18-19), as one who was all too willing to participate in the eating and drinking parties of people of all classes. Nor does he seem to have been at all concerned to enforce conventional sexual moralities (21:31). Is it the case, then, that the Pauline metaphor is in direct contradiction to the Jesus tradition? This is, of course, possible, since Paul seems not to have known much about the Jesus whom we meet in the Gospels, the narratives all being written sometime after Paul's own death. As it happens, however, there may not be such a contradiction after all. For the Pauline tradition seems to be also less concerned about these sorts of ascetic disciplines than has often been supposed.

A good place to see another possibility is in connection with a text that has the name of Paul assigned to it, even if many scholars are persuaded that it must have been written either by an associate of Paul's in his name and/or in the period not long after Paul's death. The "Paul" of Colossians writes: "If with Christ you died to the elemental spirits of the universe, why do you live as if you still belonged to the world? Why do you submit to regulations, 'Do not handle, Do not taste, Do not touch'?" (Col 2:20-21 NRSV). Here the text places the model of dying with Christ onto the cosmic frame that characterizes the point of view of Colossians as a whole. Thus, we hear of dying not to the world or to the flesh, but to "the elemental spirits (or pillars) of the universe."

Here it seems, however, that this having died (rather like Paul's talk of dying to the law in Galatians) means that the follower or adherent does not pay heed to those who counsel ascetic practices, any more than in Galatians Paul heeded the dietary restrictions that would impede fellowship with gentiles. In Colossians, the restrictions do not seem to have a specifically Mosaic basis, but are more likely to have in view rather widespread Hellenistic ascetic practices. That is, they are ascetic practices encouraged by fear of or obedience to the "pillars" of the universe. Thus, the perspective worked out in Galatians is now being applied to a quite different social and cultural context. The writer goes on to explain why it is impossible to adopt these ascetic practices: "These have indeed an appearance of wisdom in promoting self-imposed piety, humility, and severe treatment of the body, but they are of no value in checking self-indulgence [or: are of no value, serving only to indulge the flesh]" (Col 2:23 NRSV).

What the writer suggests is that anxiety about food and drink is simply the other side of the same self-preoccupation that leads to overindulgence. In each case, what is happening is that we are anxious to preserve our own life, whether through excess or through renunciation.

We should also recall that when Paul discussed differences of opinion and practice concerning what we should or should not eat or drink, he reminds his readers: "The reign of God is not food and drink, but justice, and peace and joy in the Holy Spirit" (Rom 14:17). The point is that attempts to regulate what we eat and drink have no connection to what is essential to the new reality that is coming into being. Instead, what is important is "justice, peace, and joy." Indeed, these three terms have a logical relation to one another. Without justice there can be no peace, and without peace there can be no true joy. Put another way: peace flows from justice, joy from peace. Peace without justice is the Pax Romana, the enforced quiescence of the graveyard; and joy without peace is simply feverish excitement. Neither justice nor peace depends on uniformity of opinion or practice with respect to "food and drink."

If we take this discussion out of the religious sphere, we may get a clearer sense of what is at stake. Some folk overindulge in, say, food because they fear that there is not enough and they must make sure that they get all they want. Others go on diets because they want to avoid the physical death that seems to be hastened by obesity, or the cultural death that threatens those who have less than ideal bodies. Both act out of a certain self-preoccupation, though in opposite ways. In fact, the ascetic impulse may make us more, rather than less, involved with both our bodily needs and desires and the avoidance of death. Thus, what appears to be wisdom is in fact simply a subtler version of the same trap.

If, however, we have already died (to the world, the flesh, the spirits of the universe), then neither of these motives can have a hold on us. Our anxiety can be put to rest. We can happily eat and drink whatever comes along (as long as it is equitably shared), and we can also be content with less. We need no longer be slaves, either to appetite or to diet. For both are ways of being enslaved to what Paul calls "flesh." Flesh is the name given to the self-preoccupation that is alarmed by the vulnerability of the body to death and all its surrogates.

There is, of course, an important point in asceticism. It is that much of our life under threat of death is a life lived in the acquisition of more, the consumption of more, all in the quest for more life, or what passes for life. But for those who have already died, the urgency that fuels our competition for more has also passed away. An important sign of this is something that might be termed "simplicity of life" as a way of reminding ourselves and others that life need not be defended by "hoarding up treasures on earth," nor by excess in the interest of self-assertion, self-display, or self-gratification.

This is a particularly crucial message since everything in our current world order compels us to seek to acquire and spend and consume more, in order to have and enjoy life. In the midst of the veritable feeding frenzy of acquisition and consumption (typically reaching its insane peak in relation to the alleged celebration of the birth of the Messiah), the call to simplicity of life can be both liberating and radical— radical because it "unplugs" from the existing social order, and because it requires a deep renunciation of the blandishments of the concerted voices of our global culture, but also liberating because it takes away the feverish pseudo-life that is in fact the work of death already in us.

The question of baptism

Paul's mention of baptism in connection with his argument in Romans concerning the necessary transformation in the believer's life that is signaled by "dying with [or in] Christ" has led many to suppose that the talk of dying with Christ should be understood primarily as the cultic act associated with baptism. It is true that Paul mentions baptism in this connection. But it is also true that this is only one of several metaphors that he uses in the same argument to point to the fundamental change in way of life that he supposes to follow from participation in Christ, or in the messianic reality (images like the change from one master to another for a slave, or the death of the husband for a woman). The difficulty with emphasizing baptism as the privileged occasion for participation in the death of Christ, or as the content of that participation, is that it entirely undercuts Paul's actual concern, which is with a change in behavior so that we become, as he says, slaves or instruments not of injustice, but of justice. With traditional Christianity, however, in place of a fundamentally changed style of life, what we get is a liturgical act whose effects are "invisible," or are restricted to admission into the institution. The result is an utter travesty of Paul's theology.

The careful reader of Paul should realize that baptism as such is not one of his major preoccupations. For example, in 1 Corinthians, just as he brings up the Lord's Supper only to address the question of life together in community and to oppose practices that undercut the community's embodiment of justice (1 Cor 10–11), so also he mentions baptism only to oppose quarreling over baptismal practice. Thus he writes, "What I mean is that each of you says, 'I belong to Paul,' or 'I belong to Apollos,' or 'I belong to Cephas,' or 'I belong to Christ'" (1 Cor 1:12). And then he asks, "Were you baptized in the name of Paul?" It appears that at least an initial cause of division in Corinth was that people took the precise manner of their baptism, or the pastoral agent of their baptism, too literally. Paul himself then makes clear that baptism per se is of little importance to him: "I thank God that I baptized none of you except Crispus and Gaius, so that no one can say that you were baptized in my name. (I did baptize also the household of Stephanas; beyond that, I do not know whether I baptized anyone else)" (1:14-16 NRSV). What the last parenthetical addition makes clear is that Paul simply does not consider baptism to be at all decisive. He may baptize or he may not—he doesn't really remember. The act, moment, and circumstances of baptism mean very little to him. What matters, as he goes on to say, is the proclamation of the cross and that which follows from adherence to that proclamation.

Indeed, in an odd way, Paul's uncertainty about his own baptizing of people mirrors the uncertainty in the much later Gospel of John about whether Jesus actually baptized people. Thus, in John 3:22, 26, and 4:1, we are told that Jesus was baptizing people. But in John 4:2 we have the parenthetical "correction": "(Actually Jesus didn't baptize anyone; his disciples did the baptizing.)" In the Gospel of Mark, when Jesus does talk about baptism, he clearly refers not to a cultic or liturgical act, but to literal imitation of his own fate at the hands of the structures of authority (Mark 10:38-39).

The problem is not with there being something like the practice of baptism, so long as it serves to make clear the unity of all who are participants in the messianic reality,[17] or serves as a dramatic point of identification with the change from death to life that results in a radically altered form of life. But the emphasis upon baptism typically produces exactly the opposite result. Groups of Christians divide themselves over baptismal practice and substitute baptismal participation for the sort of transformation that Paul insists is the true meaning of dying with or in Christ, dying to the law, the flesh, the world, or the elemental spirits of the universe. No wonder, then, that the cross can be reduced to a sort of fashion statement for sanctuaries or a piece of costume jewelry!

A baptismal practice that substitutes, rather than prepares us, for an imitation of the fate of Jesus is a renunciation, rather than a celebration, of the gospel. A baptismal practice that substitutes for, rather than effecting, a radical change in our form of life is a reversal of the Pauline theology of the cross.[18]

Conclusion: A life of vulnerability to the other

How then are we to live as those who have passed from death into life, as those who have already been crucified with the Messiah, and so live as those who have death behind them rather than before them?

While for centuries this has been understood as the renunciation of certain pleasures and desires, in fact the renunciation in view here is far more fundamental. It does not renounce the body and the pleasure and joy of the body, for it longs for a renewed and more lively body—a body of life—and so welcomes all that betokens this liveliness. In that sense it is not ascetic at all, but imitates the one who came eating and drinking and sharing in the pleasures of the feast and of companionship, even intimate companionship. But there is here a profound renunciation—it is the renunciation of all that seems essential to the pseudo-life that seeks to ward off death: the urgency of self-assertion, of self-preservation, of self-aggrandizement, of the competition for life and all its surrogates, as if life were to be viewed as a scarce good, and the quest for life a zero-sum game in which the advantage of the other entailed a disadvantage for me. This is the "life" always already invaded by death and living under the sign of death.

The participation in the death of the Messiah is regarded as the gateway into the transformed life that anticipates the resurrection already inaugurated in the destiny of that same Messiah. It thus means entering into the form of life that no longer has death as its future, but for which death already belongs to the past. Having died with Christ, then, means dying to all that makes justice, peace, and joy impossible.

Accordingly, Paul insists that we are already to live into the new reality of justice and peace in which we are able genuinely to welcome the other and to live in solidarity with all. In this way, we begin to anticipate that new creation that is the aim or goal of the resurrection of the Crucified.

Paul's emphasis on dying with the Messiah, or being crucified (with the Messiah) to the world, the flesh, and the law, points us back to his emphasis upon the cruciform community. What is always in view in these passages is the sort of existence that makes a new life together possible. As we have seen, it is competition and envy, division and hostility, that always endanger life together. Thus, along with the cruciform society goes the cruciform existence. Together these ways of indicating our participation in the cross of Jesus point toward a new humanity in which justice, peace, and joy are the marks of a humanity that has passed from death to life through its identification with the death—and so also the resurrection—of Jesus.

Paul is not here dealing in utopias or ideals. He is exhorting the groups of Messiah followers to whom he addresses himself to make their thought and action consistent with their commitment to the crucified and risen Messiah. He is engaged here in what Alain Badiou calls a truth process: the transformation of life and thought on the basis of commitment to the event of the death and resurrection of Jesus as the Messiah of God.[19]

We began this chapter by noticing the statement of Paul in 2 Corinthians that "we are convinced that one has died for all; therefore all have died" (5:14 NRSV). Thus, for Paul, the having died of the Messiah is something in which we all participate, in that we too have death behind us. The consequence of this, as we also noticed, is that "he died for all so that those who live might not live of themselves but from him who died and was raised for them" (2 Cor 5:15).[20] As we have seen, this theme is developed in a number of passages in Paul that indicate that the messianic life (the life in Christ or Messiah) is a life that renounces self-preoccupation in order to live in openness and vulnerability with others, and so enable the appearance of a new form of messianic sociality in which justice, peace, and joy may be actualized.

In this sense, therefore, Paul can also say in this same passage that "if any in Messiah: new creation." This extraordinarily compressed statement is typically expanded to say, "If anyone is in Messiah, (he) is a new creation," but this may actually distort the sense of what Paul is pointing toward here. It is not that you or I or someone else becomes or is "the new creation." Rather, it is that as we or they enter into this messianic way of being, the new creation truly begins. For this is not a matter of this or that individual, but rather of a transformation that includes the renovation of creation as a whole, a renovation that, to be sure, takes hold of our lives in such a way that we no longer live for ourselves, and thus broadens out to include a new way of being with, a new sociality that instantiates justice and so entails the end of the old order and the beginning of the new creation.

This new creation is not something that is merely future, nor is it unconnected with the reality we experience here and now. Rather, it is something that takes place in and through history, a history that is public and, indeed, political. It has as its decisive starting point the historical event of the cross in which the contradictions of historical-social existence come to their point of crisis. It is from this point of crisis that the new beginning is actualized. It is actualized by taking this contradiction upon ourselves, first by participating in this death, and then (and therefore) by participating in the beginning of life that has death in its past, and so is the beginning of resurrection life, life that is true life, life that is truly social life, life that signals: new creation.[21]

CHAPTER NINE

The Cross of God

What are the implications of the theology of the cross for our understanding of God? How is God, or at a minimum, our understanding of God, changed by a consideration of the cross as the decisive turning point in our history and our lives? It is to this question that we must now turn. In this chapter, we will not attempt to develop a reconstruction of the Christian doctrine of God, but only point to ways in which a focus upon the cross or the message concerning the cross has effects upon our understanding of the divine.

The perspective on the theology of the cross that has been developed in these pages takes as fundamental the public, and so political, site of the cross. We have seen that by beginning here, with the public fact of the execution of Jesus at the hands of the military power of the Roman Empire, it is possible to understand the various dimensions of the meaning of the message concerning the cross as an integrated whole. This has led to understanding the way in which Paul deploys talk of the cross in order to foster a new kind of sociality—a new way of being together—that stands in decided contrast to the structures of domination and division, and to the religious values that tend to legitimate such a social order. This new sociality fosters the emergence of a new humanity, one that anticipates a new creation. For as Paul also writes, "If one is in Christ: new creation" (2 Cor 5:17).

This new creation, however, is present under the sign of contradiction and shared suffering. It is the vulnerability of the community and of the new humanity that it fosters that is the way in which the solidarity of humanity, and of humanity with creation, is foreshadowed. But if the way of vulnerability is the constitution of a counter-politics, and thus of a new society, and if this new sociality may be understood as the reign of God, then what must become of our conception of God? Is God to be shielded from this vulnerability to suffering and death? Does the one who draws near in the mission and fate of the Messiah remain outside this way of the cross? Does the new *politeia* (polity or political constitution) of the people of God also have implications for the ways we must think of God?

When we turn to a discussion of God, this whole political dimension cannot be left behind, for as we have seen, it is the function of God-talk, and indeed of much atonement talk, to underwrite socio-religio-political orders that dominate, exclude, condemn, and inflict suffering and death, typically in the name of some god or other. If we are to think through the implications of a theology of the cross that counters these structures of domination and death, then our ways of speaking of God will have to undergo transformations no less radical than our ways of relating to one another and our world.

In order to get our bearings on the implications of the theology of the cross for our understanding of God, it will be necessary first to quickly review the ways in which this problem was broached in the patristic discussion of the incarnation and cross, and how the question was deflected in a certain way. We will then notice the reemergence of a theology or, rather, religion of the cross, first on the order of a folk piety in the Middle Ages and the initial theological expression of this in the thought of Martin Luther. While the Protestant alliance with power, and the Enlightenment emphasis upon a generic understanding of divinity, tended to relegate the reflection on the cross to a conventional doctrine of atonement, the nineteenth century witnessed a return of this theme "outside the camp" of "theology as such" in the thought of Hegel, and subsequently of Nietzsche and Freud, under the rubric of "the death of God." In the twentieth century, the century of historical horror, however, the theme of the passion of God has come increasingly to the fore. We will accordingly look at some of the ways this theme has been articulated in the thought of Whitehead, Kitamori, Bonhoeffer, Moltmann, and Altizer. In the course of these quite disparate theological proposals, the classical supposition that God cannot be implicated directly in suffering and death gives way to the possibility of taking the implications of the cross for the Christian doctrine of God far more seriously than has been typical of the Christian tradition. In general, this will mean that the theme of the suffering and even the death of God moves from outside the theological camp into the heart of Christian doctrinal discussion.

This will then return us to our theme of the political dimensions of the doctrine of the cross as this also applies to the understanding of God. It will become clear that what now makes the thought of a God who is removed from human suffering and death impossible is the very scale of public suffering and death, and the intellectual imperative to take this with seriousness. Thus, the reformulations of the suffering and death of God have a quite specific relation to the public, social, historical, and therefore political reality of human suffering. One could argue that the doctrine of God has always had a political effect. What is distinctive about this late modern revolution in the concept of God is that it reverses the complicity between the divine and the agents of human suffering that too often has characterized prior formulations of the nature of God.

The passion of God: historical perspectives

Before turning to the more radical formulations of the presence of God in the cross of the Messiah, we must first turn to a brief characterization of the way God has been understood to be related to the cross in patristic and medieval perspectives.

Toward Chalcedon

In the patristic period, the greatest challenge was to find ways to speak of the passion of Christ, or even the incarnation of the Word, in ways that both insisted that God is really involved in the incarnation, suffering, and death of the Messiah and maintained that God as such was to be understood, in keeping with the terms of Greek thought, as beyond suffering and death. Some more radical voices spoke of the death or suffering or passion of God in an unguarded manner and were subsequently labeled Patripassian. This label ascribed to them the position that the "Father" suffered and died in the cross of the Son. While this label and its association with heresy may or may not have been justified (as is normal, we have the characterizations of this position only through the depictions given by its opponents, most especially Tertullian at the end of the second century), it appears to have been an initial attempt to affirm the full presence of God in the fate of the Messiah. On the face of it, this seemed to present insuperable problems even if one maintained the resurrection, for then there would seem to be a period (part, at least, of three days), when there was no God.[1]

Theologians of this early period had to contend with apparently conflicting intellectual necessities. First, they had to find ways to insist that a Christian view of God could "make sense" within the framework provided by the forms of Greek intellectual culture. Like emergent Christianities and emergent Judaisms, that intellectual culture had sought ways to move beyond the "superstitions" of a certain folk piety of the pagan world in order to speak more fittingly of divinity as being that which was above the ordinary passions and vicissitudes of history (as had been depicted, for example, in the narratives of the gods). This, in turn, had significant appeal in a world in which chaos, suffering, and death seemed to rule. A God beyond suffering, beyond change, beyond passion, beyond death, seemed to be the only hope for escape from the world as an alien and hostile environment. In that sense, the appeal of Greek intellectual culture was that it found ways to speak of a divinity that could save people from the world of suffering and death because it was removed from that world.

Christianity, however, had a different perspective: that of a God who saves by entering into history, by becoming human, by entering into suffering and death in some way. How, then, to reconcile its way of speaking of God as related to the fate of Jesus, with the idea that God must be without passion in order to be able to help those caught up in the world of change, mortality, suffering, and death?

It is something like these conflicting necessities—that of speaking of a divine beyond suffering and of speaking of a divine related to suffering—that produced the need for talk of the two natures of Christ (the divine Son or Word and the human Jesus) as well as the three persons of the Godhead (beginning with the distinction in relation of "Father" and "Son"). In these ways, it seemed possible to prevent the passion of Jesus or of the Son from contaminating the Godhead with suffering and death, and even to insist that suffering and death really applied to the human (Jesus) but not to the divine nature of the Son. The danger of these formulations, however, was that they threatened the unity of the Godhead or of Christ, and so made the death of Christ seem like an event in which God was not seriously or fundamentally implicated. One of the effects of this emerging dogmatic formulation was to erect a sort of double fire wall between the deity and the cross, separating the cross (suffering and death of Jesus) from the divine Son, who in turn is distinguished from the divine Father. But this would make untenable the insistence of Christian proclamation that God was indeed fundamentally present in the fate of the crucified Messiah. Thus, it was agreed that one could indeed speak of the death of God, so long as one did not draw implications from this concerning the essence or being of God that would undermine the very deity of this God as defined by the transcendence of passion, and so on.[2]

The famous Tome of Leo, which rescued the Chalcedonian creedal confession, provided that there could be, in some sense, a communication or transfer of "idiom"—that is, of what was proper to one (the Son to the Father, the human to the divine nature)—and so assert the passion of God while maintaining the "apathy" of the Father.[3] This formula was remarkable for its ingenuity, since it did not actually seek to solve but to enshrine the problem as a kind of unavoidable paradox in Christian doctrine. It simply says that one cannot say either that the deity of God is compromised by death, or that the deity of God is uninvolved in the suffering and death of Jesus.

The difficulty that subsequent discussions of atonement surfaced, however, is that increasingly the implication of the "Father" or of "God" in the cross is as agent rather than as sufferer, thereby making God the effective cause of the suffering and death of the Son. If the Son is the one who suffers, and the Father the one who wills that suffering, then we have all the problems of the unjust and abusing God with which we began our reflections on the meaning of the cross.

The reemergence of the cross

For several centuries, attention seemed to be diverted from the question of the cross to that of the incarnation, a move we have seen in Athanasius's attempts to address the question of incarnation without being able to address that of the cross. From the beginning of the Middle Ages, however, folk Catholicism in the West placed a growing emphasis on the cross. It was the passion of Jesus or the Son that captured the imagination of the laity, who themselves felt abandoned to suffering and death.[4] Whether in mystics like Angela of Foligno in the thirteenth century, or in wandering bands of flagellants in the fifteenth century, there is a powerful emphasis upon the God who suffers as we do, and on the correlative suffering with this God as he suffered. This strong emphasis among the laity affects the art of the period, with increasing attention paid to depictions of the Crucified, where previously the tendency had been to depict the Son seated in glory with the Father. (This folk piety was transmitted to Latin America and took deep root there as the fertile soil in which, as we have seen, a new theology of liberation would later be born.)

What was lacking in terms of this religious identification with the Crucified was an attempt to place the cross at the center of theological reflection. It could not be long, therefore, before the whole set of questions involved in trying to think through the implications of the cross for God became more acute. One of the chief breakthroughs in this regard was the theology of Martin Luther that expressed the intuition that the Crucified is indeed God, God for us. In this way, Luther could powerfully connect theological reflection to the impulses of a kind of folk piety. In this, the recovery of the "communication of idioms" derived from Leo came into play again in a new and radical way. The Crucified is God; in the cross God does suffer and die. Indeed, Luther maintained that the basic distinction between a theologian of glory (who emphasized the victory of God in the rule of the church and its traditions) and a theologian of the cross was the essential dividing line between an evangelical faith and a triumphalist institution.[5]

The potential fruitfulness of such a distinction and the working out of its implications for a doctrine of God seemed to be short-circuited, however, by the next generations of theologians. Dogmatic controversies between the various branches of Christianity, and the need to seek the patronage of princes (not incidentally related to the "wars of religion"), were the first cause for this deflection of attention away from a theology of the cross. Indeed, it was in this time that a particularly ferocious view of the will of God as the ultimate agent of the death of the Son was developed. As the Enlightenment gathered steam, in part over disgust at the wars of religion, theological discussion emphasized the existence and nature of a "Supreme Being" as the common denominator between Christian faith and modern rationality.

Nineteenth-century reflections

In the nineteenth century, two formerly Lutheran philosophers sought to engage a theology of the cross with an even more radical seriousness than Luther himself. The first was Hegel, for whom the paradigm of incarnation/crucifixion/resurrection became arguably the very core of his speculative philosophical system. The divine mind, or Spirit or consciousness, must go out of itself and die to itself as absolute in order to enter into the world of things, time, and history. Only by abandoning itself could it become aware of itself (and thus return to itself) as consciousness or mind or Spirit. Thus, a certain "speculative Good Friday" is definitive for the divine life or consciousness itself. Even if the Good Friday of consciousness is recuperated in the returning to itself of consciousness (a kind of resurrection and ascension combined), nevertheless the cross as the denial of its own prior absoluteness affects the divine Spirit or the divine as such in an all-determining way. The fire wall between the divine and passion is broken down.

The second nineteenth-century thinker to take seriously the idea of the "death of God," and with whom this phrase is most often associated, is Friedrich Nietzsche. In his thought, what is forcefully expressed is the end of that Catholic, as well as Protestant, Christendom now eroded beyond repair by the advent of a modern and secular consciousness. In order to indicate what is really at stake in this new world of modernity, Nietzsche announces the death of God, a death that occurs in his view through the agency or the advent of a humanity now coming into its own. While Hegel's speculative Good Friday could find a sympathetic hearing among at least some theologians, Nietzsche's announcement of the death of God was regarded by all but a very few theologians as blasphemous or perhaps meaningless.[6]

Overcoming divine apathy

In spite of the speculative and prophetic voices of the nineteenth century, academic and ecclesial theology seemed to continue for a time as if nothing had happened. Yet in the twentieth century, the old insistence that God cannot suffer, still less die, was overwhelmed by an escalating succession of theological positions that increasingly take the suffering and even the death of God as their point of departure. Indeed, it is this increasingly irresistible challenge to the hegemony of the idea of the *apatheia* ("without passion") of God, and so the turn toward a kind of Patripassianism (or at least Theopassianism), that is one of the most important defining characteristics of the theologies of the late modern period.

In our epoch, so widespread has the idea of the suffering or passion of God become that it is difficult to imagine a return of the old emphasis on the apatheia of God. While this transformation in the way God is thought about does not always derive from a reflection on the cross, we can say that the entire edifice built upon the attempt to place a sort of fire wall between the cross and the Godhead has collapsed in the twentieth century. It is increasingly difficult to find serious theological perspectives that will not admit that the death of Christ has radical implications for the Godhead as well, or insist that God suffers in some sense too. This is a quite fundamental transformation in theology.

In what follows I will not attempt to examine this development in any detail, but simply offer a sort of survey of many of the ways in which the suffering, and so the passion, of God has become thinkable in our time. It is this transformation that makes it both possible and necessary to think of the cross of Jesus as also the cross of God.

Whitehead and "panentheism"

Of those perspectives that have influenced many theological positions, the first, at least chronologically, is found in the philosophical and theological reflections of Alfred North Whitehead in *Process and*

Reality, his Gifford Lectures published in 1929. Although his specu-lative metaphysics, based as it is on an engagement with the emer-gent insights of quantum physics, has continuing relevance, it is the theo-poetic insights articulated at the end of his system that have arguably had the most influence on continuing theological reflec-tion. There, Whitehead writes of a God who accompanies humanity in shared suffering: "God is the great companion, the fellow sufferer who understands."[7]

This metaphysical vision was subsequently transformed by Charles Hartshorne into the framework that he called panentheism, the view that God, while supreme and everlasting, is nevertheless ultimately related to the world and affected by whatever happens in the world, just as God affects or influences (but does not cause) what happens in the world.

It is this version of the Whiteheadian perspective that has served as the basis for much of the fruitful work by modern process theologians, especially in North America. From John Cobb and David Griffin to Marjorie Suchocki and beyond, liberal Protestantism has been signifi-cantly shaped by this vision of a God who suffers with God's world, a God who is affected by human suffering and who is engaged with that suffering in such a way as to make it an essential part of the harmony of all things, which is the divine goal.

This process perspective does not seem to have been generated directly out of a reflection on the cross. However, in the case of White-head himself, one finds indirect echoes of the cross in his contrast between the way of Jesus and that of Caesar. In part 5 of *Process and Reality*, he writes:

> When the Western world accepted Christianity, Caesar conquered; and the received text of Western theology was edited by his lawyers.... The brief Galilean vision of humility flickered through the ages uncertainly. . . . The church gave unto God the attributes which belonged exclusively to Caesar. . . . [The Galilean origin] does not emphasize the ruling Caesar, or the ruthless moralist, or the unmoved mover. It dwells upon the tender elements of the world, which slowly and in quietness operate by love.[8]

If subsequent process theology seems even less explicitly con-nected to a reflection upon the cross, there are many other theological perspectives that seem more engaged both with biblical language generally and with the centrality of the cross in particular.

Bonhoeffer and the suffering of God

While the traumas of the First World War had already spawned the crisis theology associated with Barth, Bultmann, and Tillich, and may have played a role in the reflections of Whitehead, it was in the midst of the Second World War that European theology began to reflect on the suffering of God in connection with lived historical reality.

On July 16, 1944, Dietrich Bonhoeffer wrote from his prison cell, where he had come to be because he determined to act against the tyranny that had engulfed the world in violence, "Before God and with God, we live without God. God lets himself be pushed out of the world on to the cross. He is weak and powerless in the world, and that is precisely the way, the only way, in which he is with us and helps us. Matthew 8.17 makes it quite clear that Christ helps us, not by virtue of his omnipotence, but by virtue of his weakness and suffering." He continues: "The Bible directs man to God's powerlessness and suffering; only the suffering God can help."[9] Two days later he writes, thinking of Jesus in the Garden of Gethsemane, "Man is called to share in God's sufferings at the hands of a godless world."

It must be understood that this is not the gloom of one who has given up on life, though indeed he had less than a year to live. It is the same Bonhoeffer who celebrates the love of life and who shuns the moralizing petty asceticisms of pious Christianity. Rather, it seems that it is the weakness of God that lets us be strong and brave, that summons us to the side of all who are weak, to act justly.

What can this mean? Clearly, Bonhoeffer is dealing with the question that has been there from the beginning: What sort of God can really help, *does* really help? His answer is: the one who gets exposed as weak and helpless. Not the one who is the answer to our weakness, but the one whose weakness somehow enables our strength.

These fragmentary suggestions of Bonhoeffer clearly relate the "weakness" of God to the cross, and so point in the direction of God's cross. Yet they also contain echoes of Nietzsche's intuition of the death of God in the situation of modernity, a world that, as Bonhoeffer says, has "come of age."

Kitamori and the pain of God

Among the earliest pioneers of a more biblically, and so less metaphysically, based reflection on what might be termed the cross of God is the Japanese theologian Kazoh Kitamori, who sought to take seriously the import of biblical language concerning what he termed "the pain of God."[10] He approaches the question of the pain and suffering of God from the perspective of the horrors of the Second World War. Writing under American military occupation in a Japan still reeling from the atrocities of Hiroshima and Nagasaki, as well as from a growing sense of its own implication in the horrors of the war just ended, Kitamori takes the phrase of Jeremiah 31:20 concerning God's pain (NRSV translates as "deeply moved") as his point of departure to contest the dominant Western notion of the impassibility of God. His reflections earned him the timeworn charge of Patripassianism, but the all-too-immediate resonance of his position with the historical experience of his people, and his close attention to biblical texts, ensured that his voice would be heard not only in Japan but, subsequently, in the United States as well. In the preface to the fifth edition of his book, he distinguishes the relational from the substantial identity of God, attributing "pain" to the former, rather than the latter,[11] but it is precisely this distinction that was increasingly being eroded. More recently, Kitamori's insights have been taken up and deepened by the Korean American theologian Andrew Sung Park, in his reflections on the *han* of God.[12]

Jürgen Moltmann and the crucified God

The continental theologian who has been most associated with the attempt to rethink theology, and so the character of God, from the standpoint of the cross is Jürgen Moltmann. His book *The Crucified God* not only provides a still quite useful summary of the many ways that the cross has been a part of Christian religious reflection; it also offers a way to rethink the cross, both within and against the patristic formulas of the two natures of Christ and the three persons of the Trinity. Moltmann's early attempt to rethink the cross of Jesus as the outcome of Jesus' mission and ministry, undertaken both in *The Crucified God* and then in *The Way of Jesus Christ*, has been of considerable help in my own attempt to rethink the cross of Jesus as the center of a theology. But also in this early book, Moltmann attempts to rethink how the suffering of the Son can be thought of in relation to God the Father in such a way as to provide a trinitarian theology of the cross. Although this perspective does not entirely escape the difficulties of positing God (the Father) as the one who intends the cross in some way, it does emphasize the grief of the Father in the death of the Son in such a way as to overcome the strictures against Patripassianism that have dominated theological discourse about the cross. In this context, Moltmann makes a very strong case against the tradition of the apatheia of God and argues for the passion of God, not only in the sense of grief with respect to human suffering (and anger at that which causes that suffering), but also in the sense of yearning for a world delivered from suffering, a world in which suffering is replaced by rejoicing.

Thus, it is not only God as "Son" but also God as "Father" and as "Spirit" who is present in the cross (albeit in distinctive ways), and thus present in the world that remains in the shadow of the cross—a shadow cast, however, by the resurrection light of hope for the divine future in which God will be all in all.

Thomas Altizer and the death of God

In spite of speaking of the "crucified God," Moltmann has little place for the death of God as a theological perspective. But in the United States, the death of God theology associated primarily with the work of Thomas J. J. Altizer was already making headlines. Although Altizer's books that first announced the death of God and the gospel of Christian atheism gained considerable notoriety,[13] the succession of a number of remarkable books of greater difficulty and sophistication (and thus less notoriety) has continued to deepen and extend the initial insights of those early works.

Like Moltmann, Altizer's theology is at heart a theology of the cross, even if it owes much to Nietzsche and Blake and Joyce as well, in their visionary articulations of the world of modernity as a world in which God has died. This connection is made possible by an even more radical notion of the way the very being of God is affected by the cross. Taking as a starting point the notion of kenosis or emptying, from Paul's letter to the Philippians, Altizer insists that the cross means that God not only has entered into humanity (incarnation), but has actually died.

Moreover, this death is basically not recuperated through resurrection and/or ascension, as Hegel argued, but is an irreversible event in which God dies into humanity and the world. It is this death that Christianity has all too often sought to reverse, thereby refusing the good news of what God has done for us. It is this "good news" that Nietzsche (and Blake and others) had the courage to face and announce, even if this meant a repudiation of what had come to call itself Christianity.

Obviously this position removes any barrier between the death of Jesus and the fate of God. God here does not merely share our suffering in some way, nor is it the case that the Son dies and the Father grieves, as Moltmann argues. Rather, here God dies the death of the Messiah, and this death is irreversible. This does not mean for Altizer that there is no "hope." But when Altizer speaks of something like an apocalypse in a positive sense, it is more in the Joycean terms of a "here comes everybody" that is an affirmation of life in its sheer multiplicity and solidarity.

Toward a political theology of the cross

I have sketched only the outline of the many ways in which contemporary theology has progressively removed the barriers that shielded the concept of God from the effects of the cross—in some sense, the cross of God. Moltmann has maintained, plausibly, that the doctrine of the Trinity is itself the result of an attempt to think of the cross as an event in God. However, we have seen that this doctrine has also functioned to distance God from the cross. Perhaps this is the central ambiguity of a specifically Christian doctrine of God. It does seem to be the case that along with a questioning of the apatheia of God, one of the central features of contemporary theology has been a renewed interest in trinitarian modes of thought.

Altizer, for whom trinitarian doctrine plays little role, has the divine unreservedly empty itself through the cross into the experience and history of humanity. This perspective seems to be more in keeping with certain other developments in secular contemporary philosophical thought, especially in France, which is to say that it is related to the perspective of deconstruction associated with Derrida and others.

This movement is itself concerned with what might be termed a political theology, or a political thinking, that concerns itself as well with the way "God" is thought of. Common to these emerging perspectives is the idea, derived from Carl Schmitt, that fundamental political concepts are secularized theological concepts.[14] Thus, the way we think of God has a more or less direct bearing upon the way we understand and engage the political arena.

Already in certain forms of Latin American liberation theology, we can see that the perspective advanced by Moltmann of the relation between the cross and the Trinity has produced—for example, in the thought of Leonardo Boff—the idea that the triune character of God entails a more corporate or communal view of the political.[15] Thus, the interrelation of the persons of the Trinity as equals serves as a vision of a more egalitarian social order. While this perspective already means a basic rethinking of the Trinity as a community of persons, it may be that a thinking through of the implications of the cross for our understanding of God will require an even more radical rethinking of God, whether as triune or not.

In order to see how this may be so, it may be helpful to rehearse here some of the perspectives that have gathered around this theme, beginning with Heidegger.

In a famous interview, Martin Heidegger remarked, concerning what might be termed the state of the world, that "only a god can save us."[16] Of course, this is not altogether unlike what patristic orthodox theology maintained as well when it sought to connect the cross as closely as possible to the divine reality without, however, contaminating the divine with passion in a way that would compromise the very divinity of the divine. As we have seen, this produces the paradox that God does and does not die, that God does and does not suffer.

But it is the "does not" that has predominated in the tradition, whether through the "splitting" of Christ into divine and human (which natures must somehow be sutured together without overcoming the distinction), or through the separation of the "Father" from the "Son" so that it is the latter of whom passion and death may be predicated, and not the former.

But what if we agree with Heidegger and the patristic claim that "only a god can save us," and yet let go of the attempt to protect God from change, therefore from passion, therefore from suffering, even death? For this is where the twentieth-century theology in all its varieties seems to be going. It is simply no longer possible to protect the divine from change, from being affected by that to which the divine is related. But how far does this go? Is it limited, as in process theology, to a sort of "sympathy" that "understands" suffering? That "feels our pain"?

In his essays gathered into the volume *Rogues*,[17] Derrida takes up this assertion of Heidegger in order to relate it to the political thinking that addresses the emerging global situation of empire. Near the end of the first essay, Derrida writes, "To be sure, nothing is less sure than a god without sovereignty: nothing is less sure than his coming, to be sure."[18] And in the same connection, provoked again by Heidegger's famous assertion, Derrida amplifies this invocation of a god without sovereignty near the end of the second essay, which continues and concludes his reflections on power and on hope for a radically different kind of social reality. Derrida writes, "In speaking of an ontotheology of sovereignty, I am referring here, under the name of God, the One and Only God, to the determination of a sovcreign, and thus indivisible, omnipotence. For wherever the name of God would allow us to think something else, for example a vulnerable sovereignty, one that suffers and is divisible, one that is mortal even, . . . it would be a completely different story."[19]

What is being expressed here is the supposition that only a God who can die, or who actually does die, is one who can "save" us in the current situation. For it is only in the being able to die that a conception of God can be freed from the idea or dream of sovereignty that has bathed our history in the blood of imperial ambition. In a characteristically allusive way, what is here invoked is the "theological condition" for what Derrida has often termed a "democracy to come." It is as if only with the idea of a nonsovereign God, a vulnerable God, indeed a God who can die, can humanity be rid of the dreams of invincible power that has consigned our history to violence and suffering.

In a way, this perspective may echo a theme of Irenaeus, that God becomes as we are so that we may become as God is. Of course, this is a nonidentical "repetition," for what this might mean now is that it is only because of something like the death of God on the cross that humanity can be delivered from captivity to violence, and be invited to become a new sociality of mutually vulnerable persons in solidarity with one another and the earth. Thus, the good news concerning the cross would be in some sense the gospel of Christian atheism—that is, the good news that God is emptied out into history as the coming sociality of mutual care, of justice, generosity, and joy. Thus, violent sovereignty is abolished in the cross in favor of a vulnerable *koinonia* (whether as a democracy to come, as in Derrida, or a "here comes everybody," in the Joycean idiom adopted by Altizer), and it is this alone that can save us.

When I speak, or another speaks, of the weakness of God,[20] whether in reference to Bonhoeffer, or Moltmann, or even Derrida, there is always someone who speaks out in protest on behalf of those who are themselves weak and marginalized, who asks, How can a weak God save us? What good to us is a weak God? We need a strong God, a mighty God, if we are to be delivered. How is one to reply to this? Of course, one could simply point out that this is the Feuerbachian trap, proving that God is merely a projection of our need. For clearly what has been surrendered here, even sacrificed, is the question of truth. Or one could speak of the related question of idolatry, which comes from simply worshipping a God other than the one who comes to us in the message concerning the cross.

But what is perhaps most decisive is that this assertion concerning "the God we need" has so often been the secret hinge of the history, not only of the use of "God," but also of atonement. For what is human history if not the story of the powerful constructing a divinity who answers to their needs, a God in whose image and with whose authority they can rule? This seems therefore to be a perfect example of an adage that is sometimes quoted, about not tearing down the master's house with the master's tools. For that is precisely what constructing a strong God in order to answer to one's own needs seems to be: the same old game of power, with somewhat different players. I say somewhat, for in the turning of history's spiral, those who are today on the bottom of the scale may tomorrow not be. Isn't that what happened to Israel? It "needed" a strong God when it was dominated by the powerful; yet it stuck with that God when it was more in the ascendancy. And the same is true for a certain Christian theology.

From the beginning of this book, it has been clear that the cross of the Messiah is the collision between the messianic mission of Jesus and the political structures of power. In one sense, this collision is not willed by God, for what becomes clear is that these structures are not willed by God. And the suggestion that God wills the cross is generally a cover for supposing that the structures are exonerated of the blame.[21] The structures crucify because they falsely believe that they are willed by God. And it is not accidental that so long as this death is viewed as willed by God, then death-dealing structures legitimate themselves by reference to this God. A God who wills the death of his "Son" cannot save us. That is the God who kills what he loves in order to save himself, his "justice," his glory, his reputation.

And yet the collision, and thus the cross, is perfectly inevitable historically, for the opposition between the messianic force and the structures of power is itself complete. Paul intuited that this is how it had to be—that this collision should be brought to a head, that it should be exposed for what it is—not because it was God's will that any suffer, but because it was God's will that all that causes suffering be brought to an end.[22]

One way that this has been expressed in the tradition is that God comes in Christ in order to overcome sin. The end of sin is the end of this game of violence, of collaboration in violence, of imitation of violence—a violence exercised in the name of the supposedly "strong God" it imitates. It is because of "our sin," as Paul suggests, that the Messiah is repudiated, condemned, and executed. But this does not mean because of a list of unrelated personal sins. It has rather to do with our participation in a world that rules by and collaborates in violence, exclusion, and judgment.[23] This is the pervasive reality in which we are caught up. It plays out in our relationships with people we "love," as well as in our relationships with our "enemies." It plays out in the relationship of the elite to those they control. But it also plays out among the excluded—not in the same way, but in ways that still mirror the deadly force of domination and division, even when this or that element of oppression is actively opposed. It is this scene of violence and violation that is entered by the messianic mission, and it is from this same dynamic that this mission suffers and dies.

But it suffers not simply in order to be the victim of sin, but rather to expose it and to open the way to a new reality, to participation in this same mission, in the transformation of a world of violence into a world of solidarity, of generosity, of "justice, peace, and joy" as the apostle put it. In this way, and not in terms of a degraded sacrificial system, God comes to "take away our sins," to relieve us of them and of their effects, to give to humanity and the world a whole new way of being. This new way of being, as we have seen, is one that takes on the contradiction between the new and the old, that undergoes the same contradiction and that lives beyond the contradiction in a way that has death behind it and life before it.

This way of confrontation with what is, and anticipation of what is to be, is perhaps best understood as a new sort of politics, even a counter-politics, for it plays out in the public sphere of a confrontation with the public structures of domination, exclusion, condemnation, and death, and it embodies the alternative sociality of vulnerability and solidarity in the name of the God who comes, not in sovereignty and might, but in the cross of the Messiah.

The God who comes in this way is a fundamentally different sort of God than the one who is worshipped by the religious and secular yearnings for power. It is a God who is "with us" (Emmanuel) in a far more radical way than the history of theology has yet managed to think with any clarity or consistency. Yet without such a new God or new understanding of God, there can be no new politics, no final over-coming of the structures of division and domination, no democracy to come, no reign of justice and generosity and joy.

CHAPTER TEN

After Atonement?

S ince the publication of Gustav Aulén's *Christus Victor*, discussions of the theology of the cross have taken Aulén's typology of theories of the atonement as a point of departure. This typology identified three main types: the Greco-Lutheran ransom theory, the Western view associated with Anselm and Calvin of substitutionary satisfaction, and the Abelardian and liberal perspective termed "moral influence." To be sure, Aulén recognized that these were logically distinct types that were regularly "mixed" in the work of any particular theologian. Thus, while the ransom theory, in which God defeats Satan and so rescues humanity from death and corruption, might predominate in, for example, Athanasius, Gregory of Nyssa, or Luther, there were undeniable elements of satisfaction and moral influence perspectives also to be discerned in the works of these theologians.

Although Aulén suggested that his discussion of these types was to be understood as simply indicating alternative perspectives, there is no question, as the title suggests, that he preferred the patristic and Lutheran type. However, we may also say that the effect of his work was to suggest that the substitutionary, penal satisfaction theory that was taken to be the "orthodox" view was in fact but one of three, and one that was by no means to be taken as without alternatives. Thus, the work undercut the self-evident primacy of the then-regnant view of atonement.

In spite of this, there are still many Protestants, almost certainly the majority, who suppose that something like the substitutionary satisfaction view of atonement is *the* orthodox or traditional view, any deviation from which indicates unacceptable concessions to unbelief. Even in most "mainline" denominations, those who regard themselves as "traditional" or "orthodox" propose adherence to a satisfaction or substitutionary or sacrificial view of atonement as a litmus test of theological rectitude and denominational integrity.

The work that I have undertaken in these pages demonstrates that such views of the atonement must be regarded as subversive of the gospel they think they serve. This is not because the New Testament does not make use of metaphors that are deployed as theories in these views. The New Testament uses an astonishing array of metaphors without offering any theory at all. The elevation of these fragmentary and allusive metaphors into a theory of atonement undercuts the basic thrust of New Testament reflections upon the cross. Indeed, they often result in a wholesale abandonment of New Testament perspectives.

In order to see how this is so, we need only look at the main elements of this theory. In its many permutations, this theory, or group of theories, combines in different ways at least four main elements: sacrifice, satisfaction, the forensic (or legal), and substitution.

Sacrifice: At the very beginning of this study, we indicated that sacrificial language is not serviceable for expressing well the meaning of the cross, for the good and sufficient reason that the cross abolishes sacrifice. Here René Girard is right, I believe, to insist that the story of the cross makes the very structure of sacrifice impossible.[1] Moreover, we have seen that while the idea of sacrifice generally has in view the propitiation of an angry divinity, the New Testament talk of reconciliation with God has an almost exactly opposite meaning. The reconciliation language of the New Testament suggests that it is not God but humanity that has been offended, and so must and may be reconciled to God, on account of the divine solidarity with humanity demonstrated in and through the cross and resurrection of Jesus as the Messiah of God.

Satisfaction: The idea of satisfaction has the merit that it takes divine justice with appropriate seriousness. However, it then undercuts this in at least two ways.

The most important is that it does away with the demand for justice altogether. That is, it insists that God requires justice, and then, by way of atonement, the divine demand is satisfied by something other than justice. As a consequence (albeit certainly unintended in Anselm and probably also in Luther), we have the death of the Godman itself satisfying the claim of justice, thereby letting humanity off the hook with respect to the claim. Indeed, what often happens is that justice is regarded as simply impossible and, moreover, unnecessary. A "satisfaction" substitutes for justice. But this is exactly the sort of switch that is consistently opposed by the prophets, by Jesus, and by Paul. The prophets regularly rail against those who think that by sacrifice they can escape the divine claim of justice. "I require justice and not sacrifice," says the voice of YHWH in prophet after prophet. And Jesus maintains that not those who say, "Lord, Lord," but rather those who do the will of God will be saved. The will of God is said to be justice and mercy. Moreover, Paul insists that those who have entered into the new messianic reality must actualize all the claims of justice through love of one another, for it is this alone that satisfies "the just requirements of the law." Thus, the view that Jesus' justice substitutes for ours makes a travesty of the entire biblical witness concerning divine justice.

Ultimately, the death of the innocent as the mechanism for this satisfaction is itself manifestly unjust. The mechanism by which justice is allegedly established is itself a violation of the most elementary form of justice. That it is called voluntary does nothing to mitigate the injustice of the mechanism, for it is also regarded as necessary. The use of patently unjust means to achieve allegedly just aims is enshrined as the very action of God in Christ, thereby legitimating the manifold ways in which this perspective has played a decisive role in the history of human injustice. Most recently, we have been reminded by feminist scholars of the ways in which this view has served as a template for domestic abuse—not only of women, but most particularly of children.

The Forensic: Many post-Reformation views of atonement updated this theory with ideas taken over from the legal or judicial process (the meaning of *forensic*), in order to modernize the model of satisfaction taken over, as we saw in the first chapter, from the medieval feudal system.[2] In this updated view, the human being is arraigned before the law, but though found to be guilty and under sentence of (eternal) death, the subject is pronounced innocent by virtue of a relationship to (or faith in) Christ. The very idea of penal or forensic satisfaction is a remarkable undoing of the very distinction between the law and justice that Paul is at such pains to make. It is certainly not the case that those who regularly invoke this notion suppose the law (or rather their favorite laws) to be suspended. They continue to be all too willing to use the law, or at least bits and pieces of it, to accuse and condemn whole classes of people, while at the same time using this theory to excuse themselves on the grounds that because of their belief, they are forgiven more or less automatically. Thus, domestic abusers dispense forgiveness to themselves while using the law to accuse "homosexuals," or functionaries of police states excuse themselves while condemning "subversives" to torture and death, and so on. The manifest hypocrisy here is not accidental to this view, as if somehow we could simply reform it. Rather, it seems to be intrinsic to the perspective.

What is demanded, as Paul saw, is not an abandonment of the "just requirements of the law," but rather a justice that escapes from the injustice of the law itself, a justice that is more just than the law. This happens not by declaring the guilty to be innocent, but by providing a way for the unjust to actually become just, to turn from injustice to justice.

Substitution: The idea of substitution is that Jesus substitutes for us. His death substitutes for ours as his obedience substitutes for ours. This view completely abolishes the moral seriousness of the proclamation of the cross. It makes it possible for everything to continue precisely as it was before. Moreover, this is directly contrary to the ways in which the idea of the cross is deployed in the New Testament and in the early church to make clear the meaning and cost of discipleship as a taking up of the cross. Hence the importance of Dorothee Soelle's reminder that Christ is not a substitute for, but a representative for, humanity.

But if notions of satisfaction (whether forensic or otherwise), sacrifice, and substitution, in whatever combination, will not work as an adequate way of understanding the cross of Jesus; if indeed the theories constructed on these premises seem to actually betray rather than interpret the cross, then what of the alternative theories of atonement that Aulén put forward?

Certainly, Aulén himself seems to have favored the ransom, or "Christus Victor," model of atonement theory, and this ransom theory or a modification thereof has been the one that has been the subject of most sympathetic attention over the last several years. Feminists, and those who align themselves with liberationist or political appropriations of the theology of the cross, have offered important revisions of this model as indicative of a way forward. These revisions have in common that they begin by translating the notion of the conquest of Satan into the language of fundamental structural transformation. They take seriously the way in which humanity is caught in the snares of suprapersonal destructive powers, for which, however, we have a certain responsibility. These revisions seek also to take into account the unity of humanity as the object of redemption, as opposed to the individualism that seems endemic to moral influence theories and to most versions of satisfaction theories. The work I have pursued in these pages comes closest to these contemporary revisions of ransom theory.[3]

However, the magnitude of the necessary revision of a model that was developed in terms of a trick played upon, or payment (ransom) paid to, Satan makes the connection to the patristic (and Lutheran) view rather dubious. As we have seen, this model appears as a cosmic encoding of a politically subversive text. Essential to this encoding is a mystification of the cross that reduces it to a mere symbol. Because of this, it is far better to make a clean break with the basic terminology of this model and to indicate forthrightly that what one is doing is functionally as well as terminologically quite distinct. In this way, it is possible to begin, as I have attempted to do, with the concrete reality of crucifixion as a political execution and to ground other dimensions of the theological significance of the cross in this historically concrete reality. This also obviates the problem of the injustice of God playing a trick on the devil. It is the military-political structures themselves that are demonstrably unjust, an injustice exposed in the very means by which they seek to impose their own brand of "law and order," an injustice exposed moreover in the resurrection of the Crucified that overturns the unjust verdict of the self-proclaimed defenders of divine law.

What, then, of the "moral influence" theory? In most if not all of its versions, this perspective loses the sense of corporate humanity and reduces everything to the individual. Of course, this has also happened with more recent views of satisfaction theory, even though Anselm was quite clear that what was at stake was the corporate character of humanity.[4] The individualism of this model has the distinct liability of losing the sense of the solidarity of humanity generally as the object of "salvation." Its intrinsic individualism also makes it difficult, if not impossible, to think of a community of the cross as an active vanguard of a new humanity, indeed of a new humanity as a new sociality.

Moreover, the basic thrust of the model has been to emphasize the necessity of the death of Jesus in order to demonstrate the divine love. As some feminist thinkers have made clear, this still makes God in some way the author of Jesus' death, even if in a way somewhat different from what had been maintained in the satisfaction group of theories.

What is important about this model is the way it underlines the insistence that God does not act with force to accomplish redemption, but acts by way of suasion. Of course, this was also said by those who developed alternative models: God does not force the Son to die, but the Son willingly chooses this path, or God does not "force" Satan but rather "tricks" Satan, and so on. But the moral influence view does better at suggesting that God accomplishes God's will through noncoercive means. The problem is that it then becomes unclear how these means can possibly aim at the sort of comprehensive salvation expressed in the ransom model, or at the privileging of justice that is intended by the best versions of the satisfaction model.

A principal advantage of the moral influence theory is that it makes clear that an alternative form of life is the effect of the cross. The demonstration of the love of God evokes in the adherent or faithful the determination to imitate that very love, and so in important respects to become a morally changed person. This is certainly preferable to the short-circuiting of the divine claim of justice that we find in the various versions, especially, of satisfaction theories. However, the liability here is that the "sacrificial love" allegedly demonstrated in the cross can itself be separated from the question of justice in such a way that this sacrificial love simply acquiesces to unjust structures and patterns of relationship without undermining or overthrowing them.

The way forward does not lie in choosing from among the options presented by Aulén, even if some quite remarkable work has been done in developing modifications, for example, of the ransom theory. Even less is it possible to seek to somehow combine these models, as suggested by Hans Boersma.[5]

We must face the fact that all of these models are fatally flawed. The basic problem with these theories is that they do not, and cannot, take the cross of Jesus with real seriousness. They evade the historical concrete reality of the cross and so render it superfluous. In its stead, they simply offer a death without qualities, without, indeed, the cross itself. Instead of attempting to think of the cross of Jesus with any kind of intellectual rigor, they substitute for this cross a sort of generic victimage that, rather than unleashing the transformation of the world, serves as an alibi for the perpetuation of structures of domination, division, and death.

Not only do they evade the very cross they seek to explain; they also isolate the cross (understood now simply as death or victimage) from the mission and ministry of Jesus, thereby severing the death of Jesus from the mission of affirmation of life. Death and suffering thus are liable to become ends in themselves, rather than connected as consequence to a commitment to life.

What is ultimately lost in all these theories is the divine claim and call for justice. The message concerning the cross winds up having no transformative power directed to the world, human society, or even individual comportment. Instead, all too often what happens with these theories of atonement is that they become alibis for injustice, patterns of victimage all too easily manipulated to foster either disengagement from the world that Christ came to redeem or, still worse, ways of encouraging persons to become passive victims of injustice while dispensing pardon to the perpetrators of injustice.

In view of these liabilities, it is little wonder that some have suggested that we simply ignore the cross in favor of an emphasis upon the teaching and healing behavior of Jesus as paradigmatic for his followers.[6] Yet, as I suggested in the first chapter, this would leave us unable to understand how the cross comes to have such an important place in so many of the texts of the New Testament, not only in the letters of Paul, but in the very accounts from which we seek to draw the teachings and actions of Jesus, that is to say, the Gospels.

What seems to make the cross so important for the Gospels (as well as for Paul) is that it demonstrates the fundamental conflict between a mission directed toward life and the actually existing arrangements of the world, both religious and political. What is at stake is no mere amelioration of existing arrangements, but a fundamental opposition between these arrangements and the will and purpose of God.

What God wills is the transformation of the world, announced as the coming of the divine reign of justice and generosity and joy. In no way is the death of the Messiah or "Son" the "will of God." The death of the messiah is not the only possible, still less the preferred, outcome of this conflict. Indeed, when Jesus comes announcing the arrival of the divine reign, what he calls for is *metanoia*, the turning around of the world to God, what might be termed conversion. This conversion is not simply a matter for individuals but has to do with the arrangements of power—religious, economic, and political as well. It is a complete and radical transformation. However, the powers tend not simply to capitulate, not to renounce their prestige and privilege and power. Instead, they seek to preserve themselves in the face of this claim and call. The result is that they crucify the Messiah and, indeed, those who participate with him in this messianic mission. The cross is then a rather clear-eyed view of what follows, not of necessity but predictably, from a call for radical transformation. The avoidance of the cross, therefore, leads us to underestimate the deep violence of the world in which we live, or may lead us unwittingly to collaborate in that violence by calling for less radical forms of transformation. Thus, the message concerning the cross of the Messiah seems to be essential for any theology that seeks to be clear about the true stakes involved in the mission and ministry of transformation, a mission that seeks to genuinely enact the justice and mercy of the God who comes.

What then of atonement? Is this category at all viable? Can the view that I have been putting forth in these pages be described as a doctrine of atonement? Certainly in the traditions of Western theology, the talk of atonement has generally been connected to ideas of sacrifice, substitution, and satisfaction. I have already indicated why I believe that these categories are no longer useful in coming to terms with the message concerning the cross. Not only do they represent modes of thought that no longer effectively connect with our experience of reality, but they have also served all too often to permit an evasion of central elements of the message concerning the cross. By means of such ideas, Christianity has often become the legitimation and sanctification of violence directed against the more vulnerable members of our society, and has occasioned an astonishing complacency in the face of the evil too often done in the name of Christianity.

But if we abandon these categories, do we abandon the term *atonement* for this discussion of the meaning of the cross for Christian self-understanding? As far as I can see, there are two or three reasons for not abandoning this term. In the first place, the term *atonement* has come to refer to any perspective that seeks to take the cross seriously as fundamental for a Christian perspective. Thus, for example, when Gustav Aulén wrote *Christus Victor*, he actually offered three basic types of what may be called atonement theory. Only one of these was the traditional Western view that relied on notions of satisfaction, substitution, and sacrifice. Even here, the notion of sacrifice that is often the narrow meaning of atonement is decidedly secondary for the Western theory. But in addition to this traditional Western view, Aulén offers two other views, the moral influence theory attributed to Abelard and to some proponents of modern liberal theology, and the Christus Victor model that Aulén found to be an ingredient of Greek patristic thought and of Luther. My point is not to affirm the specifics of Aulén's typology, but simply to notice that many different perspectives can be understood to be variations on atonement theory.

A further consideration has to do with the way atonement is often represented as "at-one-ment." While this is dubious as a derivation of the concept and term, and while its literal signification may be restricted to the Greek view that the immortal becomes mortal so that mortals may become immortal (a kind of literal, if restricted, deification), it may nevertheless capture the bridging of the gap of human alienation from the divine that I have emphasized as the significance of reconciliation to God. Moreover, the opening up of the various ways in which we may speak of the cross as the cross of God, and thus as signaling the coming of God to the world with the rending of the veil between the divine and the secular, gives much added weight to a certain sense of atonement as at-one-ment.

If we were to maintain this terminology, we would have to emphasize that the view put forward in these pages is not a revision of any of the existing types suggested by Aulén, but is instead a new type, or what went unnoticed in Aulén's construction of a typology. Because of the way it must begin by taking seriously the execution of Jesus as one deemed subversive of the political order imposed by Rome, we might term this something like the political model of atonement. Or when we consider the implication of religious structures in the execution of Jesus and in the maintenance of any and all forms of domination, we might term this a nonreligious or secular view of atonement.

On the other hand, it may be that the very idea of atonement has been so indelibly stamped with ideas of sacrifice and substitution and, above all, with the idea that the cross is willed by God as the instrument of salvation, that it will be necessary to jettison this term altogether and instead speak of a theology of the cross, a theological reflection provoked by the cross that is so dissimilar from what has gone before as not to be appropriately termed a theory of atonement at all.

What is at stake, then, is not a theory of atonement, but an attempt to think of the cross of the Messiah of God in its theo-political origin and ramifications. From the very beginning, we have seen that the message concerning the cross is rooted in the soil of a supremely political conflict, the conflict over how the world is to be "ordered." It is the conflict between the mission of the empire and the mission of the one whom the empire executes. Yet this mission is not restricted to the fate of Jesus. As we have seen, those who follow him must follow precisely in this way that leads into conflict with the powers that rule the earth, a conflict whose magnitude is measured by the testimony of the martyrs who follow the one Irenaeus called "the leader of martyrdom."

Of course, this conflict does not exist for its own sake. It happens because of an unremitting commitment to life for all the earth, in the face, however, of powers that promise life but deliver death instead. Thus, the fate of Jesus cannot be separated from his commitment to life, any more than it can be separated from the shared commitment of those who follow in his way, who share this mission, and so this conflict as well.

Nor can we restrict the meaning of this conflict to one that is in any narrow sense "political," at least as this is commonly understood. For as we have seen, the cross is also the consequence of a conflict with those "religious" powers and forces of privilege and exclusion that maintain their identity by denying the dignity of others. Indeed, in the ancient world no neat separation was possible between the religious and the political. What was at stake was the very "polity" of a people, whether figured as empire, as culture, or as cult. Thus, the cross of the Messiah also entails the overthrow of all the barriers that humans erect between "us and them," between friend and foe (which Schmitt declared the very essence of the political)—whether this takes the form of a division of peoples (Greek and barbarian), or class (slave and free), or gender (male and female). All of these are eminently "political" matters, even if they sometimes successfully mask themselves as religio-cultural tradition.

This is all the more true of the question of the law that is deployed to condemn "sinners," for the law is the political question par excellence. The law exists in order to make possible accusation and condemnation; and it ultimately rests, as Walter Benjamin saw, upon the right to exercise not only judgment, but the death penalty.[7] By being "found among the sinners," the Messiah broke with the power of the law and instituted a new polity, one that embraces those who had been excluded, accused, condemned, indeed executed by the "majesty" of the law. But all this happens in such a way that what is at stake is precisely the coming into being of a new sort of justice, a justice that is beyond the law but accomplishes what the law, "weakened by sin," could not accomplish.

Ultimately, the political question is the question of what Latin American theologians called "the idols of death or the God of life." For it is not only in our century that we can speak of the biopolitical as the extension of the political into the governance of life. The political always has suggested that it is the way to life, to the extension of the commonweal, the public good of prosperity, and so of more life. The difficulty is that the political, as commonly conceived, has purchased life for a few at the cost of death for many. Thus, even when we speak of the cross in its relation to human suffering and death, we have not left the sphere of the political behind.

But what, then, is the new form of human society that is brought into being through the cross, the new messianic *politeia?* We have seen that this is the primary preoccupation of Paul when he reflects upon the cross. For Paul, the cross is always deployed in such a manner as to call for a new way for persons to be together in a nonallergic being-with that is the seedbed of the new politics of the messianic people. In the overcoming of division and the struggle to affirm one's own way, Paul glimpses what it might mean to be a community or sociality of the Crucified. While Paul was able to use terms of political life, such as *ecclesia* or *synagogue,* these terms have come to signify for us not the political, but the religious separated from the political. For Paul, these are societies that are the vanguard of a new politics, the messianic politics of justice and welcome without reserve. Participation in such a new society entails becoming a new sort of person, one who has died to the world and to the contentious and self-preserving flesh in order to engage in the sharing of the spirit that empowers a new solidarity in suffering and in liveliness.

All of this is a new politics, but above all a *theo*-politics; that is, an alternative way of construing the relation of the divine to the basic political reality of human being. The divine has ever been implicated in the political, as the sanction for, and sometimes for the violent opposition to, the ruling ideologies and powers. But if we are to think of the political meaning of the cross in a new way, this is because the message concerning the cross already points toward a fundamentally different way of thinking about God. We have seen that this difference is already implicated in the talk of reconciliation, since traditionally, it is an angry and powerful God who must somehow be placated in order to be reconciled to humanity. But the message concerning the cross points in the opposite direction, toward the reconciliation of a wounded and resentful humanity to God, a God who is not the God of domination, exclusion, accusation, affliction, or abandonment, but who comes to be "God with us." And this will mean that we can no longer think of God as one who is not fundamentally present in the fate of the Executed and his followers. This in turn will mean that we must find new and more daring ways than have heretofore been conceivable to think of the death of God, the cross of God, as that which makes possible the coming of the messianic reality, or the democracy to come.

What is critical here is not a theory, whether or not termed *atonement*, but rather a confrontation with all the systems of arrogance and violence, of domination and death, of privilege and prestige, that hold humanity hostage. Even when this confrontation results in the cross, still the cross is not the final word. The final word is that even the powers of death must ultimately give way to the mission of life, so that the cross by which the powers seek to impose their will becomes instead the means of their own undoing. Ultimately, this is the meaning of the cross, that not even death can prevent the triumph of justice and generosity and joy. This is what makes the message concerning the cross into good news for humanity as a whole, indeed for the earth itself.

NOTES

1. Rethinking Atonement

1. For a more extended discussion of these mystery cults, see Walter Burkert, *Ancient Mystery Cults* (Cambridge, Mass.: Harvard University Press, 1987).

2. Gustav Aulén, *Christus Victor: An Historical Study of the Three Main Types of the Idea of the Atonement*, trans. A. G. Hebert (New York: Macmillan, 1969).

3. Athanasius, "De incarnatione," §§30–32, in *Contra Gentes and De Incarnatione*, ed. and trans. Robert W. Thomson (Oxford: Clarendon, 1971), 207–15.

4. Delores Williams, in "Black Women's Surrogacy and the Christian Notion of Redemption," notes that "most theories of atonement, classical and contemporary, are time bound (as well as ideologically bound with patriarchy) and do not respond meaningfully to the questions of people living beyond the particular time period." See Williams in *Cross Examinations: Readings on the Meaning of the Cross Today*, ed. Marit Trelstad (Minneapolis: Fortress Press, 2006), 28.

5. Although Delores Williams does not share my sense of the centrality of the cross, she does affirm something similar about method when she remarks that traditional theological practice "was to use the language and sociopolitical thought of the time to render Christian principles understandable. That fits well with the task of the black female theologian" ("Black Women's Surrogacy," 29). It is also what I am attempting in these pages.

6. See Martin Luther, "The Jews and Their Lies" (1543), in *Luther's Works*, ed. Franklin Sherman (Philadelphia: Fortress Press, 1971), 47:268–93. We will return toward the end of this study to the question of the political significance of the cross; however, we can note here that Luther's anti-Judaism results in part from a deflection of blame for the death of Christ from secular rulers to the Jews. This strategy in turn was made more plausible by Luther's apparent need to curry the favor of secular rulers (which

also resulted in the infamous call to massacre the peasants who rebelled against unjust princes).

7. Somewhat complicating this picture is the struggle of first-century Christianity to distinguish itself from more powerful and prestigious forms of emergent Judaism. Thus, the language that is sometimes employed in this struggle has often lent itself to extraordinarily negative depictions of Judaism. Grappling with this reality is something that has necessarily occupied many of the best talents of post-Holocaust biblical studies. In this essay, however, I will not attempt to deal with this entire field but will focus attention precisely on the way of understanding the cross so as to separate it from the shame of anti-Judaism.

8. For a helpful discussion of this critique, see Darby Ray, *Deceiving the Devil: Atonement, Abuse, and Ransom* (Cleveland: Pilgrim, 1997).

9. An early and forceful articulation of this critique is found in Joanne C. Brown and Rebecca Parker, "For God So Loved the World," in *Christianity, Patriarchalism, and Abuse* (Edinburgh: T & T Clark, 1989), 1–33.

10. Gregory of Nyssa, "An Address on Religious Instruction," in *Christology of the Later Fathers*, ed. Edward Rochie Hardy and Cyril C. Richardson (Philadelphia: Westminster, 1954), 268–325.

11. Thus Anselm writes: "For what justice is there in giving up the most just man of all to death on behalf of the sinner? What man would not be judged worthy of condemnation if he condemned the innocent in order to free the guilty?" See "Why God Became Man," bk. 1, ch. 8, in *A Scholastic Miscellany: Anselm to Ockham*, ed. and trans. Eugene R. Fairweather (Philadelphia: Westminster, 1961), 111. The objection raised by Boso, Anselm's interlocutor throughout, seems to haunt Anselm (who was himself remembered as a man of remarkable kindness and who severely castigated monks who unnecessarily reproved the youths in their charge). His immediate answer is that this was not imposed on the Son but undertaken freely: "He himself readily endured death in order to save men" (ibid.). But he seems to recognize that this is not yet a satisfactory answer.

12. Thus Abelard writes: "Indeed, how cruel and wicked it seems that anyone should demand the blood of an innocent person as the price for anything, or that it should in any way please him that an innocent man should be slain—still less that God should consider the death of his Son so agreeable that by it he should be reconciled to the world" ("Exposition of the Epistle to the Romans," in *Scholastic Miscellany*, 283).

13. Jon Sobrino, *Christology at the Crossroads: A Latin American Approach* (Maryknoll, N.Y.: Orbis, 1978).

14. Jürgen Moltmann, *The Crucified God: The Cross of Jesus as the Foundation and Criticism of Christian Theology*, trans. R. A. Wilson and John Bowden (New York: Harper & Row, 1974), 112–59.

15. Jürgen Moltmann, *The Way of Jesus Christ: Christology in Messianic Dimensions*, trans. Margaret Kohl (Minneapolis: Fortress Press, 1993).
16. See Michael Hardt and Antonio Negri, *Empire* (Cambridge, Mass.: Harvard University Press, 2000) and *Multitude: War and Democracy in the Age of Empire* (New York: Penguin, 2004).

2. Cross and Domination

1. Rudolf Bultmann, *Theology of the New Testament*, trans. Kendrick Grobel (New York: Charles Scribner's Sons, 1955).
2. One of the most impressive attempts to rethink the cross in the context of Latin America is in Leonardo Boff's *Passion of Christ, Passion of the World*, trans. Robert R. Barr (Maryknoll, N.Y.: Orbis, 1987); see also Jon Sobrino, *Christology at the Crossroads: A Latin American Approach* (Maryknoll, N.Y.: Orbis, 1978). A more recent study of the ways in which Latina women read the narratives about the cross and one that adds important new insights is to be found in Barbara E. Reid's *Taking up the Cross: New Testament Interpretations through Latina and Feminist Eyes* (Minneapolis: Fortress Press, 2007).
3. Athanasius, *Contra Gentes and De Incarnatione*, ed. and trans. Robert W. Thomson (Oxford: Clarendon, 1971).
4. Ibid., §1, p. 3. Further references to section and page numbers will be given in text.
5. Anselm, "Why God Became Man," in *A Scholastic Miscellany: Anselm to Ockham*, ed. and trans. Eugene R. Fairweather (Philadelphia: Westminster, 1961), 100–183.
6. Ibid., bk. 2, ch. 18, p. 177; see also ch. 11, p. 161.
7. For substantiation and elaboration of these points, see Neil Elliott, *Liberating Paul: The Justice of God and the Politics of the Apostle* (Maryknoll, N.Y.: Orbis, 1994), 93–99, and the material from the same author included in *Paul and Empire: Religion and Power in Roman Imperial Society*, ed. Richard Horsley (Harrisburg, Pa.: Trinity, 1997), 167–71.
8. The breaking of the legs of the bandits was an attempt to remove the support of the legs and thus hasten this process—a sort of euthanasia, which in John's Gospel was unnecessary in the case of Jesus since he had already died (John 19:31-33). For a description of crucifixion, see John Dominic Crossan, *Jesus: A Revolutionary Biography* (San Francisco: HarperSanFrancisco, 1994), 123–27.
9. For an example of an early approximation to this fate, see the story in 2 Sam 21:1-14 concerning the impaling of the sons of Saul by the Gibeonites. Rizpah keeps watch over the bodies of her sons to prevent the birds from feeding on them by day or the wild animals by night.

10. But note that others still call him Son of David (Bartimaeus and the Syro-phoenician woman).

11. A far more detailed reading of the Gospel of Mark from this perspective can be found in my book *The Insurrection of the Crucified* (Chicago: Exploration, 2003).

12. I will return to this question in chapter 4.

13. Albert Schweitzer, *The Quest of the Historical Jesus: A Critical Study of Its Progress from Reimarus to Wrede*, trans. W. Montgomery (New York: Macmillan, 1968).

14. Stephen J. Patterson, in *Beyond the Passion: Rethinking the Death and Life of Jesus* (Minneapolis: Fortress Press, 2004), 13–38, uses the notion of victim to focus the way in which Paul may be read as indicating the fundamental opposition between the crucified Jesus and the crucifying empire. In a subsequent chapter, he connects this as well to the image of martyr, as I will too in a subsequent section of this chapter. Patterson's book is a good example of a rethinking of the cross that takes the collision between Christ and empire as a starting point, and may be especially useful to introduce laypeople to this way of thinking.

15. See my essay "The Son of Man Strategy," in *Text and Logos: The Humanistic Interpretation of the New Testament*, ed. Theodore W. Jennings Jr. (Atlanta: Scholars, 1990), 229–43.

16. Rita Nakashima Brock, *Journeys by Heart: A Christology of Erotic Power* (New York: Crossroad, 1991), 93ff.

17. Dorothee Soelle, *Christ the Representative*, trans. David Lewis (London: SCM, 1967).

18. See my *Insurrection of the Crucified*.

19. Ched Myers, *Binding the Strong Man: A Political Reading of Mark's Story of Jesus* (Maryknoll, N.Y.: Orbis, 1988). See also Herman Waetjen, *A Reordering of Power: A Socio-political Reading of Mark's Gospel* (Minneapolis: Fortress Press, 1989).

20. Mark Lewis Taylor insists that the death of Jesus must be understood in relation not only to the "adversarial politics" of Jesus' mission, but also to the formation of "movements" of resistance in his name. *The Executed God: The Way of the Cross in Lockdown America* (Minneapolis: Fortress Press, 2001), xiii, 108.

21. Before going further into the parallels between Jesus and the members of the communities of faith founded by Paul, it is crucial that we contest the anti-Jewish interpretation of this text that has brought so much shame upon Christianity. Paul is here writing to a beleaguered minority that shares the fate of official opposition also shared by Jewish Christians in Judea. Persecution is undertaken not by Jews as such, but by the religio-political authorities in their respective communities. Taken out of its historical context, as has happened all too often, the situation of persecution

experienced by followers of Jesus, either among the Judeans or among the gentiles, turns disastrously into a license to persecute another vulnerable religious minority, the Jews. This is, quite simply, a complete perversion of the gospel.

22. The situation seems to be more one of continual torment or bullying than one of official persecution.

23. For a more extended treatment of this passage, see Elliott, *Liberating Paul*, and my own reflections in *Reading Derrida/Thinking Paul: On Justice* (Stanford: Stanford University Press, 2005), 72–77.

24. For a remarkably fruitful study of the ways in which Christian and Jewish experiences and interpretations of martyrdom interact with one another, see Daniel Boyarin's *Dying for God: Martyrdom and the Making of Christianity and Judaism* (Stanford: Stanford University Press, 1999).

25. Ignatius of Antioch, "Epistle to the Ephesians," 1.2, in *The Ante-Nicene Fathers* (Grand Rapids: Eerdmans, 1987), 1:49.

26. Ignatius of Antioch, "Epistle to the Romans," 6, in *Ante-Nicene Fathers*, 1:76.

27. Ibid., 3, in *Ante-Nicene Fathers*, 1:74.

28. Irenaeus, "Against Heresies," III.18.4, in *Ante-Nicene Fathers*, 1:447.

29. Ibid., III.18.5, in *Ante-Nicene Fathers*, 1:447.

30. Ibid., III.12.13, in *Ante-Nicene Fathers*, 1:435. See also IV.33.9, in *Ante-Nicene Fathers*, 1:508: "Wherefore the Church does in every place, because of that love which she cherishes towards God, send forward, throughout all time, a multitude of martyrs to the Father. . . . For the Church alone sustains with purity the reproach of those who suffer persecution for righteousness' sake, and endure all sorts of punishments, and are put to death because of the love which they bear to God, and their confession of His Son; often weakened indeed, yet immediately increasing her members."

31. Ignatius of Antioch, "Epistle to the Trallians," 10, in *Ante-Nicene Fathers*, 1:70.

32. Irenaeus, "Against Heresies," III.18.6, in *Ante-Nicene Fathers*, 1:447.

33. Thus JoAnne Terrell is right to insist, in "Our Mothers' Gardens: Rethinking Sacrifice," that "the martyrdom ethos in which Christianity was baptized virtually guaranteed that its central image would become the cross." In *Cross Examinations: Readings on the Meaning of the Cross Today*, ed. Marit Trelstad (Minneapolis: Fortress Press, 2006), 48; see also JoAnne Terrell, *Power in the Blood? The Cross in the African-American Experience* (Maryknoll, N.Y.: Orbis, 1998).

34. Athanasius, "De Incarnatione," §§27–28, in *Contra Gentes and De Incarnatione*, 199–203.

35. See on this the very helpful discussion of Peter Brown, *The Body and Society: Men, Women, and Sexual Renunciation in Early Christianity* (New York: Columbia University Press, 1988).

36. Athanasius, "De Incarnatione," §10, in *Contra Gentes and De Incarnatione*, 155–56.

37. Ibid., §13, 165.

38. Gregory of Nyssa, "An Address on Religious Instruction," in *Christology of the Later Fathers*, ed. Edward Rochie Farley and Cyril C. Richardson (Philadelphia: Westminster, 1954), 279.

39. Ibid., 298.

40. Ibid., 299.

41. For a contemporary and feminist appreciation of the fruitfulness of this metaphor, see Darby Ray, *Deceiving the Devil: Atonement, Abuse, and Ransom* (Cleveland: Pilgrim, 1998).

42. Athanasius, "De Incarnatione," §51, in *Contra Gentes and De Incarnatione*, 263.

43. Lactantius, "The Divine Institutes," in *Ante-Nicene Fathers*, 7:188.

44. Mark Lewis Taylor, in his book *The Executed God*, cites in the epigraph to his preface (p. xi) the words of Mumia Abu Jamal, one of the United States' most controversial death row inmates: "Isn't it odd that Christendom—that huge body of humankind that claims spiritual descent from the Jewish carpenter of Nazareth—claims to pray to and adore a being who was prisoner of Roman power, an inmate of the empire's death row? . . . That the majority of its adherents strenuously support the states' execution of thousands of imprisoned citizens? That the overwhelming majority of its judges, prosecutors, and lawyers—those who condemn, prosecute, and sell out the condemned—claim to be followers of the fettered, spat-upon, naked God?"

45. Carl Schmitt, writing in 1970, maintained that "Moltmann is right to emphasize the intense political meaning that the worship of a crucified God ineradicably contains and that cannot be sublimated into the 'purely theological.'" Carl Schmitt, *Political Theology II: The Myth of the Closure of Any Political Theology*, trans. Michael Hoetzl and Graham Ward (Cambridge: Polity, 2008), 150. Unfortunately, that sublimation has functioned rather too well. He is referring to an essay of Moltmann's titled "Political Theology" from 1969. That essay can be found in Jürgen Moltmann's *The Experiment Hope*, ed. and trans. M. Douglas Meeks (Philadelphia: Fortress, 1975), 101–18.

46. See Erasmus, "The Complaint of Peace," in *The Essential Erasmus*, ed. John Dolan (New York: Continuum, 1990), 174–204.

47. Jacques Derrida, *Cosmopolitanism and Forgiveness* (New York: Routledge, 2001), 31; see also my discussion in *Reading Derrida/Thinking Paul*, 139–40.

48. Jacques Derrida, "Globalization, Peace, and Cosmopolitanism," in *Negotiations*, ed. and trans. Elizabeth Rottenberg (Stanford: Stanford University Press, 2002), 384.

3. The Cross and Division

1. The question of reconciliation with God will be treated in chapter 6.
2. Note the absence in this formula of "male and female."
3. The question of whether it is possible for a Judaism that is reconstructed in line with a feminist perspective to retain the sense of election as designating Israel has been made with particular cogency by Judith Plaskow and, in another way, is at the heart of the "reconstructionist" program; see Judith Plaskow, *Standing Again at Sinai: Judaism from a Feminist Perspective* (San Francisco: HarperCollins, 1990), 96–107. The importance of the breaking down of walls of exclusion for feminist perspectives and possibilities will become evident below.
4. There seems to be a notable tendency within the dominant strands of Second Temple Judaism to "circle the wagons" of identity as a defensive posture relative to the cultural imperialism of dominant colonial powers that may have become most pronounced with the near submersion of Judaism in the Hellenistic cultural sphere, following the conquest by Alexander. (I have indicated ways in which it seems probable that this has affected the holiness code of Leviticus in my *Jacob's Wound: Homoerotic Narrative in the Literature of Ancient Israel* [New York: Continuum, 2005], 199–220.) It is this program of exclusivism that is especially brought into question, as we will see, by the cross. But this will not, I contend, bring into question the election of Israel as such.
5. In some ways, there is a far more important difference in Matthew's story, in that the designation of the object of the centurion's care is not a slave but his "lad." I have argued elsewhere that this should be understood as indicating that the lad is the centurion's "boyfriend," in a pederastic relationship. See *The Man Jesus Loved: Homoerotic Narratives from the New Testament* (Cleveland: Pilgrim, 2003). More recently this argument has been refined and carried in new directions in the work that I have done with my colleague Benny Tat-Siong Liew, in "Mistaken Identities but Model Faith: Rereading the Centurion, the Chap, and the Christ in Matthew 8:5-13," *Journal of Biblical Literature* 123 (2004): 467–94. It thus serves as the basis for overcoming another form of exclusion, that of gay and lesbian people.
6. A fine discussion of these "magi" is to be found in Richard A. Horsley, *The Liberation of Christmas: The Infancy Narratives in Social Context* (New York: Crossroad, 1989), 53–60.
7. We have already attended to the significance of this story for the role of Jesus' mission in opposing the powers of domination represented by the Roman occupation. The co-implication of the gentile features of the story also suggests that the dimension of the cross to which we are now attending cannot be neatly separated from the political dimension that I have argued must be viewed as basic to an understanding of the cross. For further

reflection on this, see my reading of the Gospel of Mark in *The Insurrection of the Crucified: The Gospel of Mark as Theological Manifesto* (Chicago: Exploration, 2003).

8. The accusations against Jesus and his resultant condemnation in accordance with the law will be the subject of the next chapter.

9. I should note here that this does not mean that the election of Israel comes to an end. Rather, it means that the exclusion of the non-Israelite comes to an end. See the excursus at the end of the present chapter.

10. This will have to be considered again when we come to a discussion of "the cross of God" in chapter 9.

11. We may note that Paul's several references to being crucified with Christ have in view something like a renunciation of the quest for privilege. This will be the theme of chapter 8, "Dying with Christ."

12. Athanansius, "De Incarnatione," §25, in *Contra Gentiles and De Incarnatione*, ed. and trans. Robert W. Thomson (Oxford: Clarendon, 1971), 195.

13. Gregory of Nyssa, "An Address on Religious Instruction," §32, in *Christology of the Later Fathers*, ed. Edward Rochie Hardy and Cyril C. Richardson (Philadelphia: Westminster, 1954), 311.

14. The text from 1 Peter connects the suffering of the slaves at the hands of abusive masters to the suffering of the Messiah at the hands of abusive authorities. It is astonishing that this text could have been cited to justify the abusive character of slavery, as if the perspective of 1 Peter were similarly to justify the abusive treatment of Jesus at the hands of the powerful.

15. Speaking of his master who had found religion at a Methodist camp meeting, Frederick Douglas wrote: "I believe him to have been a much worse man after his conversion than before. Prior to his conversion, he relied upon his own depravity to shield and sustain him in his savage barbarity; but after his conversion, he found religious sanction and support for his slaveholding cruelty." In *Narrative of the Life of Frederick Douglas* [1845] (New York: Dover, 1995), 32. No doubt the conversion was accompanied by much talk of the cross and singing about the blood of the Lamb!

16. John W. de Gruchy and Charles Villa-Vicencio, eds., *Apartheid Is a Heresy* (Grand Rapids: Eerdmans, 1983).

17. See Elizabeth Schüssler Fiorenza's remarkable body of work, most especially *In Memory of Her: A Feminist Theological Reconstruction of Christian Origins* (New York: Herder & Herder, 1983).

18. For an examination of the relevant texts, see my book *The Man Jesus Loved*, 171–232.

19. The long history of brilliant women's leadership is effectively assembled in Amy Oden's *In Her Words: Women's Writings in the History of Christian Thought* (Nashville: Abingdon, 1994).

20. Douglass, *Narrative of the Life of Frederick Douglass*, 71.

4. The Cross and Accusation

1. Martin Hengel seeks to clarify the origins of the view that Christ's death is somehow the basis of salvation for sinners in his book *The Atonement: The Origins of the Doctrine in the New Testament* (Philadelphia: Fortress Press, 1981), but in a different way than I propose here. He works primarily with the idea of atonement itself in its Old Testament and Jewish contexts, and with ways in which the theme of dying for others was played out in the Greco-Roman world. He does agree that the priestly and subsequent theological views of sacrifice are inadequate and that the effect of the cross in the earliest proclamation was the salvation of all humanity.

2. The reversal of the contagion of pollution finds rather dramatic expression not only in the abolition of pollution taboos in early Christianity, but also in the contagiousness of sanctity that lies at the basis of the role of relics in subsequent Christianity; see Peter Brown, *The Cult of the Saints* (Chicago: University of Chicago Press, 1981).

3. Krister Stendahl, *Paul among Jews and Gentiles* (Philadelphia: Fortress Press, 1976), 23.

4. For further discussion of the relevant texts, and for consideration of how they might relate to the situation that is normally spoken of as forgiveness, see my *Reading Derrida/Thinking Paul: On Justice* (Stanford: Stanford University Press, 2005), 128–56.

5. The Cross and Suffering

1. Jacques Ellul writes, "It is this human misery crying to heaven which can 'call God back to life,' that is to say, can move his heart to stop abandoning us. But when that day comes, it will really be the cyclone drawn in by the complete vacuum of love." *Hope in Time of Abandonment*, trans. C. Edward Hopkin (New York: Seabury, 1973), 191.

2. See the work of René Girard, who has shown that the cycle of violence is directly supported by this mechanism that depends upon the willingness to "blame the victim," and so to legitimate violence. Girard has shown that the effect of the Christian focus upon the innocence of the paradigmatic victim has the effect of breaking this cycle and so of rendering it ineffective. See René Girard, *The Scapegoat*, trans. Yvonne Freccero (Baltimore: Johns Hopkins University Press, 1986), and *Violence and the Sacred*, trans. Patrick Gregory (Baltimore: Johns Hopkins University Press, 1977).

3. The notion of a crucified people was developed by C. S. Song in his articulation of a distinctively Asian theology. The term itself is elaborated through an impressive array of Asian literary depictions of the suffering of the people, as well as their protest against unjust suffering, in *Jesus, the Crucified People* (New York: Crossroad, 1990).

4. Stuart George Hall, ed. and trans., *Melito of Sardis* (New York: Oxford University Press, 1979), 55. Delores Williams also underscores this nakedness and gives it a context of contemporary meaning. She notes that "by publicly exposing his nakedness and private parts . . . the cross thus becomes an image of defilement," which she then links to the "defilement of black women's bodies." In "Black Women's Surrogacy and the Christian Notion of Redemption," in *Cross Examinations: Readings on the Meaning of the Cross Today*, ed. Marit Trelstad (Minneapolis: Fortress Press, 2006), 31.

5. In this way, Jay B. McDaniel is correct when he asserts that "Jesus' suffering is best understood, not as the most extreme suffering that anyone has ever undergone, but as a *window to all suffering that anyone has to undergo*" (emphasis original). In "The Passion of Christ: Grace Both Red and Green," in Trelstad, *Cross Examinations*, 202.

6. Athanasius, "De Incarnatione," §8, in *Contra Gentiles and De Incarnatione*, ed. and trans. Robert W. Thomson (Oxford: Clarendon, 1971), 153.

7. Ibid., §20, in *Contra Gentiles and De Incarnatione*, 185.

8. This is also an occasion in which bodily infirmity is linked to an evil spirit.

9. In his sermon on the passion, Melito of Sardis also makes the connection between the death of Jesus and his ministry of healing, although he characteristically blames Israel rather than the Romans for this. Why was Jesus murdered in Jerusalem? he asks, and replies: "Because he healed their lame and cleansed their lepers, and brought light to their blind, and raised their dead, that is why he died" (Hall, *Melito of Sardis*, 72).

10. The many puzzles produced by this insistence on a future for the body as resurrected body, while insisting on a body no longer subject to death and corruption, are explored in Carolyn Walker Bynum, *Resurrection of the Body in Western Christianity* (New York: Columbia University Press, 1995).

11. This mirroring can work both ways, in that the suffering of Jesus can be made to reflect the suffering of the afflicted. In her essay "Imaging the Cross," Susan L. Nelson notes that the famous Isenheim altar triptych performs this function: "If the residents of the hospital at Colmar where this altarpiece was installed saw Jesus suffering their same affliction (the crucified Jesus bears the symptoms of the same St Anthony's fire from which the patients suffered), then they might also expect that they, too, would share in his resurrection." In Trelstad, *Cross Examinations*, 171.

12. Roy Stark, *The Rise of Christianity* (Princeton: Princeton University Press, 1996).

13. Rosemary Radford Ruether, *Sexism and God-Talk: Toward a Feminist Theology* (Boston: Beacon, 1983).

14. Cynthia Moe-Lobeda is correct when, in her essay "A Theology of the Cross for the 'UnCreators,'" in Trelstad, *Cross Examinations*, she says that "the earth now being 'crucified' by human ignorance, greed and arrogance is, in some sense, also the body of Christ" (194), and wonders: "How might the

cross enable God's people to (1) recognize the extent of our implication in ecological and economic injustice; (2) claim our identity as participants in God's life-giving and life-saving work on Earth; (3) embody a sense of hope . . . (4) receive the moral power . . . to transform our relation to creation" (189).

15. Delores Williams, in her remarkable essay to which I have already referred, links the defilement of Jesus' naked body to the defilement of the earth in our own time: "Worse, deeper and more wounding than alienation, defilement is the sin of which today's technological world is most guilty. Nature— the land, the seas, the animals in the sea—are everyday defiled by humans" (Williams, "Black Women's Surrogacy," 31).

16. See Gregory of Nyssa, "An Address on Religious Instruction," in *Christology of the Later Fathers*, ed. Edward Rochie Hardy and Cyril C. Richardson (Philadelphia: Westminster, 1954), 303. (Here Nyssa even supposes that Satan will be restored.) For a contemporary interpretation of the theme of the restoration of creation that is indebted to Greek Orthodox sources, see Jürgen Moltmann, *The Coming of God: Christian Eschatology*, trans. Margaret Kohl (Minneapolis: Fortress Press, 1996), 257–78.

17. Vítor Westhelle writes: "In other words, through the theology of creation we know that the cross of Christ is formally identical with the suffering of the world; through the theology of the cross the suffering in and of the world is recognized as the locus of God's creative work." *The Scandalous God: The Use and Abuse of the Cross* (Minneapolis: Fortress Press, 2006), 104.

18. The development of a liberation theology toward an ecological theology is powerfully signaled in Leonardo Boff's *Cry of the Earth, Cry of the Poor*, trans. Phillip Berryman (Maryknoll, N.Y.: Orbis, 1997).

6. Reconciliation with God

1. We recall, from the first chapter, that the talk of divine honor is the way in which Anselm sought to "indigenize" his perspective within the context of emergent feudalism.

2. See the discussion in chapter 1.

3. We should also note that in this passage there are three related ways of describing the human condition: weakness, sin, and enmity toward God. Each of these intends to show that the divine act is without condition or presupposition—that is, it is entirely gracious or gratuitous, a free gift.

4. Andrew Sung Park, *The Wounded Heart of God: The Asian Concept of Han and the Christian Doctrine of Sin* (Nashville: Abingdon, 1993).

5. Ibid., 10.

6. Considerable attention has been given to the self-legitimation of Roman imperial rule through the elaboration of the imperial cult in *Paul and*

Empire: Religion and Power in Roman Society, ed. Richard Horsley (Harrisburg, Pa.: Trinity, 1997), and *Paul and Politics: Ekklesia, Israel, Imperium, Interpretation: Essays in Honor of Krister Stendahl,* ed. Richard Horsley (Harrisburg, Pa.: Trinity, 2000).

7. The critique and, indeed, abolition of religion have been thematized by Karl Barth in *The Epistle to the Romans,* trans. Edwyn C. Hoskins (New York: Oxford, 1933), 229–70, and by Dietrich Bonhoeffer in *Letters and Papers from Prison,* ed. Eberhard Bethge (New York: Macmillan, 1971), particularly in the latter's discussion of "religionless Christianity" (280–82).

7. The Community of the Crucified

1. Most studies of the cross in Paul focus on the question of the role of God in the cross or, less commonly, on the form of individual life that is entailed by following the Crucified. It is the merit of Charles Cousar's *A Theology of the Cross: The Death of Jesus in the Pauline Letters* (Minneapolis: Fortress Press, 1990) that it gives considerable attention to what I am terming the crucified community.

2. "The Romans ruthlessly sacked and torched Corinth . . . slaughtered its men, and enslaved its women and children in 146 B.C.E.," as Richard Horsley notes in his introduction to *Paul and Empire: Religion and Power in Roman Imperial Society,* ed. Richard A. Horsley (Philadelphia: Trinity, 1997), 11. John Chow notes, "The name of the colony, *Colonia Laus Julia Corinthiensis,* stood as a constant reminder of the grace of Julius Caesar who helped to refound the colony" (John K. Chow, "Patronage in Roman Corinth," in Horsley, *Paul and Empire,* 106).

3. See Chow, "Patronage in Roman Corinth," 104–10.

4. Paul will make a similar point in Rom 1:18-32, in which he indicts Roman civilization as deserving of death and as standing under the divine wrath.

5. In the patristic period, the logic of this strategy of entrapment, whereby the enemy of humankind is led to act in such a way as to bring ruin upon itself (and liberation for humanity), is developed as the snaring of Satan, who overreaches, swallowing the incarnate God, and so must disgorge an imprisoned humanity. In chapter 9, the way in which political as well as other dimensions of the cross are projected upon a cosmic screen, or are taken to be keys to understanding the cosmic significance of the cross, will be explored further.

6. In attempting to "deconstruct" the ontotheological and ontopolitical definition of divinity, Derrida remarks that this idea of God as sovereign is entirely coextensive with the idea of omnipotence: "In speaking of an ontotheology of sovereignty, I am referring here, under the name of God, this One and Only God, to the determination of a sovereign, and thus indivisible, omnipotence." Jacques Derrida, *Rogues: Two Essays on Reason,*

trans. Pascale-Anne Brault and Michael Naas (Stanford: Stanford University Press, 2004), 157.

7. It is this sense of messianic weakness that leads Agamben to posit a strong relationship between Paul and the reflections of Walter Benjamin in "On the Concept of History." See Giorgio Agamben, *The Time That Remains: A Commentary on the Letter to the Romans*, trans. Patricia Dailey (Stanford: Stanford University Press, 2005), 138–45.

8. Epistle to Diognetes, 10:4-6, in *The Apostolic Fathers*, trans. J. B. Lightfoot and J. R. Harmer, ed. Michael W. Holmes (Grand Rapids: Baker, 1992), 549.

9. Some commentators regard this passage as an interpolation.

10. The association of the death of Jesus with the question of betrayal is, perhaps, not simply formulaic since what Paul will be concerned with is precisely another sort of betrayal: that enacted by the community of the Crucified in its very act of recollection.

11. Juvenal, Satire 10, in *Juvenal and Persius*, trans. G. G. Ramsay, Loeb Classical Library (Cambridge, Mass: Harvard University Press, 1940).

12. The abolition of structures of prestige among the followers of Jesus is made even more concrete in the Gospel of Matthew, in which Jesus tells his followers that among them none should be called teacher or rabbi or even father (Matt 23:8-10). In this way, the abolition of a gentile polity of rule is carried over into the abolition of a Judean polity as well.

13. There is a saying that is sometimes quoted as if it meant the opposite of the saying we have been looking at in Mark. In the Gospel of Matthew, also in connection with the theme of the casting out of demons: "Whoever is not with me is against me, and whoever does not gather with me scatters" (Matt 12:30 NRSV). But this saying is directed against those who are opposing the very work of exorcism because it is not done in accordance with their own rules. In this respect, the Pharisees, who are being accused of scattering, are behaving just like the disciples, and most particularly John, in forbidding one who casts out demons "because he does not follow us."

14. In a remarkably creative approach to that which makes community possible as being a reflection of the cross, Wonhee Anne Joh deploys the notion of *jeong* to emphasize the distinctive features of a new form of relationality: "One cannot succinctly define *jeong* without losing the depth of its multiple and shifting dimensions. Moreover, *jeong* embodies the invisible traces of compassion in relationships and is most often recognized when we perceive our very own self, conscious and unconscious, in the mirrored reflection of the other. *Jeong* is a Korean way of conceiving an often complex constellation of relationality of the self with the other that is deeply associated with compassion, love, vulnerability, and acceptance of heterogeneity as essential to life." Wonhee Anne Joh, *Heart of the Cross: A Postcolonial Christology* (Louisville, Ky.: Westminster John Knox, 2006), xxi; see also 120.

15. I have discussed this issue at greater length in *Reading Derrida/Thinking Paul: On Justice* (Stanford: Stanford University Press, 2005), 109–27.

16. We may have to include the many movements that appropriate messianic motifs from Christianity: the Donghuk of Korea, the Taiping of China, and the various eschatological and messianic movements in the African initiated churches. Moreover, a case could be made for including various forms of Marxism as derivative from the messianic perspectives of Judaism and Christianity.

17. In the next chapter, I will attend to the way in which Paul makes use of the notion of flesh in order to speak, not of sex, for example, but of religious differences.

18. The question of polity or politics that characterizes common faithfulness to the gospel is specifically raised by Paul in Philippians 1:27, where he urges the community to be of a polity (*politeuesthe*) that is worthy of or befitting the gospel.

19. The exhortations to slaves and to women seem significantly more "conservative" than the positions of Paul, for example.

8. Dying with/in the Messiah

1. I adopt this phrase from Jean-Luc Nancy, who seeks to develop Heidegger's idea of *Mitsein* ("being-with") into a fundamental way of "thinking being," especially of human being. See Jean-Luc Nancy, *Being Singular Plural*, trans. Robert Richardson and Anne O'Byrne (Stanford: Stanford University Press, 2000), and *The Muses*, trans. Peggy Kamuf (Stanford: Stanford University Press, 1997). For an earlier approach to this problematic, see also Jean-Luc Nancy, *The Inoperative Community*, ed. Peter Connor (Minneapolis: University of Minnesota Press, 1991). But I will leave aside for now the task of a full engagement with Nancy's project.

2. That early ascetic practices seek to prepare the body for resurrection is one of the important insights of Peter Brown in *The Body and Society: Men, Women, and Sexual Renunciation in Early Christianity* (New York: Columbia University Press, 1988).

3. Thus Brondos is correct when he maintains that "they suffer with Christ in the sense that they suffer *for the same cause and the same gospel as he did"* (emphasis in original). See David Brondos, *Paul on the Cross: Reconstructing the Apostle's Story of Redemption* (Minneapolis: Fortress Press, 2006), 171. Brondos's book helpfully demonstrates the difference between Paul's theology of the cross and subsequent theories of atonement, but he gives little attention to the corporate character of Paul's understanding of the cross that is the focus of my previous chapter.

4. In this way I am in substantial agreement with Dorothee Soelle, *Christ the Representative*, trans. David Lewis (London: SCM, 1967).

5. The italicized prepositions are not present in the Greek. We will return to the question of the appropriate preposition at the end of this chapter.

6. Scholars generally agree that 2 Corinthians is a compilation of two or more letters, even if the precise division of the existing document and attribution of passages to different letters remain disputed.

7. See chapter 2 above.

8. Emmanuel Levinas, *Totality and Infinity*, trans. Alphonso Lingis (Pittsburgh: Duquesne University Press, 1969), 305.

9. See my "Theological Perspectives on Sexuality," *Journal of Pastoral Care* 33 (1979): 3–16.

10. See my essay "Reconstructing the Doctrine of Sin," in *The Other Side of Sin*, ed. Andrew Sung Park and Susan L. Nelson (Albany, N.Y.: SUNY Press, 2001), 109–22; see also Krister Stendahl, "Paul and the Introspective Conscience of the West," in *Paul among Jews and Gentiles* (Philadelphia: Fortress Press, 1976), 78–96.

11. It is not my intention to maintain that Paul always and everywhere is completely faithful to this perspective. Undoubtedly, there are places where Paul seems to fall short of his own principles, whether because of the exigencies of the particular situations that he was addressing, or because he is in this, as in other things, still, as he himself says, seeing through a glass darkly and so not yet "face to face."

12. I have given some attention to other dimensions of these passages in *Reading Derrida/Thinking Paul: On Justice* (Stanford: Stanford University Press, 2005).

13. See Hans Walter Wolff, *Anthropology of the Old Testament*, trans. Margaret Kohl (London: SCM, 1974).

14. See, for example, Giorgio Agamben, *The Time That Remains: A Commentary on the Letter to the Romans*, trans. Patricia Dailey (Stanford: Stanford University Press, 2005); Jacob Taubes, *The Political Theology of Paul*, ed. Aleida Assman et al., trans. Dana Hollander (Stanford: Stanford University Press, 2004); and Slavoj Žižek, *The Puppet and the Dwarf: The Perverse Core of Christianity* (Cambridge, Mass.: MIT Press, 2003).

15. In *Paul on the Cross*, Brondos writes: "As believers live to Christ, they also die to the present age in the sense that they no longer identify with it" (181).

16. Alas, it is not just "the world" that regards these structures as having an ultimate ground. Protestant theology has regularly linked these very structures to what it calls "orders of creation," in order to make them the central regions of theological and ethical reflection. This, it seems to me, flies in the face of the Pauline *hos me*, "as if not."

17. In *Loyalty to God: The Apostles' Creed in Life and Liturgy* (Nashville: Abingdon, 1992), I pointed out that early Christian baptism and the creed that accompanied it served to dramatize the loyalty unto death that was made concrete in the experience of martyrdom.

18. A similar concern was evidenced by John Wesley, who emphasized the transformation worked by the "new birth" that he also associated with baptism, in accordance with the doctrine of the Church of England. He found no acceptable way to reconcile the apparent contradiction that some were baptized without displaying the effects he insisted were essential to regeneration or new birth.

19. See Alain Badiou, *Saint Paul: The Foundation of Universalism*, trans. Ray Brassier (Stanford: Stanford University Press, 2003). There Badiou writes: "Paul's general procedure is the following: if there has been an event, and if truth consists in declaring it and then in being faithful to this declaration, two consequences ensue. First, since truth is evental, or of the order of what occurs, it is singular. It is neither structural, nor axiomatic, nor legal. No available generality can account for it, nor structure the subject who claims to follow in its wake. Consequently, there cannot be a law of truth. Second, truth being inscribed on the basis of a declaration that is in essence subjective, no preconstituted subset can support it; nothing communitarian or historically established can lend its substance to the process of truth. Truth is diagonal relative to every communitarian subset; it neither claims authority from, nor (this is obviously the most delicate point) constitutes any identity. It is offered to all, or addressed to everyone, without a condition of belonging being able to limit this offer, or this address" (14).

20. It is here necessary to alter the choice of prepositions with which this text is frequently translated. In the Greek, the preposition in the phrase "no longer live for/unto/from themselves but for/unto/from the [one] having died and been raised for/to/from them" is not present but rather is simply "understood." The choice of a preposition therefore will depend on how one makes sense of the passage.

21. There is something of a parallel here with the dialectical materialism of Marx, Engels, and Lenin. For them, the new sociality comes into being in the crisis of the old and bears the marks of the old as it comes into being.

9. The Cross of God

1. This view can still be seen enacted in the custom in Mexico for folk to celebrate Holy Saturday as the day when the demons (rather impish ones, admittedly) are given free reign. And it is interesting that this custom appears in cultures where folk piety most seriously evokes the death of God in street portrayals of the passion of the Christ.

2. Thus, Melito of Sardis, whose second-century poetic homily on the cross has already been cited, also demonstrates an early version of this *communicatio*

idiomatum when he writes, "The impassible suffers. The immortal dies." In *Melito of Sardis*, ed. and trans. Stuard George Hall (New York: Oxford University Press, 1979), 80.

3. The text of Leo's Tome (ca. 448) is found in *Christology of the Later Fathers*, ed. Edward Hardy (London: SCM, 1954), 360–70. One of the key passages asserts: "Accordingly, while the distinctness of both natures and substances is preserved, and both meet in one person, lowliness is assumed by majesty, weakness by power, mortality by eternity . . . the inviolable nature has been united to the passible" (§3, p. 363). Thus it is correct that "the Son of God is said to have been crucified and buried" (§5, p. 366).

4. Rita Nakashima Brock points toward what may be the beginning of this process when she suggests a connection between the "33 year terror campaign" directed against the Saxons and the appearance of the first crucifix in the West (the Gero cross), around 960–70 in Saxony. "The Cross of Resurrection and Communal Redemption," in *Cross Examinations: Readings on the Meaning of the Cross Today*, ed. Marit Trelstad (Minneapolis: Fortress Press, 2006), 241–51.

5. For a very fruitful interpretation of Luther's emphasis on what it means to be a theologian of the cross, and an application of this to the contemporary situation, see Vítor Westhelle, *The Scandalous God: The Use and Abuse of the Cross* (Minneapolis: Fortress Press, 2006). Luther's decisive formulation of the distinction is found in his "Heidelberg Disputation of 1518," §§20, 92, and 93, in *Luther's Works*, ed. Franklin Sherman (Philadelphia: Fortress Press, 1971), 33:39–58.

6. Nietzsche was defended by the theologian Franz Overbeck, who himself had a decisive influence upon Karl Barth (as the many references to Overbeck in Barth's commentary on Romans indicates). It may, then, be no accident that Barth's early theological work was regarded as nihilistic (a favorite way of characterizing Nietzsche) by the defenders of a kind of liberal mainstream theological consensus in Europe.

7. Alfred North Whitehead, *Process and Reality: An Essay in Cosmology* (London: Macmillan, 1929), 532.

8. Ibid., 520–21.

9. Dietrich Bonhoeffer, *Letters and Papers from Prison*, ed. Eberhard Bethge (New York: Macmillan, 1972), 357–62.

10. Kazoh Kitamori, *Theology of the Pain of God* [1946], 5th ed. (Richmond, Va.: John Knox, 1958). The book was translated due to the attention that Carl Michaelson had drawn to it and other Japanese innovations in theology.

11. Ibid., 16.

12. Andrew Sung Park, *The Wounded Heart of God: The Asian Concept of Han and the Christian Doctrine of Sin* (Nashville: Abingdon, 1993).

13. The book that gained the most attention and that continues to be a fundamentally important articulation of his position is Thomas J. J. Altizer, *The Gospel of Christian Atheism* (Philadelphia: Westminster, 1966).

14. Carl Schmitt, *Political Theology: Four Chapters on the Concept of Sovereignty*, trans. George Schwab (Chicago: University of Chicago Press, 2005), 36.

15. Leonardo Boff, *Trinity and Society*, trans. Paul Burns (Maryknoll, N.Y.: Orbis, 1988).

16. Martin Heidegger, "Only a God Can Save Us," trans. Maria P. Alter and John D. Caputo, *Philosophy Today* (Winter 1976): 267–84.

17. Jacques Derrida, *Rogues: Two Essays on Reason*, trans. Pascale-Anne Brault and Michael Naas (Stanford: Stanford University Press, 2005).

18. Ibid., 114.

19. Ibid., 157.

20. John D. Caputo, *The Weakness of God: A Theology of the Event* (Bloomington: Indiana University Press, 2006).

21. Although this has not been traditionally said of the Jews; that is, they are not typically exonerated because they played a necessary role in this macabre game.

22. Douglas John Hall, in his book *The Cross in Our Context: Jesus and the Suffering World* (Minneapolis: Fortress Press, 2003), rightly maintains: "The brutal death of Jesus of Nazareth is not to be attributed to some heavenly blueprint. . . . It is not *God's* vindictiveness, *God's* 'plan' " (103). It is, rather, he maintains, the wrath of the powers of domination, and thus it is only in hindsight that "faith is allowed to see the hand of God in this human tragedy." Of course, the "hand of God" here is to be seen in the reversal of the intention of the powers.

23. In this sense, I agree with S. Mark Heim when he says, "God used our sin to save us from that sin." In "Saved by What Shouldn't Happen: The Anti-Sacrificial Meaning of the Cross," in *Cross Examinations: Readings on the Meaning of the Cross Today*, ed. Marit Trelstad (Minneapolis: Fortress Press, 2006), 224.

10. After Atonement?

1. The appropriation of Girard's views for a discussion of atonement is a basic element in the work of S. Mark Heim. See "Saved by What Shouldn't Happen: The Anti-Sacrificial Meaning of the Cross," in *Cross Examinations: Readings on the Meaning of the Cross Today*, ed. Marit Trelstad (Minneapolis: Fortress Press, 2006), 211–24.

2. Douglas John Hall suggests that the attraction of this view also has to do with the growing middle-class ethos in which the language of debt and transaction made a good deal of intuitive sense. *The Cross in Our Context: Jesus and the Suffering World* (Minneapolis: Fortress Press, 2003), 106–7.

3. Among the most important and helpful of these revisions of the "Christus Victor" approach are those of Darby Ray (already cited) and the more recent work of J. Denny Weaver in *The Nonviolent Atonement* (Grand Rapids: Eerdmans, 2001). Weaver terms his approach a "narrative Christus Victor," which refers to his incorporation of the ministry of Jesus into the story of the cross and resurrection. The limitation of this approach is that it focuses so exclusively on the political cross of confrontation that it does not do justice to the other dimensions of the cross that have been elaborated in these pages.

4. In quite a dramatic way, Karl Barth managed to overcome the individualism of modern satisfaction theories by making Christ substitute for humanity as a whole in such a way as to suggest a universal redemption.

5. In his book *Violence, Hospitality, and the Cross: Reappropriating the Atonement Tradition* (Grand Rapids: Baker Academic, 2004), Hans Boersma maintains, "The various atonement theories all have a place within the Church, and we need not exclude the one at the expense of the other" (119). Boersma seeks to make use of some aspects of the views of Levinas and Derrida to elaborate his understanding of the cross, a project with which I am sympathetic; but his discussion is marred by a peculiar attachment to ideas of violence that he confusedly links to Derrida. This, together with an insistence that the violence of the Old Testament must be positively appropriated into Christian theology (91), mars an otherwise intriguing attempt to rethink atonement within a traditional evangelical perspective. He defends the association of God with violence by saying, "We can only shield God from the violence of the cross at the cost of parting ways with the tradition of the church" (43). Of course, it is precisely that tradition that must be reevaluated.

6. See, for example, Delores Williams, "Black Women's Surrogacy and the Christian Notion of Redemption," in Trelstad, *Cross Examinations*, 32.

7. Walter Benjamin, "Critique of Violence," in *Reflections: Essays, Aphorisms, Autobiographical Writings*, ed. Peter Demetz (New York: Schocken, 1978), 277–300.

BIBLIOGRAPHY

Abelard, Peter. 1961. Exposition of the Epistle to the Romans. In *A Scholastic Miscellany: Anselm to Ockham*, ed. and trans. Eugene R. Fairweather, 276–87. Philadelphia: Westminster.

Agamben, Giorgio. 2005. *The Time That Remains: A Commentary on the Letter to the Romans*. Trans. Patricia Dailey. Stanford: Stanford University Press.

Altizer, Thomas J. J. 1966. *The Gospel of Christian Atheism*. Philadelphia: Westminster.

Anselm of Canterbury. 1982. Why God Became Man. In *A Scholastic Miscellany: Anselm to Ockham*, ed. and trans. Eugene R. Fairweather, 100–183. Philadelphia: Westminster.

Athanasius. 1971. *Contra Gentes and De Incarnatione*. Ed. and trans. Robert W. Thomson. Oxford: Clarendon.

Aulén, Gustav. 1969. *Christus Victor: An Historical Study of the Three Main Types of the Idea of the Atonement*. Trans. A. G. Hebert. New York: Macmillan.

Badiou, Alain. 2003. *Saint Paul: The Foundation of Universalism*. Trans. Ray Brassier. Stanford: Stanford University Press.

Barth, Karl. 1933. *The Epistle to the Romans*. Trans. Edwyn C. Hoskins. London: Oxford University Press.

Benjamin, Walter. 1978. Critique of Violence. In *Reflections: Essays, Aphorisms, Autobiographical Writings*, ed. Peter Demetz, 277–300. New York: Schocken.

Boersma, Hans. 2004. *Violence, Hospitality, and the Cross: Reappropriating the Atonement Tradition*. Grand Rapids: Baker Academic.

Boff, Leonardo. 1987. *Passion of Christ, Passion of the World*. Trans. Robert R. Barr. Maryknoll, N.Y.: Orbis.

———. 1988. *Trinity and Society*. Trans. Paul Burns. Maryknoll, N.Y.: Orbis.

———. 1997. *Cry of the Earth, Cry of the Poor*. Trans. Phillip Berryman. Maryknoll, N.Y.: Orbis.

Bonhoeffer, Dietrich. 1971. *Letters and Papers from Prison*. Ed. Eberhard Bethge. New York: Macmillan.

Boyarin, Daniel. 1999. *Dying for God: Martyrdom and the Making of Christianity and Judaism*. Stanford: Stanford University Press.

Brock, Rita Nakashima. 1991. *Journeys by Heart: A Christology of Erotic Power*. New York: Crossroad.

———. 2006. The Cross of Resurrection and Communal Redemption. In *Cross Examinations: Readings on the Meaning of the Cross Today*, ed. Marit Trelstad, 241–51. Minneapolis: Fortress Press.

Brondos, David. 2006. *Paul on the Cross: Reconstructing the Apostle's Story of Redemption*. Minneapolis: Fortress Press.

Brown, Joanne C., and Rebecca Parker. 1989. For God So Loved the World. In *Christianity, Patriarchalism, and Abuse*, 1–30. Edinburgh: T & T Clark.

Brown, Peter. 1981. *The Cult of the Saints*. Chicago: University of Chicago Press.

———. 1988. *The Body and Society: Men, Women, and Sexual Renunciation in Early Christianity*. New York: Columbia University Press.

Bultmann, Rudolf. 1955. *Theology of the New Testament*. 2 vols. Trans. Kendrick Grobel. New York: Charles Scribner's Sons.

Burkert, Walter. 1987. *Ancient Mystery Cults*. Cambridge, Mass.: Harvard University Press.

Bynum, Carolyn Walker. 1995. *Resurrection of the Body in Western Christianity, 200–1336*. New York: Columbia University Press.

Caputo, John D. 2006. *The Weakness of God: A Theology of the Event*. Bloomington: Indiana University Press.

Chow, John K. 1997. Patronage in Roman Corinth. In *Paul and Empire: Religion and Power in Roman Imperial Society*, ed. Richard A. Horsley, 104–25. Harrisburg, Pa.: Trinity.

Cousar, Charles. 1990. *A Theology of the Cross: The Death of Jesus in the Pauline Letters*. Minneapolis: Fortress Press.

Crossan, John Dominic. 1994. *Jesus: A Revolutionary Biography*. San Francisco: HarperSanFrancisco.

de Gruchy, John W., and Charles Villa-Vicencio, eds. 1983. *Apartheid Is a Heresy*. Grand Rapids: Eerdmans.

Derrida, Jacques. 2001. *Cosmopolitanism and Forgiveness*. Trans. Mark Dooley and Michael Hughes. New York: Routledge.

———. 2002. Globalization, Peace, and Cosmopolitanism. In *Negotiations*, ed. and trans. Elizabeth Rottenberg, 371–86. Stanford: Stanford University Press.

———. 2004. *Rogues: Two Essays on Reason*. Trans. Pascale-Anne Brault and Michael Naas. Stanford: Stanford University Press.

Douglass, Fredrick. 1995. *Narrative of the Life of Frederick Douglass*. New York: Dover.

Elliott, Neil. 1994. *Liberating Paul: The Justice of God and the Politics of the Apostle*. Maryknoll, N.Y.: Orbis.

Ellul, Jacques. 1973. *Hope in Time of Abandonment*. Trans. C. Edward Hopkin. New York: Seabury.

Epistle to Diognetus. 1992. In *The Apostolic Fathers*, trans. J. B. Lightfoot and J. R. Harmer, ed. Michael W. Holmes, 529–55. Grand Rapids: Baker.

Erasmus. 1990. The Complaint of Peace. In *The Essential Erasmus*, ed. John Dolan, 174–204. New York: Continuum.

Fiorenza, Elizabeth Schüssler. 1983. *In Memory of Her: A Feminist Theological Reconstruction of Christian Origins*. New York: Herder & Herder.

Girard, René. 1977. *Violence and the Sacred*. Trans. Patrick Gregory. Baltimore: Johns Hopkins University Press.

———. 1986. *The Scapegoat*. Trans. Yvonne Freccero. Baltimore: Johns Hopkins University Press.

Gregory of Nyssa. 1954. An Address on Religious Instruction. In *Christology of the Later Fathers*, ed. Edward Rochie Hardy and Cyril C. Richardson, 268–325. Philadelphia: Westminster.

Hall, Douglas John. 2003. *The Cross in our Context: Jesus and the Suffering World*. Minneapolis: Fortress Press.

Hall, Stuart George, ed. and trans. 1979. *Melito of Sardis*. New York: Oxford University Press.

Hardt, Michael, and Antonio Negri. 2000. *Empire*. Cambridge, Mass.: Harvard University Press.

———. 2004. *Multitude: War and Democracy in the Age of Empire*. New York: Penguin.

Heidegger, Martin. 1976. Only a God Can Save Us, trans. Maria P. Alter and John D. Caputo. *Philosophy Today* 20 (4): 267–84.

Heim, S. Mark. 2006. Saved by What Shouldn't Happen: The Anti-Sacrificial Meaning of the Cross. In *Cross Examinations: Readings on the Meaning of the Cross Today*, ed. Marit Trelstad, 211–24. Minneapolis: Fortress Press.

Hengel, Martin. 1981. *The Atonement: The Origins of the Doctrine in the New Testament*. Philadelphia: Fortress Press.

Horsley, Richard A. 1989. *The Liberation of Christmas: The Infancy Narratives in Social Context*. New York: Crossroad.

———, ed. 1997. *Paul and Empire: Religion and Power in Roman Imperial Society*. Harrisburg, Pa.: Trinity.

———. 2000. *Paul and Politics: Ekklesia, Israel, Imperium, Interpretation; Essays in Honor of Krister Stendahl*. Harrisburg, Pa.: Trinity.

Ignatius of Antioch. 1987. Epistles. In *The Ante-Nicene Fathers*, vol. 1, 49–126. Grand Rapids: Eerdmans.

Irenaeus. 1987. Against Heresies. In *The Ante-Nicene Fathers*, vol. 1, 315–567. Grand Rapids: Eerdmans.

Jennings, Theodore W., Jr. 1979. Theological Perspectives on Sexuality. *Journal of Pastoral Care* 33:3–16.

———. 1990. The Son of Man Strategy. In *Text and Logos: The Humanistic Interpretation of the New Testament*, ed. Theodore W. Jennings Jr., 229–43. Atlanta: Scholars.

———. 1992. *Loyalty to God: The Apostles' Creed in Life and Liturgy*. Nashville: Abingdon.

———. 2001. Reconstructing the Doctrine of Sin. In *The Other Side of Sin*, ed. Andrew Sung Park and Susan L. Nelson, 109–22. Albany: SUNY Press.

———. 2003. *The Insurrection of the Crucified*. Chicago: Exploration.

———. 2003. *The Man Jesus Loved: Homoerotic Narratives from the New Testament*. Cleveland: Pilgrim.

———. 2005. *Jacob's Wound: Homoerotic Narrative in the Literature of Ancient Israel*. New York: Continuum.

———. 2005. *Reading Derrida/Thinking Paul: On Justice*. Stanford: Stanford University Press.

Jennings, Theodore W., Jr., and Benny Tat-Siong Liew. 2004. Mistaken Identities but Model Faith: Rereading the Centurion, the Chap, and the Christ in Matthew 8:5-13. *Journal of Biblical Literature* 123 (3): 467–94.

Joh, Wonhee Anne. 2006. *Heart of the Cross: A Postcolonial Christology*. Louisville, Ky.: Westminster John Knox.

Juvenal. 1940. Satire 10. In *Juvenal and Persius*, trans. G. G. Ramsay, 193–221. Cambridge, Mass.: Harvard University Press.

Kitamori, Kazoh. 1958. *Theology of the Pain of God.* 5th ed. Richmond, Va.: John Knox.

Lactantius. 1987. The Divine Institutes. In *The Ante-Nicene Fathers,* vol. 7, 9–223. Grand Rapids: Eerdmans.

Leo the Great. 1954. Tome. In *Christology of the Later Fathers,* ed. Edward Rochie Hardy and Cyril C. Richardson, 359–70. Philadelphia: Westminster.

Levinas, Emmanuel. 1969. *Totality and Infinity.* Trans. Alphonso Lingis. Pittsburgh: Duquesne University Press.

Luther, Martin. 1971. Heidelberg Disputation of 1518. In *Luther's Works,* ed. Franklin Sherman, vol. 31, 39–58. Philadelphia: Fortress Press.

———. 1971. The Jews and Their Lies (1543). In *Luther's Works,* ed. Franklin Sherman, vol. 47, 137–306. Philadelphia: Fortress Press.

McDaniel, Jay B. 2006. The Passion of Christ: Grace Both Red and Green. In *Cross Examinations: Readings on the Meaning of the Cross Today,* ed. Marit Trelstad, 196–207. Minneapolis: Fortress Press.

Moe-Lobeda, Cynthia. 2006. A Theology of the Cross for the "UnCreators." In *Cross Examinations: Readings on the Meaning of the Cross Today,* ed. Marit Trelstad, 181–95. Minneapolis: Fortress Press.

Moltmann, Jürgen. 1974. *The Crucified God: The Cross of Jesus as the Foundation and Criticism of Christian Theology.* Trans. R. A. Wilson and John Bowden. New York: Harper & Row.

———. 1975. Political Theology. In *The Experiment Hope,* ed. and trans. M. Douglas Meeks, 101–18. Philadelphia: Fortress Press.

———. 1993. *The Way of Jesus Christ: Christology in Messianic Dimensions.* Trans. Margaret Kohl. Minneapolis: Fortress Press.

———. 1996. *The Coming of God: Christian Eschatology.* Trans. Margaret Kohl. Minneapolis: Fortress Press.

Myers, Ched. 1988. *Binding the Strong Man: A Political Reading of Mark's Story of Jesus.* Maryknoll, N.Y.: Orbis.

Nancy, Jean-Luc. 1991. *The Inoperative Community.* Ed. Peter Connor. Minneapolis: University of Minnesota Press.

———. 1997. *The Muses.* Trans. Peggy Kamuf. Stanford: Stanford University Press.

———. 2000. *Being Singular Plural.* Trans. Robert Richardson and Anne O'Byrne. Stanford: Stanford University Press.

Nelson, Susan L. 2006. Imaging the Cross. In *Cross Examinations: Readings on the Meaning of the Cross Today,* ed. Marit Trelstad, 165–80. Minneapolis: Fortress Press.

Oden, Amy. 1994. *In Her Words: Women's Writings in the History of Christian Thought.* Nashville: Abingdon.

Park, Andrew Sung. 1993. *The Wounded Heart of God: The Asian Concept of Han and the Christian Doctrine of Sin.* Nashville: Abingdon.

Patterson, Stephen J. 2004. *Beyond the Passion: Rethinking the Death and Life of Jesus.* Minneapolis: Fortress Press.

Plaskow, Judith. 1990. *Standing Again at Sinai: Judaism from a Feminist Perspective.* San Francisco: HarperCollins.

Ray, Darby. 1997. *Deceiving the Devil: Atonement, Abuse, and Ransom.* Cleveland: Pilgrim.

Reid, Barbara E. 2007. *Taking up the Cross: New Testament Interpretations through Latina and Feminist Eyes.* Minneapolis: Fortress Press.

Ruether, Rosemary Radford. 1983. *Sexism and God-Talk: Toward a Feminist Theology.* Boston: Beacon.

Schmitt, Carl. 2005. *Political Theology: Four Chapters on the Concept of Sovereignty.* Trans. George Schwab. Chicago: University of Chicago Press.

———. 2008. *Political Theology II: The Myth of the Closure of Any Political Theology.* Trans. Michael Hoetzl and Graham Ward. Cambridge: Polity.

Schweitzer, Albert. 1968. *The Quest of the Historical Jesus: A Critical Study of Its Progress from Reimarus to Wrede.* Trans. W. Montgomery. New York: Macmillan.

Sobrino, Jon. 1978. *Christology at the Crossroads: A Latin American Approach.* Maryknoll, N.Y.: Orbis.

Soelle, Dorothee. 1967. *Christ the Representative.* Trans. David Lewis. London: SCM.

Song, C. S. 1990. *Jesus, the Crucified People.* New York: Crossroad.

Stark, Roy. 1996. *The Rise of Christianity.* Princeton: Princeton University Press.

Stendahl, Krister. 1976. *Paul among Jews and Gentiles.* Philadelphia: Fortress Press.

Taubes, Jacob. 2004. *The Political Theology of Paul.* Ed. Aleida Assmann, Jan Assmann, Hent de Vries, and Mieke Bar. Trans. Dana Hollander. Stanford: Stanford University Press.

Taylor, Mark Lewis. 2001. *The Executed God: The Way of the Cross in Lockdown America.* Minneapolis: Fortress Press.

Terrell, Joanne Marie. 1998. *Power in the Blood? The Cross in the African-American Experience.* Maryknoll, N.Y.: Orbis.

————. 2006. Our Mothers' Gardens: Rethinking Sacrifice. In *Cross Examinations: Readings on the Meaning of the Cross Today*, ed. Marit Trelstad, 33–49. Minneapolis: Fortress Press.

Waetjen, Herman. 1989. *A Re-ordering of Power: A Socio-political Reading of Mark's Gospel*. Minneapolis: Fortress Press.

Weaver, J. Denny. 2001. *The Nonviolent Atonement*. Grand Rapids: Eerdmans.

Westhelle, Vítor. 2006. *The Scandalous God: The Use and Abuse of the Cross*. Minneapolis: Fortress Press.

Whitehead, Alfred North. 1929. *Process and Reality: An Essay in Cosmology*. London: Macmillan.

Williams, Delores. 2006. Black Women's Surrogacy and the Christian Notion of Redemption. In *Cross Examinations: Readings on the Meaning of the Cross Today*, ed. Marit Trelstad, 19–32. Minneapolis: Fortress Press.

Wolff, Hans Walter. 1974. *Anthropology of the Old Testament*. Trans. Margaret Kohl. London: SCM.

Žižek, Slavoj. 2003. *The Puppet and the Dwarf: The Perverse Core of Christianity*. Cambridge, Mass.: MIT Press.

INDEX

SCRIPTURE INDEX

Made in the USA
San Bernardino, CA
16 November 2013